Blessed Among Women?

Blessed Among Women?

Mothers and Motherhood in the New Testament

ALICIA D. MYERS

OXFORD
UNIVERSITY PRESS

OXFORD
UNIVERSITY PRESS

Oxford University Press is a department of the University of Oxford. It furthers the University's objective of excellence in research, scholarship, and education by publishing worldwide. Oxford is a registered trade mark of Oxford University Press in the UK and certain other countries.

Published in the United States of America by Oxford University Press
198 Madison Avenue, New York, NY 10016, United States of America.

First issued as an Oxford University Press paperback, 2020

Library of Congress Cataloging-in-Publication Data
Names: Myers, Alicia D., author.
Title: Blessed among women? : mothers and motherhood in the New Testament/ Alicia D. Myers.
Description: New York : Oxford University Press, 2017. | Includes bibliographical references and index.
Identifiers: LCCN 2017000253 (print) | LCCN 2017039302 (ebook) | ISBN 9780190677091 (updf) |
ISBN 9780190677107 (epub) | ISBN 9780190677084 (hardcover : alk. paper) |
ISBN 9780190097011 (paperback : alk. paper) |
Subjects: LCSH: Women in the Bible. | Mothers in the Bible. |
Motherhood—Religious aspects—Christianity.
Classification: LCC BS2445 (ebook) | LCC BS2445 .M94 2017 (print) |
DDC 220.8/3068743—dc23
LC record available at https://lccn.loc.gov/2017000253

To my mom, sister, and grandmas.
All amazing women, who also happen to be mothers.
By them I am truly blessed.

Contents

Preface

THIS PROJECT HAD its beginnings in a seminar on women in early Christianity through the Medieval period taught by Beth Allison Barr at Baylor University. Exploring Jesus's odd exchange with his mother in John 2 for this class took me down a path of maternal constructions in the ancient Mediterranean world. Even though I was fascinated by the topic, I knew I already had a dissertation idea selected and had better stay the course to finish my degree. But, all this meant I also knew what my second book would be once the time came. What I did not realize at the time was how personal the work for this second book would become over the next eight years.

Mothering and motherhood were never simple ideas for me. As I grew up, it was my older sister who seemed to have inherited the maternal instinct, while I was always awkward and wary around small children—and downright fearful of infants. She wanted dolls, and I received them too, though I often was a bit baffled at what to do with them. But my sister helped me. She was the delight of our younger cousins, while I was unsure, and jealous of both the attention they received and the ease with which my sister could make them laugh and soothe their tantrums. Eventually, I crafted a narrative for us both: she would be the mother, and I would remain childless—not out of any acknowledged "defeat"—but rather due to what I interpreted as the very clear fact that I had no idea what to do with children, even though I, of course, was still one myself.

Life, however, has a way of upending our narratives, no matter how carefully they are wrought.

Changes came first for me. Married younger than I had ever planned, I was twenty-eight and suddenly "ready" (if such a thing could ever really be true) to start thinking about having children. A doctoral program prevented this reality for a time; but what was newly clear, and very surprising for me, was a strong desire to be a mother, though certainly not without fear over what that might mean.

Changes came next for my sister. She was recently married too, and I assumed she would soon be the mother I had always expected her to be. When news came of her pregnancy, we were overjoyed and eagerly awaited the new arrival: a baby girl, Libby. Once again, my sister would be the one to be the mother, and she could help me figure out all those complicated things when my time came.

This story, however, was not meant to be.

The summer after graduating from my doctoral program, my husband and I moved north as I accepted my first tenure-track appointment. The very week my husband and I moved into our new house, my sister, now twenty-four weeks pregnant called with tragic news: her daughter had died. Breath ceased. Sorrow welled and overflowed. There was never a reason why.

We grieved and still grieve for Libby.

Suddenly motherhood was even more complicated than I had ever thought. Of course, it was not that death had not touched my family and friends in this way before. I know women who have had multiple miscarriages. And my grandmother had lost her third son, Richard, in delivery when his umbilical cord became wrapped around his neck. But my grandma never spoke of Richard. I only learned of his existence when I was ten, from stories my father then began to share with me. When I was in high school, we would drive my grandma to Richard's grave on Memorial Day. There was grief, but it was never opened wide. There were also the stories of my mother's and grandmother's difficult deliveries, placental abruptions, and emergency C-sections, but living children and mothers in the end. In an age of consumerized motherhood, Babies-R-Us (TM), and Baby Gap (TM), I attributed these events to the medical limitations of years past; the reality of fetal death was far from my mind. Surely, the stories of my sister and me would be different. And, of course, they were, but not as I had expected or planned.

After Libby's death, my husband and I decided to start our family. I desired life. I was quickly pregnant and, though anxious and at times terrified, experienced a trouble-free pregnancy and labor. I birthed our son, living, and was soon absorbed into other realms of motherhood—debates over infant-feeding, and the physical realities of such a task, lack of sleep, fear at his unpredictable cries and smallness, and joy at the brightness of his little eyes and strength of his tiny grasp. I was learning about motherhood. And my sister was still there to guide me, though not in the way either of us had imagined. I still missed Libby even as I watched my own child pass milestones.

The next challenge came, unexpectedly, at eight months when my little boy contracted a variant of Guillain-Barré syndrome that left him paralyzed and on a ventilator for three weeks. My husband and I spent days and nights with him in the PICU, changing diapers, moistening lips chapped from the intubation. I pumped and filled bags for the feeding tube, and we waited for his eyes to open. Thankfully, they would open, and his tiny body would eventually thaw. A year later, after countless hours of therapy, he was medically cleared; a regular twenty-month-old and two parents with a harrowing story to tell.

All of these events have informed the writing of this book. I returned to my topic three months after my son was born, and was researching portions of it up until his illness jerked me into an alternative world. I returned to it again as he regained strength, publishing the first portions of it shortly after his second birthday. My sister gave birth to her son in this time, and we rejoiced at two living boys, healthy and happy. A move to a new university took my family across the country. Another year found both my sister and me pregnant again, joyful, though not without well-founded anxieties. I went on to birth my second son, while my sister again suffered loss, this time at fourteen weeks. This book now approaches completion as my house is filled by four-and-a-half-year-old and eleven-month-old sons. My sister's is full of her three-year-old son's laughter. But both of our houses feel the loss of the two who are not present.

I cannot, therefore, pretend that this book, and the deep questions about the constructions of mothers and motherhood both ancient and contemporary that it explores, are not personal. They are profoundly so. The joys, challenges, and deep sorrows of the past eight years have changed me. They have also driven me, repeatedly, back to this research and back to writing. The pages of this book, the topics examined, and the words chosen resonate with my own story. Just as the maternal characters and maternal imagery of the New Testament reflect actual bodies, so too, does this book reflect my own. Viscerally felt through my own experiences of motherhood, and sisterhood, this book is at least partially an attempt to wrestle with the past eight years, and the various narratives I had cast for myself and my sister, as well as with the narratives that have been foisted upon us.

It is also a book that speaks to the broader realities of maternal constructions that affect us all, regardless of gender and parental status. After all, we are all "of woman born." And, as such, the stories and cultural constructions of mothers have impacted all our lives. The images of mothers and metaphors of motherhood reach across divides, elicit immediate responses that can draw groups together or push them apart, due to the power they contain. Indeed, it is the personal aspects of mothers and motherhood that cause such connection and rupture, making these characters and motifs potent signifiers in religious writings and contexts, including the New Testament. The New Testament and early Christian writings employ maternal characters and imagery not only because mothers were physically present in the midst of these communities, and in the lives of the authors and audiences, but also because their physical presence elicits memories and embodied metaphors of connection, suffering, love, joy, and loss that communicate theologies in ways no other imagery could, or can.

Maternal bodies are profound, theological bodies. They can demonstrate intimacy and vulnerability, as well as perseverance, long suffering, and even ambition. Whether or not you are a mother or parent yourself, or have ever desired to be one, the image of a mother can reach into your heart, rousing you to hear and to see in ways otherwise impossible. It exposes emotions and conflicts, personal and social. The pause that mother-language creates in us invites us to once again investigate these images and metaphors in the New Testament, as well as in our contemporary contexts. This book is one pathway in that investigation. It certainly has been for me.

I have a number of people to thank for their help with this project over the years. First, to my family who has walked with me through the personal and professional challenges and joys. To my husband, for his constant support and steadfast love. He has joined me on this journey of life, and parenthood, with compassion and a wonderful sense of humor. To my sons, who have taught me so much. To my sister, for being my best friend and for allowing me to share just a bit of her story here; we are still figuring out this motherhood-thing, and life-thing, together. To my parents, my mom and dad, who have always encouraged me, no matter where life has taken all of us. And to Dorothy Rasley, my grandma, and greatest inspiration in my life. A head nurse specializing in epidemiology with fantastic optimism, I wish she were still alive to read this book. I hope she would be proud.

Next, I must thank colleagues and friends who have encouraged my work, read portions, and offered feedback to help me improve along the way: Derek Hogan, Lisa Hess, Felicia LaBoy, Lydia Hoyle, Tom Dozeman, Barry Jones, Tony Cartledge, Cameron Jorgenson, Lindsey Trozzo, and Mikeal Parsons. To Beth Stovell and Ruth Sheridan for giving me an opportunity to craft an article on breastmilk in 1 Peter and Hebrews 5 ("*Pater Nutrix*: Milk Metaphors and Character Formation in Hebrews and 1 Peter," in *Making Sense of Motherhood: Biblical and Systematic Perspectives*, ed. Beth Stovell [Wipf & Stock, 2016], 81–99). And to Wipf & Stock and the *Catholic Biblical Quarterly* for granting permission to reuse portions of work previously published and now developed more fully in this book ("Pater Nutrix" [Wipf & Stock, 2016]; "'In the Father's Bosom': Breastfeeding and Identity Formation in John's Gospel," *CBQ* 77 [2014]: 481–97). John David Penniman was also gracious in allowing me to read his book *Raised on Christian Milk: Food and the Formation of the Soul in Early Christianity*, Synkrisis Series (New Haven: Yale University Press, 2017) prior to publication. I also thank Steve Wiggins at Oxford University Press for his excitement for this project, his guidance, and quick communication throughout the process. Finally, I must also thank my students, at United Theological Seminary and Campbell University Divinity School, whose interest in this topic and questions helped me to probe more deeply and think through the implications of my study. It is my hope that this book causes us all to consider again the constructions of mothers and motherhood that continue to bless (and even to curse) us as we all wrestle with our own stories, the ones we craft as well as the ones we are given.

Abbreviations

Unless otherwise noted in the list below, the abbreviations used in this work cohere with those listed in the *Society of Biblical Literature Handbook of Style*, Second Edition (SBL Press, 2014).

CMG	*Corpus Medicorum Graecorum*
GALEN	
AA	*Anatomical Procedures*
HNH	*Commentary on Hippocrates's On the Nature of Man*
Hipp. Aph.	*Commentary on Hippocrates's Aphorisms*
Nat. Fac.	*On the Natural Faculties*
PHP	*On the Opinions of Hippocrates and Plato*
Sem.	*On Seed*
MM	*On the Therapeutic Method*
MMG	*Therapeutics to Glaucon*
UP	*On the Usefulness of Parts*
HIPPOCRATES	
DYG	*Diseases of Young Girls*
Gen.	*On Generation*
Glands	*On Glands*
JSCS	*Journal of Septuagint and Cognate Studies*
Perp.	*Martyrdom of Perpetua and Felicitas*
RUFUS OF EPHESUS	
Onom.	*On the Naming of the Parts of the Human Body*
Ruf. ab. Orib. Coll. Med. lib. inc.	*On Girls' Regimen and On Women's Regimen*
SORANUS OF EPHESUS	
Gyn.	*Gynecology*

1

Introduction

MOTHERHOOD AND WOMANHOOD IN NEW TESTAMENT CONTEXTS

IN ONE OF THE most well-known scenes from Luke's Gospel an aged, once-barren but now pregnant Elizabeth rushes to greet her young, virginal but now pregnant relative, Mary (1:36). Upon hearing Mary's greeting, the still gestating John "leaped in her [Elizabeth's] womb (*koilia autēs*)" (1:41) and a holy Spirit seemingly bubbles up to prompt her prophetic words to Mary, "Blessed are you among women, and blessed is the fruit of your womb (*koilias sou*)" (1:42, NRSV). Few in the Gospel audience would seem to disagree with Elizabeth's assessment, not least because it is described as coming from a holy Spirit by the narrator (1:41). Those listening to Luke's story have also just heard the holy origins of Mary's conception in 1:26–38, as well as what is often described as her obedient and faithful response in verse 38: "Behold, the slave of the Lord. May it be to me according to your word."[1] Mary also affirms Elizabeth's description in her song of praise that follows, "My soul magnifies the Lord, and my spirit rejoices in God my Savior, for he has looked with favor on the lowliness of his slave. Surely, from now on all generations will call me blessed" (1:46–48).

Nevertheless, such quick assent to Elizabeth's proclamation can cause readers to miss the larger ambivalence of Luke's presentations of Mary, other mothers, and motifs of motherhood more generally in both the Gospel and Acts. In spite of her verbose entrance in the first few chapters of Luke's story, for example, Mary virtually disappears from the remainder of the tale, only referenced opaquely in Luke 8:19–21 and 11:27–28 before turning up among the rest of Jesus's disciples awaiting the holy Spirit in Acts 1:14. Luke's words from Jesus in 11:27–28 are particularly troublesome for a simple acceptance of Mary's "blessed" status. As Jesus taught about an "unclean spirit" returning to torment its host, "a woman in the crowd raised her voice and said to him,

'Blessed is the womb (*koilia*) that bore you and the breasts (*mastoi*) that nursed you!' But he said, 'Blessed rather are those who hear the word of God and obey it!'" (NRSV). Beverly Roberts Gaventa is right to note that Mary might well be included among "those who hear the word of God and obey it," but that the open-endedness of Jesus's phrase leaves the tension unresolved (see also Luke 8:19–21).[2] If Mary is blessed, it is because of her faithful obedience and not because of her status as Jesus's mother.

Luke's maternal ambiguity is not an isolated occurrence in the New Testament (NT), but works in tandem with additional portrayals of Mary, other mothers, and maternal motifs in the rest of the canon. These maternal presentations, whether episodic characterizations in the other Gospels (e.g., Matt 1–2; Luke 1–2; Mark 3:20–35; John 2:1–11; 19:25–27), brief but powerful metaphors for apostolic ministry in Paul's letters (1 Cor 3:1–3; Gal 4:19; 1 Thess 2:5–8), or instructions for women to marry and raise children in the Pastorals (1 Tim 2:15; 5:9–15; Titus 2:3–5), they are often ambivalent and even conflict across the NT. In addition to these explicit maternal references, the NT writings likewise interact with ancient understandings of women and motherhood whenever they use familial or household language to describe theological and social dynamics in the early believing communities.[3] Indeed, while mothers and motherhood are rarely the primary subjects of discussion in the NT, they frequently surface both explicitly and implicitly to support various theological claims in these texts. On a deeper level, the ways in which mothers and motherhood are presented point to the assumed gendered anthropologies in NT writings, which not only shape views concerning the behavior of believers in communities, but also the theologies presented.

When we move immediately to agree with Elizabeth's words of blessing, or to welcome the intimate nurture of maternal images in the NT, we not only overlook the ambiguity of these maternal presentations in their larger contexts, but we risk continuing to sanction problematic understandings that collapse the categories of femininity, or ideal womanhood, with motherhood in the Christian tradition and beyond in western societies.[4] Not only does this collapse pressure women (and men) to conform to traditionally gendered roles, but I will argue that it does so by perpetuating the subtle, yet pervasive, equation of masculinity with perfection that was rampant in the ancient Mediterranean world. When order and perfection are masculine, salvation is portrayed as a process of masculinization for both women and men. In this gendered construction, motherhood becomes a means of masculinization; it is a path for salvation, giving purpose to the otherwise inexplicable femininity of female bodies in the cosmos. In addition to the obvious problems of this soteriology for women (and men) unable or not desirous of having children, this scheme of salvation likewise mutes the contested territory of gender identity in NT and early Christian contexts by normalizing parenthood and (re)locating salvation in the production of children rather than the parousia of Christ.

This book, therefore, seeks to problematize such simple acceptance of maternal motifs in the NT by using gender analysis to uncover the ambivalence toward mothers and motherhood that was common in the ancient Mediterranean world and that is repeatedly reflected in the NT writings, such as Luke's Gospel. Exploring this ambivalence will contribute to the growing awareness of embodiment to all theologies, including those perpetuated by NT writings, that has led to increased attention to maternal motifs among recent interpreters. Furthermore, it will expose the deeply entrenched assumption of motherhood as ideal womanhood in western societies that traces its roots back to the Greco-Roman world from which the NT emerges. Rather than simply endorsing motherhood, NT and early Christian writings offer differing paths of ideal discipleship, and salvation, for women. In this way, the presentations of mothers and maternal motifs in these writings act as a poignant arena for the battles over gender identity and salvation debated by and embedded in Christian theologies. Although salvation is repeatedly construed as masculinization by early Christians, what type of masculinity, and how that masculinity was achieved for female bodies in particular, is rife with conflict. Motherhood is not the only, or even necessarily the desired, option.

Before diving into the topic at hand, however, the groundwork needs to be laid. In what follows, I will offer an overview of two relevant areas of research: (1) recent contributions on mothers and maternal motifs in the NT, which highlight the inescapable connection between anthropology and theology often overlooked by earlier scholars; and (2) the persistent association of motherhood with ideal womanhood not only in the contexts from which the NT comes, but which persists in contemporary western contexts, even those seemingly liberated by feminist ideas.

Mothers, Anthropology, and Theology in the New Testament

In recent years, a growing number of studies have acknowledged the importance of maternal language in the NT, particularly the mother metaphors used by Paul. Such studies have not only raised awareness of the pervasiveness of maternal language in the NT, but they have also sought to establish the place of such language in theological conversations. Scholars such as Gaventa and Susan Eastman emphasize that maternal images are a key part of the theologies presented in the NT writings and should, therefore, not be dismissed as mere ornamentation.[5] Instead, interpreters need to recognize the connection between theology and anthropology made explicit by maternal language, which highlights the embodied nature of biblical authors and their audiences who were flesh and blood people trying to live faithful lives according to their understandings of God. Connecting authors, characters, and audiences with maternal language in particular paints vivid scenes before the eyes of those hearing the texts, creating calls for unity when maternal bonds are reinforced or causing shock at their surprising disruptions. These images not only reflect and shape audience members' views of one another, but also of the Divine. Rather than simple decoration, then, maternal images and characters evoke the necessarily embodied nature of theology—that is, the need to communicate, comprehend, and live it out among the vicissitudes of daily, and very fleshly, life. As Jennifer Glancy writes, "bodies were understood to be vessels of truth."[6] With repeated and varying appeals to maternal bodies, bodies that were emphatically constructed as vessels in the ancient world, the NT highlights the importance of maternity in early Christian theologies.

Janet Martin Soskice writes on the significance of maternal components of the NT while writing on kinship language in the NT and early Christianity more broadly. She emphasizes not only the saturation of the Christian Bible with such language, but also the theological importance and risk it holds.[7] Soskice quickly acknowledges the problematic history of kinship language in Christian theology as means of reinforcing established power structures. But she finds within the biblical tradition, and some classical Christian authors, a "spirit of freedom in the anthropology" that upends the expectations of the first century and late antique Roman world, such as Jesus's reestablishment of his familial bonds on the basis of obedience rather than biology in Matt 12:47–50 or Luke 11:27–28.[8] For Soskice, kinship language, perhaps especially that of motherhood, encourages readers of biblical texts to have a relational theology, one that is "all about birth, growth, and change."[9] This change not only affects believers who are metaphorically reborn and formed by God, but also affects the God who births and forms believers. Instead of exalting an impermeable and disinterested God, therefore, the kinship and maternal images of the NT underscore the vulnerability, emotional investment, and physical attachment that exists between Creator and creation, and that is felt in the very flesh of Jesus Christ as well as of his followers. Soskice explains that the embodied and relational theology that results from kinship language "open[s] up for us an *eschatological anthropology* wherein our constant becoming is our way of being children of God."[10]

The relational and nurturing theology Soskice attributes to kinship language resonates with studies that focus more specifically on mothers and motherhood in the NT, particularly in the writings of Paul. Paul uses maternal language to describe himself in 1 Thess 2:5–8, 1 Cor 3:1–3, and Gal 4:19–20, and uses language of birth more broadly in several more passages (1 Thess 5:3; Rom 8:22). With language similar to that of Soskice, Gaventa suggests that Paul's maternal language emphasizes "nurture over a period of time" rather than simply the moment of conversion of his congregations.[11] Moreover, Gaventa describes the birthing and nursing language used by Paul as being "substantially connected to the apocalyptic nature of Paul's theology" signifying not only the formation of Christ in his audiences, but also God's deliverance (i.e., birthing) of all creation by means of the work of Jesus Christ (Rom 8:18–23).[12] Paul's maternal language, therefore, is a crucial component of his interpretation of his work as apostle: namely as one who births and nourishes newly formed and ever-developing communities of believers. But, as particularly vivid metaphors rooted in Jewish eschatological and apocalyptic traditions, Paul's maternal language is also "substantially connected to the apocalyptic nature of Paul's theology."[13] Paul uses this language not only because it is especially emotional, but also because it resonates with his Jewish faith to communicate his apocalyptic theology.[14] Such language, therefore, is not an extra flourish, but rather part of the very substance of Paul's theological perspective. "[R]etreiv[ing] these texts from their place in the footnotes of Pauline studies," Gaventa reminds readers that Paul's theology is not found "only in his use of prepositional statements." Instead, "Paul speaks theologically when he says, 'All have sinned and fallen short of the glory of God.' He *also* speaks theologically when he says, 'I am in labor until Christ is formed in you.' "[15] Paul's metaphorically maternal body is also a theological one.

Eastman, too, highlights the apocalyptic aspects of Paul's maternal imagery and notes its importance in uniting his audiences. Rather than exploring all of these metaphors in Paul, Eastman focuses her study on Gal 4:12–5:1, which emphasizes birth metaphors rather than the nursing or nurturing found in 1 Corinthians and 1 Thessalonians. Eastman also highlights the connection between Paul's maternal language and his theology, but uses a different method than that of Gaventa. Based on the work of Ursula Le Guin, Eastman seeks to recover Paul's "mother tongue," his private, relational, and conversational language, in her reading of Paul's theology in Galatians.[16] This approach enables Eastman to resist the rupturing dualisms found in the "father's tongue," particularly those between theology and anthropology, the divine and human, and the flesh and spirit. While the father's tongue seeks to inform from above with "objective" truths—or in Gaventa's words "prepositional statements"—the mother's tongue remains embodied and vulnerable in relationship.[17] For Eastman, recognition of Paul's unwillingness to speak *only* as a father demonstrates his own awareness of embodied vulnerability and its importance in his theological message.[18] In fact, Eastman argues, rather than a general description of his apostolic office, Paul's description of "birth pangs" in Gal 4:19 points to his literal corporeal suffering for the sake of his allegiance to Jesus. Building on traditions of "birth pangs" and barren mothers from Jeremiah and Isaiah,

Eastman suggests that Paul's maternal descriptions remind the Galatians of "the paradoxical nature of God's power mediated through suffering" as well as "God's enduring care for the community of faith."[19] The maternal language of Galatians, then, communicates both affirmation of past commitment from Paul and God in order to reinforce or reclaim hope in the promises that are yet to be fulfilled.[20]

Although aspects of their arguments differ, the works of Gaventa and Eastman serve to highlight the importance of Paul's maternal imagery in his writings and thus invite interpreters of the NT to take seriously maternal language whenever it appears. Instead of dismissing Paul's maternal and embodied statements as ornamental, Gaventa and Eastman have demonstrated the theological importance of Paul's maternal constructions, as well as the maternal and anthropological implications of his theological constructions. Paul's attention to embodied, and especially the embodied *female* experiences of motherhood, can upset traditional images of the masculine and self-controlled leader.[21] Moreover, they emphasize not only Paul's own presence and connection to his audiences, but also God's presence and commitment to them. Rather than dividing Paul's divine arguments from the human, therefore, Gaventa and Eastman highlight the divine within Paul's very human language, as well as the human in his divine pronouncements. Indeed, they argue, certain aspects of Paul's theology are overlooked when we ignore his graphically embodied speech.

Having established the importance of maternal characters and motifs beyond ornamentation for NT interpretation, these studies pave the way for continued research into these themes. This book, therefore, will explore maternal images and characters both in and outside the letters of Paul that have occupied these earlier studies, and will also include additional information on the construction of maternal bodies in ancient Mediterranean medical and philosophical literatures. Although earlier scholars have indicated the importance of corporeality to NT theologies communicated through motherhood motifs, they have not given significant attention to *how* maternal bodies themselves were constructed and interpreted in ancient Mediterranean contexts. This study addresses this gap in the literature and, in so doing, identifies the corporeal justification of motherhood as ideal womanhood that pervades Mediterranean antiquity. Such a discovery brings increased attention to the gendered nature of soteriological language in the NT and early Christian writings, as well as that of their later interpreters. As Soskice, Gaventa, and Eastman have shown, maternal language is theological. What this study will explore is the gender constructions that inform this theological language, especially the assumption of salvation as masculinization that they often betray.

Cults of Motherhood: Matrons Ancient and Contemporary

The intertwining of motherhood with proper femininity was a mainstay of Mediterranean antiquity. This fact is explored in detail in Chapter 2, but for now it is sufficient to note that both Jewish and Greco-Roman authors regularly assume female deficiency alongside the purposing of such deficiency by means of legitimate reproduction in motherhood. The emphasis on reproduction in rabbinic texts is well-known and although women were not necessarily required to fulfill the command to "be fruitful and multiply" their participation was required for any man to realize it.[22] Capturing the Roman perspective, Rebecca Flemming offers this summary of the second-century physician, Galen: procreation is "the main explanation of why woman is, and is as she is, it being for the best in the sense that humanity thus comes as close to immortality as possible."[23] For many of these authors, who were overwhelming elite and male, the purpose for women is nothing less than motherhood.[24]

It is not surprising, then, that motherhood is a powerful rhetorical tool in the ancient Mediterranean world. Augustus, in particular, capitalizes on reproductive power in order to solidify his constructions of ideal manhood ("masculinity") and womanhood ("femininity") in his burgeoning Empire. By fulfilling their culturally identified goal of becoming mothers, freeborn and freed women exhibited their virtuous submission to their husbands. Motherhood effectively demonstrated their recognition of inferiority beneath their men, as well as their acceptance of the maternal telos prescribed for them. Yet, the public displays of maternal submission in the Augustan age also offered select women increased agency through the recognition of their feminine virtue. In showing proper submission by becoming mothers, these women were awarded public acknowledgment. Moreover, men who fathered legitimate children through their wives likewise demonstrated their own virtue—that is, their masculinity—by controlling the weaker feminine and purposing her for her "natural," maternal, end. In this way, constructions of mothers and motherhood in the ancient Mediterranean world were at once used to justify and showcase female inferiority even as they offered both women and men paths to increased legitimacy in the ever-contested spheres of gender construction: "real" women were mothers, and "real" men made them.

Such was the case even in many early Christian circles. In her recent monograph *Birthing Salvation*, Anna Rebecca Solevåg notes the connection between childbearing and salvation in Greco-Roman world, as well as the debates that surrounded such a connection among early Christians.[25] The Pastoral Epistles accept the dominant cultural view and actively advocate for women to become mothers. Yet, this was not the only perspective offered. In contrast, the *Acts of Andrew* and *The Martyrdom of Perpetua and Felicitas* push against the traditional maternal ideal for women, although in diverse ways. It is through allegiance to Christ rather than husbands or fathers that the women in these tales experience salvation. Nevertheless, a consistent feature of all these writings remains an assumed inferiority of all things female, and this results in thorough hierarchies, including between female characters themselves. Solevåg emphasizes the importance of class to constructions of womanhood as motherhood in ancient writings, noting that childbearing is only truly salvific to females capable of being recognized as "real" women in the ancient Mediterranean world: namely, freeborn and freed women.[26] Slaves and "other" females are either hopelessly lost, expendable, or relegated to an inferior salvation.[27]

At its heart, the deep ambivalence toward mothers and motherhood in the ancient Mediterranean world reflects its entrenched misogyny, or what Dale Martin calls "the entire ancient complex of the devaluation of the feminine."[28] In other words, it is a consequence of aligning perfection with masculinity. Such a worldview, however, is hardly a bygone artifact relegated to the ancient Mediterranean context. In her work examining the transformation of "American motherhood" in the late nineteenth to the late twentieth centuries, Rebecca Jo Plant traces the radical shifts in the perception and lives of American mothers after the Victorian era. In this time period, white, middle-class women gained greater access to public life outside the homes that constrained their Victorian counterparts.[29] Yet, at the same time, these women were still expected to become mothers. Unlike their Victorian foremothers, however, postwar era mothers were also expected to have attachments outside of their children *and* outside of the home, lest they harm their children's developing autonomy. Particularly dangerous was maternal attachment to sons, whose masculinity could be stunted if entangled in the emotional cords of a mother's pathological love. Plant writes that as Americans "increasingly came to view 'masculinity' as a coveted trait in its own right, . . . women could play little if any role in cultivating manhood, except in the negative sense of knowing when to snip the apron strings."[30]

Plant observes that in postwar America, women were (and continue to be) caught in this "vicious double bind."[31] On the one hand, they have greater access to the public arena—access that was fought for and won on the basis of Victorian ideals of female moral superiority and "Mother Love" predicated on their location in the home.[32] On the other hand, this greater access to the public arena undermines their status as detached parties. Ironically, then, the limited access won by these women simultaneously removed the foundation that legitimatized their space in the public arena: namely, their assumed disinterested stance toward public life. Now involved in the public arena, women could not be "disinterested citizens" and their private sphere where "mother knows best" was now open to critique in new ways.[33] While in the Victorian era, mother was seen as the morally superior "angel of the house" who birthed and reared men for the good of God and country, mothers in the postwar era lost their moral superiority and the emotional doting over children was often interpreted as manipulative and ambitious. Rather than bringing forth soldiers for the state, these women emasculated their sons through their intense attachment to them that was the result of their own stunted autonomy as housebound wives.[34] Thus, in postwar America women were expected to become mothers not because of their unique ability to bear and raise men for society, but out of a sense of "deep personal fulfillment" as women.[35] Such fulfillment, however, needed to be checked, lest it interfere with the developing autonomy of their children.

According to Plant, the shift from motherhood as civic responsibility to personal fulfillment traps many American women. No longer is motherhood recognized as automatically socially beneficial and meriting some degree of special status on the basis of self-sacrificial love and nurture as it was in the Victorian era; rather, motherhood is its own reward. Women should become mothers because it is naturally fulfilling for them to do so, if they are "truly 'feminine'" that is.[36] Moreover, women should exercise their motherhood on the basis of instinct, with prescribed detachment, rather than the ever-present and overly devoted Victorian relic. The mother (or "mom"), therefore, who expects acknowledgment for such instinct and fulfillment is pathological and selfish.

Although Plant's history focuses on American, white, middle-class women of the modern era, many of her observations resonate with perceptions of mothers and motherhood from the ancient world. As in the Roman world, only certain women are permitted the option of becoming "real" women, based on racial and socioeconomic assumptions of the era. In American narratives, the default view is of the white, middle-class woman; in ancient Rome, it is often the elite freeborn woman. Philosophies, theologies, social structures, and policies reinforce the narrative of necessary reproduction for all women, while simultaneously stifling "real" motherhood for women outside the ideal. While all women are expected to reproduce, not all of them will enjoy recognition as "real" women, who embody "ideal" womanhood. In other words, because non-white and working-class women in America, or female slaves in Rome, can never be "real" women in accordance to the expectations of dominant cultural narratives, they can never be "real" mothers, even when they birth children. As Patricia Hill Collins summarizes in her analysis of motherhood in contemporary American society, "the mother glorification targeted toward middle-class White women coexists with a heterogeneous collection of social policies designed to retain the image of motherhood as vitally important for all women while simultaneously discouraging selected groups of women from becoming mothers because they fail to attain the standards of 'real' mothers."[37] Similarly, in the Roman world Augustus established laws to reward women (that is, free and married female citizens) when they birthed living children; in this way, their fulfillment of the maternal narrative is acknowledged and assessed. Left unnoticed, however, is the fact that the entire Empire rested on the labor of slaves, birthed by those who were never acknowledged as "real" women or mothers by the Empire and the elite men they helped to nurse and rear.

Moreover, like Roman mothers, American mothers occupy a precarious space. Motherhood is at once an avenue to some legitimacy (by this means a woman is "truly feminine" or, as in the Victorian era, she serves the state) *and* a role that must be closely monitored (lest a mother become excessive in her love, and therefore, her ambition).[38] Motherhood is both entirely "natural," and carefully policed—by physicians, moralists, politicians, courts, and the public gaze. When we recognize the misogyny that underlies this ambivalence, however, we see that it cannot be otherwise. Since motherhood is the expression of a woman's virtue of *being feminine*, it necessitates her close monitoring. This is because it is precisely the *being feminine* that is routinely required of "women" that makes them so dangerous. Put succinctly, women are problematic because they can never be truly masculine. The best they can hope for is being put to use by the masculine, and motherhood is one powerful manifestation of that purposing.

It is no wonder, then, that mothers and motherhood continue to be main topics of debate in western societies, dramatically impacting the lives of all women regardless of their race, class, or maternal status. Collins argues that, "[s]ince the 1980s, the American nation-state has increasingly defined ideas about what it means to be American through ideas of Whiteness, Christianity, wealth, masculinity, and herterosexuality."[39] It is in this context that conflicts over reproductive rights and the use of contraceptives that occupy political campaigns and the United States Supreme Court are described as debates over "religious liberty."[40] In these debates, Christians of various theological stripes and political leanings appeal to NT texts, some of which will be explored in this book, to support their views. Conservative Christians actively instruct girls and women to attain motherhood as the expression of their true femininity, and Catholic doctrine continues also to highlight assumptions of marriage and motherhood with its teachings against contraception, articulated in such works as Paul VI's encyclical *Humanae Vitae*. The "motherhood" endorsed in these writings and contexts, however, is very limited. Offering his critique of contemporary "American Christianity, especially Protestantism," Martin concludes that, "[c]oupled with the obscene emphasis on patriotism and nationalism, the emphasis on the family in American Christianity and popular culture approaches idolatry." According to Martin, "traditional families" (i.e., heterosexual, reproductive units) are "universally recognized" to typify "Christian values" in the United States.[41] For many contemporary, Protestant women in the United States, motherhood is often an expected role—and even a performance of their Christian faith.

Returning to American society outside of these strictly Christian writings one can also find a consistent tension over ideal womanhood and motherhood in the public arena. A quick look at the 2008 United States presidential campaign illustrates this point, not least because of the role of the "religious right" and reactionaries against them in American society. Tracing the employment of Sarah Palin's maternal identity in the campaign, Lindal Buchanan concludes that "motherhood is still golden in the public forum" as a cultural institution that evokes ideals of "love, care, children, protection, morality, self-sacrifice, home, and nation."[42] As such, the maternal Palin was a persuasive image of trust for the McCain campaign. Her maternal identity, however, had a flip side that restricted her "through its embedded and inequitable gender presumptions (holding, for example, that mothers belong in the private rather than the public sphere) and thereby undermine[d] her run for political office."[43] Palin's feminine credentials as a mother were at once an asset for her *and* a hindrance; when advertised, her maternity communicated trust but also traditional assumptions of submission to masculinity. Just as she submitted to her husband at home, she could be trusted to submit to John McCain as his Vice President.

Palin, of course, is not the only woman to find herself in the midst of this ambivalence. Buchanan also examines the use of maternal signifiers for former First Lady, Michelle Obama. Describing herself as the "Mom-in-Chief," Obama played into the same "broad cultural ideals and gender stereotypes" that Palin did.[44] Not only does this result in the same problems faced by Palin, but it also uncovers how maternal constructions "subsume the specificity and uniqueness of individuals" with their culturally construed claims of universality.[45] By putting on "the cloak of maternity," Obama is theoretically able to relate better to the public generally—including those who might be alienated (or threatened) by her race, education, professional accomplishments, or socioeconomic class. Yet, it also leads to the diminishment of these aspects of her identity, thereby underplaying their significance and perpetuating the ideal that motherhood trumps all other aspects of "real" female identity. Unfortunately, then, the construction of Obama as "Mom-in-Chief" can perpetuate the normativity of white, heterosexual, middle-class, and Christian presentations of ideal womanhood in the United States.

The pervasiveness of this ideal is striking, even among women at home in neoliberal contexts that highlight the importance of female agency. After conducting a study on the identity construction of Canadian women (ages 18–26) of various ethnic backgrounds from a university setting in 2003–2004, Heather A. K. Jacques and H. Lorraine Radtke argue that, "disentangling ideals of womanhood from ideals of motherhood is virtually impossible."[46] Indeed, rather than liberating women from traditional expectations of "intensive mothering" that posit the incompatibility of career and motherhood, Jacques and Radtke note how the women they interviewed consistently posited traditional gendered stances.[47] Focusing on U.S. mothers, Jodi Vandenberg-Daves comes to a similar conclusion, because—as she argues—ideal motherhood in the United States is "an intensively privatized ideal" where "a mother is enveloped, emotionally and physically, in the 'sphere' of her childrearing, and she is vested with unique responsibility for children's moral development."[48] In such a construction, no woman can have both career and be a "real" mother. Furthermore, the emphasis on choice in feminist theory only seems to constrain women further. When forced to choose, "good" women should choose to be real mothers.

Rather than being freed by the idea of autonomy, therefore, the women interviewed in Jacques and Radtke's study consistently elevated the personal "choice" to be a mother over a professional. In this process, they repeatedly ignored the culturally constructed pressures placed on women not only to become mothers, but to exercise their motherhood in socially idealized ways (i.e., the intensive, stay-at-home mother). In other words, these women did not recognize the cultural constraints placed on their perceived autonomous choices. They did not note the cultural narrative that their personal, feminine fulfillment was to be found in motherhood, and not, for example, in a professional occupation. Rather, they simply described their *choice* of motherhood over and against careers as though such a choice were unmitigated by society. The women, therefore, not only reinforced the normativity of motherhood as true womanhood, but they isolated themselves by identifying such a construction as their own choice and by assigning various levels of value to those choices. As Vandenberg-Daves explains, "the debates [over motherhood and careers] themselves have tended to pit women against women and to suggest that mothers have far more choice than most actually do."[49] Moreover, since the choice in favor of motherhood is perceived as natural and fulfilling for them as women specifically, Jacques and Radtke noticed that the women they interviewed described very little expectation for a male partner's parental responsibility. They persisted in locating male fulfillment and purpose with careers outside the home that would "provide" for the family.[50] Jacques and Radkte conclude: "Ironically, then, neoliberal discourses of individualism and choice serve to support rather than undermine women's traditional mandate."[51]

That "motherhood remains both a contested identity position and a persistent ideal of womanhood"[52] is further demonstrated in the rhetoric surrounding pregnancy, childbirth, and infant feeding. Jane Clare Jones, for example, explores the heated debates over "ideal" and "industrialized" labor that set advocates of "natural childbirth" against medically induced and caesarean births. By using language of what is "natural" and not, participants in these debates stigmatize each other, alienating women from one another by means of what Rebecca Kukla calls a "maternal achievement test" of unmedicated labor and discussions of "childbirth satisfaction."[53] These disputes spill over into postpartum life for women who must navigate the challenges of breastfeeding, exclusive pumping, and formula feeding for their infants alongside other trials of infant and self-care after birth. Tracing the history of breastfeeding advocacy in particular, Erin N. Taylor and Lora Ebert Wallace note that "the link between breastfeeding and femininity that is assumed in the accounts of many breastfeeding advocates means that non-breastfeeding mothers are also less feminine, deficient not only as mothers, but also as women."[54] In language that is surprisingly similar to the second-century philosopher, Favorinus of Arles, whom I will discuss in Chapter 3, Taylor and Wallace conclude that, "[t]he message that all women can breastfeed implies that any woman who cannot or does not is shameful, an *incomplete* woman."[55]

The brief overview provided here only scratches the surface of contemporary cults of motherhood in western societies. In fact, an entire area of scholarship on "maternal theory" is blossoming in women's studies as scholars continue to explore how motherhood (and what types of motherhood) contribute to the identity formation of women both by themselves and by the larger societies of which they are a part.[56] At play in this formation are questions of what is "natural" for women to pursue as "women"—and whether motherhood, physical or metaphorical, has an immutable location in that gendered identity. Yet, the pervasive understanding of femininity as inferior to masculinity that is perpetuated by social constructions of motherhood needs also to be exposed. As Buchanan writes, "the code of motherhood is part of the larger discursive formation of gender and so reiterates its governing constructs of male and female, masculinity and femininity."[57] Motherhood remains bound up with ideas of justifying—and therefore, "saving"—female deficiency by means of the masculine purposing of reproduction. It is no wonder, then, that women's bodies are visceral locations of contention in public policy, daily life, and religious settings. Awareness of these realities brings a new edge to interpreting maternal characters and metaphors in the NT and early Christian writings, writings whose influence persists in explicit and implicit ways in western societies. When salvation is masculinization, the physical reality of femaleness is a problem that must be resolved, not only for women, but also for men who must purpose them.

Maternal Theologies, Maternal Bodies: Method, Argument, and Overview

The task of this book, therefore, is not only to continue exploring maternal language in the NT by extending the analysis beyond Paul's letters, but to do so while incorporating additional information on the corporeal constructions of women and mothers from the ancient Mediterranean world. In this way, this study will investigate the gender assumptions and debates at play in the theologies communicated by maternal language in the NT and early Christian writings. This study will investigate both written and material sources primarily from the Hellenistic and early Roman imperial eras (ca. 323 BCE–211 CE). It will also explore Aristotelian and Hippocratic texts that fall outside these dates due to the significant influence they had upon authors writing in the Hellenistic age who often borrow, combine, and reshape Hippocratic and Aristotelian ideas in their formulations of femininity, the female body, and motherhood. Since the Hippocratic corpus and Aristotelian works form the foundation of various Roman syntheses, I will highlight their initial constructions before turning to their later, Roman counterparts, many of whom postdate the majority of NT writings.

Rather than arguing for direct literary and iconic dependence between these materials and the NT, this study employs audience criticism, which seeks to identify shared cultural understandings from the contexts of the NT and early Christian writings. Emerging from the literary theories of H. R. Jauss, Peter Rabbinowitz, and Gian Biagio Conte, audience criticism has found a home in NT scholarship among interpreters seeking to locate ancient expectations in order to understand better a number of NT motifs and rhetorical techniques.[58] Admittedly, recovery of an absolute understanding of women, mothers, and motherhood from the ancient Mediterranean world is impossible, not only because such understandings were variable in antiquity, but also because surviving data is highly skewed toward elite, male constructions. Exploring these representations while remaining aware of their limitations, nevertheless, offers an avenue to cultivate what Charles Talbert calls the "conceptual world" of ancient audiences.[59] Although not a complete "conceptual world," the evidence provides glimpses into ancient expectations that point toward the rhetorical and theological implications of maternal language in these writings.

The conceptual world revealed through such an analysis repeatedly shows an ambivalence toward mothers and motherhood that is grounded in a larger suspicion of women in the ancient Mediterranean world. As naturally deficient, women were given purpose through becoming mothers, but such purposing did not on its own resolve their troublesome tendencies. Instead, women and mothers remained weak points for men throughout their lives and, therefore, required continued masculine oversight. In such a context, motherhood is the purpose for female bodies, but it is not a complete solution to their femininity. Even as a mother, a woman must be watched and controlled. Unlike a man, she can never achieve full masculinity.

In many instances, NT works themselves reproduce this dominant maternal narrative (e.g., 1 Cor 11; 1 Tim; Titus). Nevertheless, these writings also repeatedly press against it with claims of Jesus's unique identity and mission, including his willing suffering on behalf of others and his impending return. Although God's representative, Jesus's life and teachings run the risk of appearing feminine in the Roman world that claimed masculinity was displayed through power and the production of sons in well-ordered households. In contrast to the dominant masculine narrative, Jesus's own origins are questionable in each Gospel, and he repeatedly offers antifamilial sayings that he has come to "set a man against his father, and a daughter against her mother, and a daughter-in-law against her mother-in law; and one's foes will be members of one's household" (Matt 10:35// Luke 12:51–53). According to such a teaching, a woman is no longer made secure by bearing children and remaining in a household, but like her husband, faces threats even from within. Rather than familial security that Roman masculinity idealizes, believers are to find security in following Christ, whose work ushers in a new, eschatological age. As Elizabeth Clark writes, "In this eschatological context . . . Christians understood that Jesus had called them to lives in which traditional values (including those pertaining to the family) were displaced by an ethic of radical allegiance to God alone."[60]

Thus, while NT works regularly assume female deficiency, their affirmation of this deficiency is also a part of their attempts to reframe ancient ideas of "masculinity" and "femininity" to align with presentations of God's salvific work through Jesus, the suffering and yet victorious Christ. Like other marginalized Jewish groups, early Jesus followers argued for salvation in apparent weakness, or femininity, by making use of irony and apocalyptic perspectives to argue for God's initiation of a new era. Although hidden from the majority culture affirming Roman masculinity, early Christians argued that God's new era was ushering in the "real" masculinity, the final and perfect age of peace. Salvation, therefore, remains a process of masculinization for all believers, and the cosmos, even though the type of masculinization is indecipherable to many outside the movement itself.

As a part of this new era, new families of believers were formed based not on biological or household relationships, but on shared confessions of Jesus as God's Christ. The extensive fictive kinship of early communities necessarily affects the presentations of women and mothers in NT writings, especially as the completion of God's apocalyptic work remained unrealized. Caught in the already-not-yet tension, NT authors faced the continued need for and reality of mothers, not to mention the potentially problematic presence of female believers more generally, all while articulating claims of a (soon-to-be) redeemed creation that would no longer require biological reproduction. The NT and early Christian writings, therefore, offer divergent depictions of mothers and maternal motifs as a part of the debates over gender identity inherent to their assumption that salvation is masculinization. In addition to being theological language, therefore, maternal language in the NT and early Christian writings exposes the debates over gender identity for Christ-followers, male and female—debates that are still felt in contemporary western societies.

In order to make this argument, this book will begin with an overview of how ancients understood maternal bodies in Chapter 2. This chapter investigates constructions of gender (masculinity and femininity) before turning to popular origin stories for women that justify and reinforce the need for female inferiority to be controlled by men through pregnancy and motherhood. Finally, the chapter will explore the anatomical and physiological presentations of female bodies, noting how even medical literature endorses pregnancy and lactation as the primary functions for the female body, many arguing that the masculinized state of pregnancy is the most healthful state for all women. Throughout these diverse literatures a single theme for women becomes clear: a woman must be a mother who bears her husband's (or master's) children, otherwise she not only fails at her purpose for existence, but she jeopardizes herself, the men in her household, and even the cosmos itself.

With this foundation in place, the next three chapters will examine three additional themes that demonstrate not only the pervasiveness of this understanding of women in the ancient Mediterranean world, but the ambivalent ways in which NT writings interacted with it as a part of their reframing of gender identity in developing Christian circles. Chapter 3 will build on the physiological constructions of the female body to describe how ancient theories of conception, generation, and childbirth interact with presentations of mothers and motherhood in the Gospels and Acts, focusing on the character of Mary, the mother of Jesus. Chapter 4 will explore understandings of breastmilk in Mediterranean antiquity in order to provide significant background on milk metaphors used in the Gospel of John, several NT letters (1 Thess 2:5–8; 1 Cor 3:1–3; Heb 5:12–16; 1 Peter 2:1–3), and perpetuated in early Christian traditions (e.g., *Odes of Solomon*). Chapter 5 will turn to social representations and legal codes surrounding mothers in households during the Augustan age as a means to interpret the competing traditions of ideal womanhood in the Pastoral Epistles, the household codes (Col 3:18–4:3; Eph 5:21–6:9; 1 Pet 2:9–3:12), and several especially pertinent extracanonical texts (*Acts of Thecla*; *Acts of Andrew*; *Martyrdom of Perpetua and Felicitas*).[61] Although not every NT passage or early Christian writing that discusses mothers is explored in this book, the passages and topics discussed should provide a lens for additional reflection on the remaining portions. Chapter 6 will conclude this study with a discussion of how gender debates of these early Christians manifest themselves in their maternal language, as well as how their persistent soteriology of masculinization complicates a straightforward appropriation of such language. In other words, rather than simply accepting Elizabeth's proclamation of Mary's "blessed" state, we should ask why and how.

As I will show, maternal language in the NT and early Christian writings is not only theological, but also indebted to ancient gender constructions and their complex reshaping by early Christians. Examining this language in light of anatomical, physiological, and social constructions of women and maternity in the ancient Mediterranean world demonstrates their deep connections to the assumption that perfection is masculine, which I will show undergirds the soteriological schema in many NT and early Christian works. Female bodies are a contentious focal point for these soteriologies, made even more so as the delayed parousia forced communities to wrestle with how actual women were to live without threatening the masculinity of the growing, Christian movement. Rather than offering a homogenous approval of motherhood, these writings depict different options for women disciples, some of which diminish biological motherhood in favor of the metaphorical motherhood of Jesus or his apostles, while others hold fast to a literal maternal ideal.

Instead of acknowledging this tension, however, Christian traditions and the western societies influenced by Christendom, have instead often assumed maternity as the pinnacle of womanhood. Indeed, as I illustrated above, this depiction is so engrained that it remains a mainstay of western cultures far outside specifically Christian, or even religious, settings. Exploring the ambivalence of mothers and motherhood in the NT and early Christian writings exposes the persistent equation of perfection with masculinity on which this maternal depiction rests. Having stripped these gender assumptions bare, we not only have a better appreciation for the theological dimensions of the maternal language in the NT and early Christian works, but we can move beyond an unexamined acceptance of female inferiority in order to begin appreciating mothers, motherhood, and women without these hierarchical bonds. Such a move opens us up to viewing the fluidity of gender as a part of identity construction among ancient Christians, providing insight into how this fluidity continues in contemporary contexts.

2

Maternal Bodies

CONSTRUCTING WOMEN IN MEDITERRANEAN ANTIQUITY

AS THE BODIES from which all persons emerge, maternal bodies hold a special place in theological and philosophical traditions from the ancient world. Nevertheless, few studies have examined the anthropological assumptions undergirding maternal characters and metaphors used in the NT.[1] Interpreters, therefore, often approach these characters and metaphors with perhaps unconscious assumptions of anatomy, physiology, and embryology that are much more at home in the contemporary rather than the ancient world. Doing so, however, risks eliding contemporary constructions with ancient ones with the result that readers either miss out on significant interpretive implications or, worse, they continue to import what are oftentimes problematic ancient anthropologies into Christian theology and contemporary, western societies. Before moving on to examine the relevant NT writings, therefore, the present chapter provides an overview of ancient constructions of femininity and the female body. In particular, this chapter will demonstrate the intertwining of female identity with motherhood that results from these constructions. With the myopic focus on freeborn, elite females clear in many of these writings, ancient elite, male authors insist that to be a "woman" is to be a "wife" (*gynē*) and to be a "woman/wife" is to be a "mother." Motherhood thus operates as the fulfillment of female purpose, giving reason for her difference and deficiency in comparison to the male norm.

Sexes among the Sects: Debates on the Female in Greco-Roman Medicine

For the past several decades, Thomas Laqueur's study *Making Sex* has dominated the study of gender construction in the ancient world. According to Laqueur, unlike contemporary assumptions of humanity as dual-sexed or dual-gendered—male and female—the ancient world was a "unisex" one. For the Greco-Roman world and, indeed until the eighteenth century, there was really only *one* true sex/gender: the male.[2] The female is not a unique being meriting full discussion, but rather an inverted male and useful only to highlight assumed male normativity, which is equated with his superiority.

More recently, classicists such as Helen King have seriously challenged this prevailing view due in large part to the emphasis on female difference described by ancient Greco-Roman authors, even when such difference allows for similarities.[3] Among ancients who stress female difference are Hesiod, with his narrative of Pandora's late and separate creation, and the Hippocratics, who craft an entire branch of medicine to unravel and control baffling female bodies. For the Hippocratics, female bodies are physiologically opposite male bodies, due to their physically loose flesh that causes them to be colder and to absorb excess moisture that is either released each month in menstruation, used in the formation of a fetus, or in the production of breastmilk. As Rebecca Flemming notes, the importance of "sexual differentiation" is, therefore, crucial for Hippocratic practitioners such as the author of *Diseases of Women* who concludes: "The healing of diseases of women differs greatly from the healing of men's diseases" (*Mul.* 1.62).[4]

Nevertheless, ancient authors do highlight female similarity to maleness and even assign names from male body parts to female body parts to reinforce symmetry. Ovaries, therefore, are described as "testicles," debates rage over the existence of female ejaculation and semen, and women are portrayed as mutilated men, whose genitalia are stunted, having never developed to the presumed superior external location.[5] King and her colleagues are right to note, however, that this symmetry is not without its limits—precisely because physicians had to grapple with the unique experiences of female bodies in menarche, menstruation, pregnancy, childbirth, lactation, and menopause. Reflections and constructions that include females and femininity regularly remark on these unique female experiences because they, too, can be used to reinforce assumptions of male normativity and superiority that are often the focus of the authors.[6]

Roman medical authors were influenced by other physicians in the years between Classical Greece and Imperial Rome, most significantly the dissections leading to the anatomical works of Herophilus of Alexandria and Erasistratus of Chios in the Hellenistic era. Flemming, however, contends that "[t]he Roman medical authors none the less considered themselves part of a tradition that extended back to Hippocrates and beyond."[7] Indeed, Galen characterizes Hippocrates as the model physician, even though Galen rejects the mechanistic outlook of the Hippocratics and betrays Aristotelian perspectives in his embryological theory.[8] In the Roman era, Hippocratic and Aristotelian ideas were combined and reshaped, not only in conversation with one another, but also with additional medical theories and medicinal practices. As a result, the Hippocratic emphasis on sexual differentiation remained a center of debate long after the more systematic work of Aristotle pronounced the female nothing more than a "deformed male" whose difference is located in inability rather than physiology (*Gen. an.* 2.3.737a28). Yet, even for Aristotle, female deficiency ultimately renders the female simultaneously similar to *and* opposite of the male; she is a deformed male, but that deformity makes her his opposite—she is cold and he is hot (*Gen. an.* 4.1.766a20). This paradoxical position remains in the writings of Galen in the second century CE due to the consistent debates over the nature of female difference in the medical literature of the Roman world and as a result of the persistent influence of both Hippocratic and Aristotelian thought that Roman physicians blend together and react to in their own works.[9]

In his *Gynecology*, for example, the second-century physician, Soranus of Ephesus, stakes his own position in this debate. The question at hand is whether or not women had "conditions particularly their own" that warranted specific treatments (3.*pref.*1).[10] In other words, he is arguing whether or not there truly were anything to be properly described as the "diseases of women" that occupied the Hippocratic mind. As a methodist, Soranus does not think this can be the case. Like other physicians of the methodist branch, Soranus argues that all human bodies suffer disease as a result of an imbalance of three "manifest generalities": flux, constriction, or a mixture of the two.[11] Remedies, therefore, came from of balancing these conditions. He does, however, allow for the exception of female bodies in the experiences that are "peculiarly" female: namely, "conception, parturition, and lactation" (3.*pref.*3). Indeed, it is the fact that these experiences necessitate separate consideration that Soranus composes his *Gynecology* in the first place (3.*pref.*1–5). That Soranus believes it necessary to argue for female similarity to the male at all, however, illustrates that there was debate over this during his lifetime; not everyone thought women and men were but "one sex."

The debate over sexual differentiation among Roman physicians is an indication of their larger debates concerning the nature of the human body as well as the origin (and, therefore, treatment) of diseases. Different sects of Roman physicians championed varying epistemologies that ranged from an emphasis on the individual patient's experiences, to an emphasis on unseen systems or conditions that were thought to epitomize the human experience generally (i.e., the theory of four humors that dominates Galen's work). The former position generally coheres with most empiricist physicians (*empirikoi*) who, therefore, largely conclude there *were* specific "female diseases" on account of female difference, while the latter coheres with most rationalist physicians (*logikoi* or "dogmatists") who conclude the opposite.[12] Yet, the range of views that span the great divide between these extremes demonstrates the liveliness of debate among Roman physicians. Galen, for example, is an eclectic, who retains a humoral theory and values dissection and vivisection for the acquisition of knowledge like the dogmatists, but who also emphasizes a purpose to human beings and their bodies in line with Aristotle, that cannot be identified through dissection alone. As Flemming concludes, "[w]oman is thus caught up in a whole host of ongoing disputes in the fluid and changeable conceptual world of Roman medicine," a world that can hardly be epitomized as representing a homogenous, single-sex mode of thought.[13]

In spite of the great variance of ideas around the female body, and female disease, in the ancient Mediterranean world, there is at least one consistent thread: the assumption that maleness, as recognized by "masculine" traits, was assumed indicative of full personhood, orderliness, and therefore, perfection. While Laqueur's assertion that this paradigmatic function of maleness overshadowed any gender difference is highly problematic, Flemming's observation bears out: the "generic" is male, while the "specific" is female.[14] As she explains elsewhere in summarizing the views of Aristotle: "It is not so much that the female is inferior as that the inferior is female."[15] True for Aristotle, this statement is axiomatic throughout Mediterranean antiquity as preserved by elite, male authors and commissioners of art and architecture who regularly seek to define masculinity and to deride any deviance from their ideal as "femininity."[16] To be human in the fullest sense, then, was to be a man, and to achieve perfect manliness was to approach divinity.[17] As "impenetrable penetrators," real men were both anatomically male and were able to assert power, or control over themselves and others. Manly men could "defend their bodies" against any type of penetration or assault *and* assert the right to penetrate (and assault) others.[18] The relative worth of these others, then, must be compared with the real men who were the paragons of (at least potential) perfection: that is, of "masculinity." In such a hierarchy, the goal was to demarcate a man from the rest or, as Jonathan Walters describes it, the man from the un-man.[19] Although necessary for the reproduction of ideally masculine men, therefore, women were necessarily and permanently deficient in their own [hu]manness.

[Hu]man or Un[hu]man: Masculinity in the Greco-Roman World

In such a context, it is perhaps unsurprising that the image of the phallus was ubiquitous as an emblem of power—protective, aggressive, reproductive, and otherwise. Yet, in spite of the permeation of phallic imagery on amulets, adorning architecture, and lining street corners, manliness was not a matter decided by one's genitalia alone.[20] Colleen Conway writes, "the core of masculine identity resided not in the body per se but rather in what one did with, and allowed to be done to, one's body."[21] More precisely, masculinity resided in one's ability to exert control over one's self and others. For this reason, Jennifer Glancy explains that although male slaves were anatomically "complete," they were not *masculine* because they could neither control the boundaries of their own bodies nor those of others, even if they begot children. A male slave was never called a *vir*, a "man," but always remained a *puer*, a "boy."[22] "Symbolically," she writes, "no slave had a phallus."[23] Just like female slaves, male slaves were "surrogate bodies" for their owners, standing in to receive insults, punishment meant for their masters and acting as the locus of sexual penetration. Focusing on the powerlessness of male slaves in particular, Shane Butler comments on an anecdote of one such slave's self-castration, which was at least figuratively associated with the removal of his penis. In accord with Glancy, Butler explains that the slave's penis was not a phallus because "it did not signify the sexual and political domination exercised by adult male Roman citizens." His penis was only a "meaningless loose end" and this "slave of Caepio is to be thanked for neatly trimming [it] away."[24]

A "real" man, therefore, exhibited the virtue of self-control (*sōphrosynē*), which included the control of his own body—dress, mannerisms, emotions, speech, ability to move about, and so forth—as well as the control of those in his established sphere. Plato, for example, describes the "just" (*dikaios*) man as on who "regulates well what is really his own and rules himself. He puts himself in order" until "he becomes entirely one, moderate (*sōphrona*) and harmonious."[25] Aristotle similarly explains that the "function of a good man" is "the exercise of the soul's faculties and activities in association with rational principle (*logos*)" which he equates with conformity to "excellence" (*aretē*, *Eth. nic.* 1.7.15). According to Michael Satlow, this emphasis on self-control is also found in a number of Jewish writings especially Sirach (18:30; 31:25), as well as later rabbinic texts, which he writes "points to a relatively uniform construction of manliness that was pervasive in Jewish and non-Jewish, Semitic and Greek elite groups in late antiquity . . . to exercise that (nearly) distinctly manly attribute of self-control in order to pursue Torah study, wisdom, or philosophy."[26] So important was self-control for demarcating masculinity that rhetoricians and physiognomists underscore the ability to decipher manliness through a male's self-presentation.[27] Quintilian emphasizes the importance of exhibiting masculinity in rhetorical performance, writing that boys should be trained in voice and gestures, along with rhetorical techniques and moral character (*Inst.* 11–12). For Quintilian, only this complete package makes a good man, and only a good man can be an orator: "I am not only saying that the orator must be a good man, but that *no one* can be an orator *unless* he is a good man."[28]

The collapsing of masculinity with order and rationality (*logos*) in philosophical writings indicates the usefulness of this anthropology for those in positions of power. In addition to wives and children, elite men would necessarily add additional family members in their households, as well as slaves and other properties, under their control. Ruling men, however, exerted their control over other men, from advisors to soldiers and artisans, as well as all other subjects in their realm.[29] These ruling men were expected to be exemplars of masculinity in order to merit truly masculine followers. Obedience to the masculine man highlights the virtue/manliness of his male followers because they are conforming to the rationality (*logos*) and perfection embodied by their leader. Conway's analysis of Octavian Augustus identifies his use of these assumptions in imperial propaganda in statues, coins, biographical writings, and his own record of achievements in the *Res Gestae*. Combating charges of vice, sexual promiscuity and penetration, as well as a weak constitution, the emperor responded with the "cultural creation of 'Caesar Augustus,'" the *divi filius* (son of a god).[30] With the careful cultivation of his masculine persona, Augustus set himself up to be the "ideal man" for all Roman men to follow and he is fittingly honored with the title "father of the country."[31] For Augustus, such perfection culminates with the recognition of his divinity as the final affirmation of his manliness.

Rulers like Augustus needed to promote their masculinity precisely because it was an unstable identifier; it was always up to others to evaluate. As Maud W. Gleason explains, "gender identity is not a transhistorical constant, but a social construct, a series of stressed and unstressed possibilities, of subterfuges perpetually in the making."[32] Degrees of masculinity and femininity are constantly being constructed, assessed, and maintained by individuals and by society as a whole. The failure of a "man" to act masculine opened him up to attack since following "feminine" thinking was equated with disorder, imperfection, and deficiency. A man only followed a man more masculine than himself, and a ruler's "penetrative" status revealed a nation's vulnerability to conquest as well. Gender, then, is a performance—albeit a performance based on perspective and on very specific rules about who had access to various roles. The elite, freeborn male occupies center stage in the surviving literature, whether Greco-Roman or Jewish. He is "the [hu]man," the norm, the ruler, the rightful leader who must pursue masculinity and virtue to retain the order and safety of all those less masculine than himself: lower status freemen, women, children, slaves, and foreigners. Pursuit of masculinity is equated with the pursuit of virtue; femininity is failure and vice.[33]

What Makes a Woman? Femininity, the Female Body, and Motherhood

While authors and imagery in the Greco-Roman world focus on the male body, and especially the phallus, as the emblem of power and control, they center their construction of female bodies on the uterus. Such utero-centricity is an outworking of male normativity. In her study of Roman women and medicine, Flemming explains: "Humanity's unity breaks down around women, not men, as the emergence of Hippocratic gynaecology indicates. It is the female who thus differs from the male rather than the reverse."[34] Medicine as a whole is androcentric *precisely* because, as demonstrated above, a "human" in the fullest sense was assumed to be a man: one who exhibits consistently masculine behavior and possesses a phallus (not just a penis). Special accommodations and study had to be made for the female, whose relationship to the male was one of difference and deficiency—though the degrees of either varied among ancient writers. The locus of such difference was a woman's uterus, breasts, and the menstrual blood associated with both that resulted in her unique experiences of menstruation, pregnancy, childbirth, and lactation. The prescribed "normal" activities of a woman's reproductive organs, especially her uterus, were therefore critical to the construction of her gendered identity, even as they were the telltale indicators of her deficiency in all things biological, moral, civic, and cosmic.

Pandora and Eve: Hellenistic Interpretations on the Origins of "Woman"

Views defining the female, femininity, and womanhood abound in mythologies surrounding the creation of women in the ancient Mediterranean world. As narratives constructed to explain the appearance and purpose of women, as well as the dangers and benefits their presence presents men, these stories reinforce male normativity in the Greco-Roman world by providing etiological justifications for masculine control. In the following section, two such stories will be examined: the story of Pandora from Hesiod and that of Eve in Genesis. While these are not the only narratives of origin in Mediterranean antiquity, they are the most well-known and the most influential in the contexts that are the focus of this study.[35] Surveying these two narratives, one question comes to the fore: If the man is human, then *what* is the woman?

Hesiod offers his explanation of what is "woman" in two versions of the Pandora myth, narrated in his *Theogony* and *Works and Days*. Given as a "gift" in retribution for Prometheus's theft of fire from Olympus, Pandora is a separate and later creation than men, made not for their benefit but as an unavoidable punishment. Bidding the gods gather in his judgment against mankind, Zeus "laughed aloud" as each god worked to craft the deception he commands.

> Forthwith the famous Lame God molded clay in the likeness of a modest maid (*parthenō aidoiē ikelon*), as the son of Cronos purposed. And the goddess bright-eyed Athene girded and clothed her, and the divine Graces and queenly Persuasion put necklaces of gold upon her, and the rich-haired Hours crowned her head with spring flowers. And Pallas Athene bedecked her form with all manners of finery. Also the Guide, the Slayer of

> Argus, contrived within her lies and crafty words and a deceitful nature at the will of loud thundering Zeus, and the Herald of the gods put speech in her. And he called this woman (*gynaika*) Pandora, because all they who dwelt on Olympus gave each a gift, a plague to men who eat bread. (*Op.* 69–82 [Evelyn-White, LCL])

Sending the "sheer, hopeless snare" to Prometheus's ill-fated brother, Epimetheus, Zeus's will is enacted. In a few words, Hesiod describes their marriage as Epimetheus takes Pandora as "his own," and it is too late when he finally recognizes the evil hidden beneath the façade of a virgin dressed in bridal finery. The "gifts" (*dōra*) given to *Pandora* (lit. "all-gifts") are ultimately deceptive. In the "likeness" of an enticing maid, she appears harmless, having been gifted with beauty and charm. But, she also brings other "gifts" to mankind when she opens a box, or literally a "jar" (*pithos*), which held other "gifts" from the gods to men. With her act of opening, she unleashes all manners of disease and toil, leaving only hope inside as a mercy from Zeus (*Op.* 83–105).

King highlights the deception emphasized in Hesiod's version from *Works and Days*. Unlike the separation of *parthenos* and *gynē* that is standard in Hippocratic texts—the *parthenos* being a marriageable virgin and the *gynē* a "fully reproductive" (that is, non-virginal) woman—Pandora exists as a combination of these realities in order to trick Epimetheus.[36] She masquerades in virgin dress although she is, in reality, a woman. And upon opening her "jar," she releases all sorts of evils upon mankind. Significantly, Pandora herself seems to be the "jar" that she opens; there is no separate description of a jar given to her to carry. In blunt fashion, then, King describes Hesiod's Pandora as "a late creation, a construct, an artifice, an illusion, containing a bitch-mind and a womb-jar."[37]

Froma Zeitlin argues the artificiality of Pandora's sexual innocence is further underscored by Hesiod's description of her opening of the jar. As will be shown below, the Hippocratics often use the image of a jar to describe the womb. This jar filled each month with excess blood before it emptied via menses or was filled with a growing fetus. Yet, the opening of a bride's "jar" was not her own act. Rather, it was the man/husband's role as the penetrator.[38] A *parthenos* was to know nothing of sex before her wedding night, lest she be placed under suspicion concerning the source of such expertise, as it does for the false virgin/bride Pandora.[39] Pandora's opening of her own womb exposes her "bitch-mind" (*kyneon noon*, *Op.* 66), greedy for all things that Classical Greek society claims belong to her husband, including her womb/sexuality.[40] In this way, she brings chaos by endangering her husband's property through her conspicuous consumption and the potential illegitimacy of his heir. Moreover, as the source of "the race of women," Pandora sets the precedent for females (and femininity) and stands as a bold warning for all men (*Theog.* 585–90). Although alluring and an unfortunate necessity for reproduction, a woman is a trap. She is a foreign creature, part of a separate species that dresses like a virgin and feigns submission while pillaging a man's property and undermining his legacy.

Alongside Pandora, and more important for those participating in the burgeoning movement of Jesus followers in the NT, are the stories of Gen 1–3. These oft-debated chapters contain two stories of the creation of humanity. Their history of interpretation, particularly in more Hellenized circles, is instructive for understanding the construction of women in NT contexts. The first creation narrative begins in Gen 1, culminating in the creation of the *adam*, or as Phyllis Trible translates, the "earth creature."[41] Genesis 2–3, then, abruptly picks up a new narrative of Adam and Eve's creation, placement in the Garden, commission and, of course, "fall." The first chapter of Genesis describes the creation of the *adam* as the crowning moment of the entire creation saga with the following words:

> So God created *ha-adam* (*ton anthrōpon*) in his image,
> in the image of God he created him;
> male and female he created them (*autous*).
>
> (Gen 1:27 LXX)

What follows are commands to "be fruitful and multiply" and to steward the entire creation (vv. 28–30). Genesis 2 offers an additional, or alternative, creation account in which God "formed *ha-adam* (*ton anthrōpon*) from the dust of the *adamah* (*gēs*, earth)" and gave "him" life by breathing into his nostrils (v. 7). It is this *adam* alone that the Lord places in the Garden of Eden and commands not to eat from the "tree of the knowledge of good and evil" (vv. 15–17). The separate creation of the "helping partner" or, in the LXX, the "helper corresponding to him" (*boēthon kat auton*) happens later.[42] In Gen 2:18–25, the Lord separates the woman (*gynaika*) from the man (*andros*) by removing one of his ribs and "building" her from it. The term for "building" in the LXX is *ōikodomēsen*, which has clear connections to the house (*oikos*) and room imagery used for women's bodies in the biblical and rabbinic literature discussed in the next section. At her sight, the man rejoices, names her "woman" (*gynē*), and describes their reunion as one flesh in marriage (vv. 23–25).

Far from Hesiod's "sheerless snare," the female/woman is included as a part of God's plan for creation alongside the male/man in both creation accounts in Genesis. Moreover, her presence is marked with positivity—either facilitating the command to multiply in Gen 1 or having the unique ability to "partner" with the man in Gen 2. Their parity results in unity as "one flesh," language that highlights cooperation and mutuality rather than competition or domination. Nevertheless, there are stark differences in the time and manner of the woman's "building" in the two stories: is she part of the original "earth-creature"—the male/female of

Gen 1:26–27—or is she a later creation, built from one of the man's constituent parts as in Gen 2?

As Daniel Boyarin notes, the existence of these two creation narratives in Genesis results in a classic hermeneutical dilemma, one that develops along a number of trajectories in the Hellenistic and Roman worlds.[43] Interpreters are left to solve the apparent problem of the differences, differences that Genesis leaves in tension. The solution of choice was often harmonization. Thus, Rabbi Samuel suggests that God creates an androgynous *adam*, who was subsequently divided: "Said R. Samuel bar Nahman, 'When the Holy One, blessed be he, created the first man, he created him with two faces, then sawed him into two and made a back on one side and a back on the other'" (Gen. Rab. 8.1.3).[44] While this interpretation provides room for the "female" even at the initial moment of humanity's creation, it is significant that this androgyne is still a "man" referred to with masculine pronouns. The masculine is still operative and subsuming of the female. Even so, this rabbinic interpretation is arguably friendlier than those offered by several other Jewish interpreters in the Hellenistic and Roman worlds who are explicitly misogynistic. Briefly tracing the interpretation history of these stories, we will see how a growing emphasis on Gen 2–3 in Hellenistic Jewish circles enabled many male readers to craft Eve into another Pandora-like misfortune for mankind.

Writing widely on Gen 1–3, Philo of Alexandria offers a thoroughly Hellenized reading that incorporates Platonic and Stoic ontologies into his interpretation of these stories as a seamless, chronological unity.[45] For Philo, the narratives of Genesis communicate the creation of three creatures over a period of time. First is the ideal "man" of Gen 1, who "was an idea or type or seal, an object of thought (only), incorporeal, neither male nor female, by nature incorruptible" (*Creation* 44.134).[46] This creation is none other than God's *Logos*, rationality, reason, and order that exists as a perfect reflection of God's image. By identifying this "man" with God's *Logos*, Philo reveals his assumption that perfect rationality is masculinity, laying the foundation for any departure from this "perfection" to be interpreted as gender slippage toward femininity. The second creature in this scenario is the "man" of Gen 2. He is similar to the archetypal *Logos*-man of Gen 1, but differs as a combination of "dust and clay" and a soul, which is a portion of God's image—that is, a portion of *Logos*—received when "the Divine Breath was breathed into his face" (*Creation* 48.139; Gen 2:7). The result is a man whose "nature was a combination of the corruptible and incorruptible" (*QG* 1.4).[47] Despite his corruptible components, however, Philo emphasizes that "the first man, earth-born" was "most excellent in each part of his being, in both soul and body, and greatly excelling those who came after him" as a result of being created in the image of God's *Logos* (*Creation* 47.136). With a rightly ordered soul and body, his "mind in the dominant part as king," this man perceived his surroundings by means of his body and named the creatures of creation as an exercise of his rationality and his office as king (*Creation* 48.140–52.148).

The third creature is the woman/wife. "Since nothing in creation lasts forever," Philo explains, "it was unavoidable that the first man should also undergo some disaster. And the beginning of his life being liable to reproach was a woman/wife (*gynē*)" (*Creation* 53.151). Specifically, the disaster Philo describes is the awakening of pleasure and physical desire that occurs when the man and woman behold each other. For Philo, the woman is the symbol of the physical senses, the one who is more susceptible to the lure of pleasure as a result of being formed from the man's corruptible body rather than from God's perfectly masculine *Logos*. "Femininity," then, is identified as the fleshly inclinations, the physical senses, and the desire for pleasure that act to prevent the right rule of the masculine *Logos* from which she was separated at her creation.[48] It is for this reason, Philo concludes, that the serpent chooses to deceive the woman and not the man:

> But the woman was more accustomed to be deceived than the man. For his counsels as well as his body are of a *masculine* sort, and competent to disentangle the notions of seduction; but the mind of a woman is more *effeminate*, so that through her *softness* she easily yields and is easily caught by the persuasions of falsehood, which imitate the resemblance of truth. (*QG* 1.33; emphasis added)

These ideas are reinforced in Philo's interpretation of the judgment scenes of Gen 3 that follow Eve's deception. It is the man who thinks first to cover their shame with clothes as he is the originator of "every good feeling and action" in contrast to the woman who "being imperfect and depraved by nature, made the beginning of sin and prevaricating" (*QG* 1.43). God addresses Adam and not Eve in Gen 3:10 because "God did not condescend to put any question to the woman at all, looking upon her as the cause of the evil which had occurred" (1.45). As the "outward senses," the woman is blameworthy and more "accustomed to be deceived than to devise anything of importance out of her own head" (1.46). In giving herself up to the "seduction" of the serpent, she introduces destruction into the world (1.47).[49]

As in Hesiod's Pandora myth, Philo emphasizes the woman's late appearance and foreign nature. These aspects reinforce the man's control of her as well as her inferiority to him. A later creation, she is not of "equal dignity with the man" and is to be ruled over as one who is younger than her husband—a perpetual child beneath her lord. The man is to "take care of his wife, as of a necessary part of himself" and she "should requite him in return with service, as of a portion of the universe" (*QG* 1.27). Describing her nature, Philo underscores her difference, writing: "[S]he was made out of man, not out of the earth, as he was; nor from seed, as all mankind after them; but of a certain intermediate nature; and like a branch brought out of one vine to produce another vine" (1.28). In other words, she is a vessel, contingent on the man and purposed in reproduction, but yet different from him in her very nature. Adam, then, names her according to her unique nature and purpose. She is "Eve" (Life) as the maternal "fountain of all generations," but she is also "Eve" since "she did not derive existence of her substance out of the earth but out of a *living* creature" (1.52; emphasis added). Her late arrival and liminal ontology establish her status as a "necessary evil" (1.49). The masculine man, governed by his *logos* (rationality), must rule over this separated feminine part of his once-unified-whole in order to prevent disaster. As Philo summarizes: "Every good thing should be represented under the power of the man, and death and every evil under that of the woman" even though it is only through her that subsequent life shall come (1.37). Only when the feminine "flesh" is contained by the masculine *logos* again can Philo's androgynous (meaning, ideally masculine) Adam/man fulfill his created purpose. Salvation is re-masculinization.

Philo's interpretations of Gen 1–3 reflect a broader shift in the post-exilic and Hellenistic eras from identifying Gen 6 as the story sin's origins, to focusing on Gen 3. In contrast to the *Book of Jubilees* and the *Book of Watchers*, where chaos enters the created order when lustful angels seduce the "daughters of men," later Hellenistic Jewish works insist that it is in the eating of the forbidden fruit that disobedience first begins to take root (cf. *4 Ezra*; *Wisdom of Solomon*). While Eve is not always the center of blame—indeed she is excised from *4 Ezra*'s retelling—she begins to take on this role as early as in the writings of Ben Sirach who, in the midst of his tirade against "wicked" wives, writes: "From a woman sin had its beginning, and because of her we all die" (25:24). Later, the Greek *Life of Adam and Eve* (*GLAE*) develops this tradition by supplying narratives of life outside the Garden of Eden, including a retelling of the story of the expulsion of Eve at the time of Adam's death.[50] As in Sirach, it is again the woman, here explicitly Eve, who is to blame for the introduction of sin, suffering, and death for Adam and his offspring. She takes full culpability for not only the original seduction of Gen 3 (*GLAE* 9.2; 10.1–11.3; 14.2; 19.1–21.6; 29.8–9), but also a second one when Satan arrives in the "form of an angel" to interrupt her penance (29.15–17). As in Philo, the sin to which Eve succumbs is "desire," resulting in a sexualization of her sin her that explains the "demonic" origins of Cain reflected in a number of later rabbinic and Christian texts.[51] As Vita Daphna Arbel argues, the sexualization of Eve's sin is not a new invention in the *GLAE*, but rather an intertwining of traditions around Gen 6 with those of Gen 3 (cf. *1 En.* 37–71; Gen. Rab. 20.5.5).[52] In all these stories, women are seduced by disgraced angels, overtaken by their "desire," and it is their uncontrolled sexuality/wombs that is the conduit for chaos. Like Pandora, their illicitly opened "jars" may have the potential to offer "hope" in the form of legitimate male offspring, but when left to women these womb-jars are vessels for evil as a result of women's inherent femininity, their proclivity for pleasure.[53]

In answering the question posed at the outset of this section concerning woman's identity, interpretive traditions surrounding Eve and Pandora offer similar answers: Woman is a later creation from man, and while she is similar and alluring in appearance—designed to draw man to her—she ultimately brings disaster as a result of her difference from the man and, especially, her unwillingness to submit to him. While Hesiod's Pandora is straightforward in its misogyny, the stories of Gen 1–3 are developed in this manner during a shift to emphasizing Gen 2–3 in the Hellenistic and Roman eras. Although God's initial plan for Eve was good, she veers from her purpose as a helpmate by succumbing to her weakness for physical pleasure. Philo even goes so far as to characterize such disobedience as the inevitable result of her separation from the masculine man in Gen 2; her very existence as "feminine" is defined as deficiency, and divided from the man she lacks any inherent ability to live an ordered (that is, masculine) life. These traditions, therefore, reinforce and justify assumptions concerning woman's secondary status and troublesome nature on a cosmic level. The warning for men to act masculine by exercising their divinely ordained control rings clear. Lest they bring further ruin to mankind, men must control their own feminine leanings toward pleasure *and* control the femininity that surrounds them, particularly in the form of women whose very nature is weakness and openness to (sexual) corruption and vice.

The focus on Pandora and Eve's tendencies for sexual deviance evident in these narratives reflects the utero-centricity of the milieu. Proper use of the womb-jar comes with the man/husband's control—depositing of his seed for the reproduction of (ideally, male) children. In this way, women experience a type of redemption through motherhood; she has allowed her womb to be used for its (and her) intended purpose. Identity as woman becomes aligned with the functions of the uterus so that in dominant philosophical and medical literatures women are often regarded as little more than "vessels," conduits for the perpetuation of male seed.[54] While the experience would of course vary widely for women along class lines, the production of male offspring was consistently identified as the key locus of female value. Being a mother thus becomes intertwined with the identity of womanhood as a naturally inevitable consequence of a woman's femininity unless unusual circumstances intervene.[55] Yet, even if motherhood opens an avenue of a sort of "redemption," this should not be seen as overcoming the assumed feminine tendency toward vice. As we will see in subsequent chapters, even legitimate sons can fall prey to "bad" mothers. Rather, the collation of motherhood and womanhood fuels male normativity that aligns a woman's uterus with her identity. In the end, then, a woman's sexuality eclipses any other dimension of her being.

Jars and Houses: Constructing the Female Body

The interest in the uterus comes sharply, and graphically, into focus in the construction of female bodies in Greco-Roman medical literature. Indeed, the Hippocratics argued that the uterus was responsible for all the "diseases of women" as a result of it "chang[ing] from its original position" (*Loc. hom.* 47.345).[56] As the key differentiating anatomical feature between male and female, as well as the means by which full womanhood was achieved in the birth of children, the uterus occupies a central place in the imagination of Greco-Roman medical writers. These authors focus on the proper position of the uterus, the appropriate amounts and consistency of monthly menstrual flows, the relationship between the uterus and various "tubes" (i.e., veins, *phlebia*) in the female body that were believed to be connected to it, and the need for regular intercourse with a husband. For the Hippocratics in particular, a healthy woman was a pregnant one.[57] Although not medical treatises, Charlotte Elisheva Fonrobert notes that rabbinic texts operate in the same "cultural matrix" as these writings and demonstrate similar preoccupations, metaphors, and emphases on a woman's need to maintain and examine her uterus for the production of children.[58] Reflecting the same utero-centricity demonstrated in the origin stories above, these medical texts construct the female body—and indeed the female life—around the uterus: the "jar" and "house" whose constant absorption and transmission of blood placed women at the liminal juncture of life and death, purity and impurity.

While texts differ in the particulars, most ancient Mediterranean medical authors understand the distinction between male and female bodies to lie in their absorption, retention, and expulsion of moisture as made evident in menses. Lesley Dean-Jones notes that there is consistency among the Hippocratics that female bodies are moister than their male counterparts.[59] Thus, in order to explain the absence of large breasts on the male, the Hippocratic author of *On Glands* writes:

> In males it is largely the compactness and density of their bodies that contribute to the smallness of these glands [i.e., breasts]; for the male is close-pressed like a thick carpet both in appearance and to the touch. The female, on the other hand, is rarefied and porous like a flock of wool in appearance and to the touch: it follows that this rarefied and soft tissue does not reject moisture. (16.573)[60]

In addition to porousness, female bodies were also commonly regarded as colder than male bodies, resulting in and contributing to their greater fluidity. The Hippocratic work the *Nature of Women* demonstrates the association between temperature, porousness, and moisture explaining,

> The most important factor in human affairs is the divine; then the natures of women (*gynaikōn*), and their complexions. . .. The person who manages these things correctly must begin from divine factors, and distinguish the natures of women, their ages, the seasons, and the places where they happened to be; for *cold places promote fluxes, while hot ones are drying and constipating*. (1.312; emphasis added)

Temperatures also figure into the foods prescribed for women in the *Nature of Women*. They are to avoid hot, drying foods when promoting fluxes, and to avoid cold, moist foods when trying to curtail them.[61]

Aristotle, likewise, suggests that female bodies have more moisture than male bodies. Yet, while he reflects the common practice of including "the fluid substance [and] the solid" in the "elements" that make up all animals, he focuses on the other two elements, "the cold, and the hot" in his discussion of male and female (*Part. an.* 2.1.646b21–2.3.650b13).[62] Reflecting what Flemming identifies as a universal belief among ancient medical authors, Aristotle writes that the human body is made out of blood, which is itself the "final concoction" of food (*Part. an.* 2.4.651a14).[63] While both females and males can concoct, or heat, food in order to make it useful to the body as blood and then, flesh, only males are able to create the necessary heat to concoct blood into semen. As naturally colder beings, females are left with excess blood in their bodies that collects in their uterus until it is either formed into a fetus by the implantation of male semen, or expelled as menstrual discharge. As evidence for his theory, Aristotle explains that the menstrual discharge "remains bloodlike" as a result of the female's inability to heat the blood sufficiently to create semen. For Aristotle, then, "[m]ale and female are distinguished by a certain ability and inability. Male is that which is able to concoct, to cause to take shape, and to discharge, semen possessing the 'principle' of the 'form'; . . . Female is that which receives the semen, but is unable to cause semen to take shape or to discharge it" (*Gen. an.* 4.1.765b9–15).[64] Since Aristotle presupposes that "Nature" has a purpose for all things, female deficiency and inability have purpose in the production of children. Nevertheless, his definitions are also biological justifications for male superiority, agency, and activity over the "female" and the "feminine," which Aristotle considers to be inherently passive and inferior.[65]

The pre-imposed hierarchy of male superiority underpinning both Hippocratic and Aristotelian writings reinforces male normativity in the ancient Mediterranean world, and continues as a mainstay among medical authors in the Roman Imperial era. Thus, while various medical sects emerged in the Roman world, they nevertheless agreed on several fundamental factors.[66] First, the male body was generically "human" and all bodies that varied from this norm—especially the female, but also the castrated or hermaphroditic, etc.—were marked by their difference. Focusing specifically on women, Flemming writes that in the Roman world: "Women differed from men, not vice versa; and that difference was inevitably damaging."[67]

Second, Roman physicians repeated Hippocratic and Aristotelian conclusions by regarding female bodies as cold and wet in contrast to the superior male body that was hot and dry. Emphasizing the pervasiveness of this thought, Rufus of Ephesus writes, "The bodies of women are wetter and colder, as everyone would agree."[68] How to handle a woman's cold wetness, however, was a matter of some debate. Rufus suggests that women require a "hotter regimen," but Soranus and Galen argued that this "somatic economy" was regulated by the body itself, and therefore required no special regimen unless disease prevented proper expulsion of excess moisture.[69] Moreover, for the methodists the amount of excess moisture in each woman could vary, depending on her own experience, body condition, and climate. Thus, contrasting the Hippocratic conclusions that menstruation and pregnancy are required for female health, Soranus and other methodists argued that menstruation, pregnancy, and lactation were negative for some women who were naturally drier, or more masculine, than others.[70] Indeed, Soranus writes that menstruation does not help the health of women, but is needed only for childbearing (*Gyn.* 1.6.27–29). Nevertheless, although there were areas of difference and debate among Roman physicians, they agree that the occurrence of regular bleedings of some sort revealed the female body, and therefore the female herself, to be vulnerable, penetrable and passive, and requiring domesticity.

Third, repeating Aristotle's emphasis on a telos giving purpose to nature, a number of Roman medical authors, especially Galen, perceive the meaning behind female "imperfection" to be the providential provision for reproduction of men. In his *On the Usefulness of Parts* Galen argues extensively for the reason behind female imperfection, explaining,

> Now just as mankind is the most perfect of all animals, so within mankind the man is more perfect than the woman, and the reason for his perfection is his excess of heat, for heat is Nature's primary instrument. Hence in those animals that have less of it, her workmanship is necessarily more imperfect, and so it is no wonder that the female is less perfect than the male by as much as she is colder than he. . . . So too the woman is less perfect than the man in respect to the generative parts. For the parts were formed within her when she was still a fetus, but could not because of the defect in the heat emerge and project on the outside, and this, though making the animal itself that was being formed less perfect than the one that is complete in all respects, provided no small advantage (*chreia*) for the race; for there needs must be a female. Indeed, you ought not think

> that our Creator would purposely make half the whole race imperfect and, as it were, mutilated, unless there was to be some great advantage in such a mutilation.

He goes on to explain, such "mutilation" enables the female to "retain the semen and to nourish and perfect the fetus."[71] Most of the time such reproduction was interpreted as healthful for women, along the line of Hippocratic reasoning. Even when Soranus bucks this trend, however, he cedes that women *will* marry and *will* produce children because to do so is useful for society, even if it is ultimately harmful to female health (*Gyn.* 1.11.42). As a result, the "medical woman" of the Roman world remains constructed by and through her reproductive organs. The marks that distinguish her from male normativity, thereby betraying her innate frailty, also act as her only means of justifying the existence of such frailty through the birth of children.

As the collection point for the blood created and stored by female bodies, then, the uterus occupies a key place in ancient constructions of ancient female physiology. According to Dean-Jones, the Hippocratics understood the female body to be made up of a "network of channels leading to the womb."[72] This series of channels, or veins, traced from the mouth and nostrils, throughout the body's limbs and organs, until they emptied into the womb. These veins transported blood, seminal fluids, and even acted as potential pathways for a wayward uterus to travel when not restrained by sufficient moisture or the weight of male semen.[73] Aristotle, Soranus, and Galen likewise picture the uterus as "the terminus for many veins," although they are skeptical of a womb's ability to travel.[74] In a healthy female body, blood flowed through the veins and collected in the uterus, which medical authors often pictured as an upside down jar or wineskin. The womb-jar was, then, filled with either excess blood to be discharged each month, or it grew to nourish a fetus upon the implantation of male seed. The uterus is described by the Hippocratics and Soranus as pulling blood toward it "like a cupping vessel," while Aristotle dissents from this popular interpretation since he saw the uterus as a definitively passive organ parallel to its feminine container (Soranus, *Gyn.* 1.3.9; Aristotle, *Gen. an.* 2.4.737b.28–34).[75] While not actively drawn into the uterus, Aristotle nevertheless agrees that blood gathers in the uterus each month before it is discharged (*Gen. an.* 1.13.725b3).

Rabbinic sources often use the image of a "house" or "chambers" instead of a jar in their brief euphemistic comments on female genitalia.[76] Such language resonates with interpretations of Genesis, which describe the "building" of the woman from the man's rib/side noted above. As a "building" or "house" (*oikos*), a woman has various rooms or chambers that she maintains, the most important being her genitalia, which must remain ritually pure to ensure the conception and generation of healthy (and, again, ideally male) children. This "house" language extends to women being described in terms of cities and fortresses and to the cities themselves, which are personified as women in Israel's Scriptures and throughout the ancient Near Eastern, Hellenistic, and Roman eras. As an example of this conceptual phenomenon, Cynthia Baker quotes Song of Songs 8:8–10:

> We have a little sister and she has no breasts.
> What shall we do for our sister when suitors besiege her?
> If she is a wall, we will build a silver turret upon her.
> If she is a door, we will bolt her with beams of cedarwood.
> *I am a wall and my breasts are towers.*
> *But for my lover, I am a city of peace.*[77]

Baker suggests that the "conflation of the woman/wife and house" occupies an important place in Palestinian rabbinic traditions, developing beyond the common Jewish idea that a woman/wife is necessary for the completion of a household as the means for procreation and household management, to the construction of "*the house within the woman*."[78] Thus, Baker concludes that "in a number of rabbinic constructions, a house is not *where* a woman/wife is, but rather a house is, in part, *who* and *what* she is."[79] Moreover, the woman/wife is the "caretaker" of this house just as she is of the larger domicile. "[T]he pious wife will not only 'examine the house' but will have 'the house in order' to receive her husband when he comes home (so to speak); and she will 'clean the house' properly after he does just that."[80] A "clean house" helped to ensure proper intercourse and facilitated the goal of pregnancy so that the male could fulfill the command to "be fruitful and multiply." Like contemporaneous Greek and Roman constructions, the metaphor employed for the female body again highlights female dependency on the male and existence for the sake of the male, conflating her identity with the "house" she was to manage.

Ancient physiological and anatomical constructions also theorize a primary pathway in the female body, which linked the mouth/nostrils to the uterus and vagina. Relying on the work of Paola Manuli, King describes this pathway as the *hodos*, a "road" that placed the female head in a corresponding relationship with her genitalia.[81] Although King admits that there is "no explicit anatomical description of this tube" among ancient medical authors, "its existence is implied in many ways, through vocabulary, and through context."[82] Such vocabulary includes the description of the uterus's "mouth" and "throat" that opened and closed depending on menstruation, penetration, pregnancy, and parturition. The uterus also has "shoulders," the broad section below the "sides" but above the "neck" or "trachea." All of these parts are protected by the "lips" that enclosed them.[83]

Prescribed therapies also indicate a belief in the *hodos* running through the female body. Hippocratic odor therapy regularly prescribed fumigations to repel or attract the uterus so it would return to its normal position, indicating its ability to "smell" as nostrils do. For example, the author of the *Nature of Women* instructs, "When the uterus causes suffocation [by advancing upward], hold all sorts of evil-smelling fumigations under the patient's nostrils: pitch, sulfur, horn, lamp wick, seal oil, castoreum; below her genitalia (sc. fumigate with) fragrant ones" (26.343). King also notes a pseudo-Aristotelian text that describes the uterus "breathing in" male semen during intercourse.[84] Not surprisingly, then, an indicator of menstruation included a sore throat, and a bloody nose could be interpreted as redirected menstrual flow that could not otherwise vacate the body below.[85]

Fumigations and suppositories were also frequently used in fertility tests to determine if a woman's passage was open enough to accept male semen for pregnancy. One recipe recommended by the *Nature of Woman* is as follows:

> Test for fertility: boil a head of garlic and apply it to the uterus; on the next day have the woman examine herself by palpating with a finger; and if her mouth smells, the sign is positive. If not, make another application. (96.414)

Dean-Jones suggests that the "model of a tube connecting the head to the vagina perhaps explains why the [Hippocratic] gynaecology includes a specific cure for bad breath in women" alongside its various fumigations and suppositories promoting menstruation and pregnancy.[86] This theory might also provide more context for the admonitions restricting a woman's access to indulgent foods and wine. While food and wines were regulated to impact the amount of excess blood present in a woman's body, an additional motive appears to be that limiting the opening of one mouth might help restrain the inappropriate "opening" of the other. Thus, in his *On Girls' Regimen*, Rufus of Ephesus writes that wine should be kept from girls "so that the seething in her nature and in that of the wine do not become allies. Drinking water contributes to moderation (*sōphrosynē*), wine makes [girls] more intemperate."[87]

The width of a woman's *hodos* was necessarily affected by intercourse, pregnancy, and childbirth. Stretched by penetration, and eventually by pregnancy and childbirth, the *hodos* of a non-virginal woman varied from that of a virgin. Thus, a woman's voice was believed to deepen after defloration.[88] Such widening, when occurring in expected cultural contexts, was considered a positive and natural progression in the life of a female as she moved from child to virgin/bride to wife/woman and mother. According to King, such was the program of ancient medical literature, which

> aimed to transform incomplete, immature girls into complete, reproductive women; in Greek terms, to make a *parthenos* into a *gynē*, a term

> covering both "woman" and "wife." To be a *gynē* in the fullest sense it was also necessary to have given birth: the first menstrual period demonstrates the readiness of the body, in terms of both the availability of blood from which a foetus can be formed, and the possibility of male semen gaining entry to the womb, while the lochial flow after birth completes the process, also "breaking down" the woman's flesh so that excess blood can rest in the open spaces created.[89]

Indeed, so crucial was this process for the health of a female that she was put at risk if it were delayed.

In the short document *Diseases of Young Girls* (*DYG*, *Peri partheniōn*) the Hippocratic author argues that virgins (*parthenoi*) had a greater quantity of blood in their bodies near the time of their first menstrual period (*DYG* 14–15). If unable to exit through the "mouth" of the womb, the blood can travel upward and rest upon the heart and diaphragm, causing suffocation, hallucinations, and at its worst, prompting suicide (*DYG* 15–37). Instead of desiring a husband, the afflicted virgin "desires death like a lover," and, as further evidence of the linkage between the head and the vagina, she moves to strangle or drown herself, thereby cutting off sexual access to her "mouth" and "neck" bloodlessly and permanently.[90] Not surprisingly, the optimal cure for this disease was marriage, which was to occur as close to menarche as possible (*DYG* 40–44).[91] Yet, even this could not guarantee female health if a woman does not conceive and complete the process of widening through childbirth (*DYG* 44–45; Hippocrates, *Steril.* 1.414–15). And widened passageways could also potentially increase the risk of suffocation by a travelling uterus if a woman stopped having sex with her husband, especially if she has already given birth to several children and is suffering the dryness that comes with age. Female precariousness requires male involvement throughout her life.

Overall, then, the anatomical and physiological construction of the female body that emerges from medical literature is one of instability in need of male stability. Flemming argues that, like their Greek counterparts, Roman medical writers perceived the female body to be inherently "excessive" as a result of her colder and wetter state, thus requiring monthly menstrual flows in order to regulate itself if not pregnant or lactating.[92] The root of her difference is the extra moisture collected and retained by her body, necessitating the existence of a vagina, uterus, and breasts that are otherwise absent from the male norm. This contrasting, and in Aristotle and Galen's words "opposite," nature of the female and her body showcases her deficiency, which requires maintenance and male regulation for completeness.[93] Indeed, without a husband the female body endangers itself, suffocating from excess blood or even suffering from the wanderings of a wild womb traversing through her body without the taming weight of her husband's semen. Such factors support King's conclusion of an ancient medical agenda to map a female's life from childhood to motherhood in as short a time span as possible. Even authors who acknowledge the dangers of early marriage emphasize the need for a woman to marry so that she might produce children for her own health, or at least for the health of society, as the fulfillment of her created or natural purpose.[94] Outside the world of freeborn and elite women, these interpretations of the female body could also be used as justification for sexual exploitation of females in general, since sex was "for her own good"—weighting the womb, facilitating necessary menstrual flows, and completing a female's development to become a "reproductive woman" even if she would never be acknowledged as "wife." Not only does the medical literature reinforce male superiority and control of the female bodily as well as socially, but it likewise secures the priority of motherhood as the "natural" consequence of female existence. As the meaning behind her difference and deficiency, reproduction of (male) children is epitomized as the rightful goal of the female body, and therefore, for women themselves; motherhood is firmly intertwined with definitions of a "woman/wife" (*gynē*).

Wo/man-Made: Maternal Bodies and the New Testament

The construction of women, as of men, in Mediterranean antiquity was a continuous enterprise. With male normativity assumed and reinforced throughout the dominant literature of the culture, masculinity was firmly identified with orderliness, rationality, control, and perfection. As biologically female, girls and women were unable to achieve full personhood. Their very nature prevented such a feat; even if certain women are praised for displaying masculine virtues, others were chastised for acting inappropriately male. As incomplete persons, perpetually stunted and childish, females required the oversight of men. Thus, interpretations of the Pandora and Eve narratives current in the first centuries of the Roman Empire highlight the women's late creation and tendency toward vice, which is sexualized in the unsanctioned opening of jars and mouths outside of a man/husband's control. Only when the man controls her can the potential of "hope" within a woman be realized: only then can (male) children be born and a man's legacy secured.

The anatomical and physiological constructions of female bodies surveyed in the medical literature likewise emphasize the need for masculine control. Cold and wet, female bodies exist in a precarious state of flux—taking in, retaining, and expelling blood monthly as a result of their innate imperfection. This biological instability correlates to the moral vulnerability outlined in the origin narratives to provide yet another avenue to justify masculine control. As in the narratives of Pandora and the Hellenistic renderings of Eve, the female is reduced to her reproductive ability, either "correctly" or "incorrectly" used. Maintenance of her "jar" or "house" through careful tracking of menstruation and self-examination leads to her own health and (or at least) to civic health by ensuring the reproduction of men. Unwilling to let feminine "imperfection" exist for no reason, our ancient authors affirm her presence for the purposes of reproduction. She has the honor of making more men, who despite their innate completeness cannot replicate on their own. In a twist of logic balanced on the assumption of male superiority, female ability is inability, the existence of her uterus is the inversion of a penis, the presence of her vagina a point of rightful penetration, and her breasts indicate her intake of moisture rather than her ability to provide it.

This, then, is part of the complex picture of women as mothers in the ancient Mediterranean world, the world that fostered the writings that would eventually form the NT. Mothers and motherhood are necessary components of human life—precariously powerful as the acknowledged telos for female deficiency. Motherhood, then, was the end to which all "natural" women were to aspire *and* it was necessary for the survival of the truly human beings: men. As deficient and inferior, susceptible to vice and corruption, a woman simultaneously contained the *only* means to preserve masculinity in her conveyance of male/masculine seed through her uterus and her breasts. Tempered and formed by innate male heat, our authors inform us, the female can be made useful; rather, she *must* be made useful for the continuation of the *real* genus that is mankind. This operative misogyny was rife with challenges, captured in sentiments such as those expressed by Metellus Numidicus, who famously quipped, "If we could all get on without a woman/wife, Romans, we all would avoid that annoyance; but since nature has decreed that we can neither live very comfortably with them nor at all without them, we must take thought for our lasting well-being rather than the pleasure of the moment" (*Noct. att.* 1.6.2).[95] Since she cannot be dispensed with, a woman/wife must be controlled and used for her purpose: the perpetuation of men.

Yet, as we will see, this sentiment is an oversimplification and, indeed, overly negative interpretation of surviving data. While elite women were not regarded as "equal" to men in any sense, they were able to approach legitimate (if liminal and easily polemicized) positions of power *because* of their role as mothers.[96] Indeed, the *need* for women to conceive, gestate, birth, and suckle children resulted in a preoccupation of their roles among medical authors, philosophers, historians, dramatists, composers of epics, and in iconic representations. Their influence over sons, in particular, as well as their double-sided role as necessary and deficient, marks their appearance in a number of works. While always presented as inferior to the ideal *man*, ideal mothers can and do figure as key participants in history and legend, wielding power and influence as projections of the masculine performances of male family members.[97] Mothers feature as a potential commonplace for praise and blame not only for themselves, but also for the "proper" male subjects of our ancient authors: while good women produced good/masculine sons, bad women produced effeminate ones, who not only brought chaos to their families, but to the nation as well. Indeed, while our elite, male authors repeatedly emphasize the need for women in reproduction, it is clear that they likewise needed women in order to construct the "feminine" over which they claimed dominance, even while their very existence was predicated on women's unique attributes: physical and psychological.

Mothers and motherhood, therefore, surface as simultaneously celebrated and potentially problematic beings and metaphors in the larger Greco-Roman world, NT writings included. Focusing on the unique person of Jesus, NT authors were forced to deal with issues of his origins, including his relationship with his mother, as part of this common *topos* for praise or blame. They also faced questions concerning the construction of their own believing communities, which were often characterized with family metaphors but nevertheless existed outside blood-kinship bonds. Outside biological kinship groups, upon whom were these communities dependent and who can claim their birth or formation/education at the breast? The constructions of mothers and ideas of motherhood in the NT, therefore, have direct bearing on the theologies offered in these writings, paving the way for persistent debates in the early centuries of Christianity and in current contexts. Not surprisingly, the ambivalence of Greco-Roman authors is reflected in NT writings, mothers appearing simultaneously as models of piety and as potential distractions which must be distanced. As the early Jesus-believers moved toward worshiping Jesus as the "incarnate one"—the embodiment of the divine—their depictions of mothers and motherhood were shaped to reinforce particular theological arguments. These arguments, like those of our elite, male authors above, generally focus on other, more masculinely construed topics, such as Jesus's identity, the hierarchy of various assemblies, and the revelation of God's order through Christ.

Nevertheless, in construing these topics as masculine (i.e., reflecting God's "order"), NT authors regularly utilize traditionally feminine components including suffering and maternal language.[98] Thus, Paul describes his commitment and suffering for the Galatians with explicitly feminine language of passive childbirth (4:19–21). In this way, NT writings utilize and subvert constructions of gender and identity in the Greco-Roman world as a means of communicating the apocalyptic vision of God's final victory in a new age. Indeed, the decreased emphasis on biological reproduction in apocalyptic theology creates space for women, mothers, and men to participate in ways that conflict with dominant cultural expectations. By presenting Jesus's crucifixion and resurrection, the outflowing of God's Spirit, and the initiation of the eschaton as indicative of God's redemption of all humanity, NT writings often imply that women, too, are made complete by Christ rather than by motherhood (or at least not by motherhood alone). As we will see, while such an emphasis can lead to the distancing of biological mothers in the Gospels and Acts, it likewise creates space for male authors, such as Paul, to adopt maternal metaphors as descriptions for themselves and for Jesus. Since these early Jesus-believing communities de-emphasized biological relationships, they created room for the formation of new families begotten, birthed, and nourished by God and apostle. As we will see, in these families, the space occupied by female bodies, literal and metaphorical, is repeatedly contested as NT authors wrestle with ways to communicate God's salvific (masculinizing) action through Jesus.

3

Conceiving Christ and Community

MARY, MOTHERS, AND GOD'S HOUSEHOLD IN THE GOSPELS AND ACTS

MARY, THE MOTHER OF JESUS, is perhaps the most obvious starting point for a study on mothers and motherhood in the NT. Indeed, she has garnered the majority of attention given to biblical women throughout Christian history and scholarship.[1] As the mother of Christ, such attention is certainly understandable as interpreters and theologians wrestle with her unique position among not only women, but also humanity.[2] When Mary does appear in the Gospels, she is a significant *and* an ambiguous character. As noted in the introductory chapter, her presence is simultaneously necessitated by and often problematic to Jesus's existence and ministry.[3] This chapter will show that Mary's ambiguity in the Gospels and Acts is likewise reflected in similar ambiguity surrounding biological mothers and motherhood generally in these stories, as well as the unconventional uses of maternal imagery in additional NT texts. Indeed, the ambiguity of mothers and motherhood is heightened by the apocalyptic expectations and tensions present in these writings; after all, if God's reign has truly "drawn near," what need is there for biological reproduction generally and for mothers in particular (Mark 1:14–15; Luke 21:34–36)?

Rather than emphasizing the need for procreation and married alliances among the free and property-owning classes that was ubiquitous in this milieu, these early stories of Jesus and his followers actively push against childbearing, and therefore, against the creation of biological mothers. Instead, these stories prioritize the formation of a family or household (*oikos*) of God over existing (and even future) families built on biological and long-standing kinship relationships.[4] In her study on the Gospel of Matthew, Marianne Blickenstaff concludes that "[a]s he does with biological fatherhood, Matthew subordinates biological motherhood to fictive parenthood in the Kingdom of Heaven."[5] Followers of to grow God's household (and not their own) by "making disciples of all nations" who become their siblings and fellow children of God.[6] The diminishing role of traditional family/household systems has significant ramifications for the understandings of mothers, motherhood, and womanhood. Women, like their male counterparts, are to find their telos in the family of God on the basis of their obedience and faithfulness to the will of their heavenly Father rather than in becoming literal mothers themselves.[7] Blickenstaff's observations bear out in a number of other NT writings as well, including the other Synoptic Gospels, each of which contains rhetoric similar to Matthew, and Paul's encouragement for unmarried life in 1 Corinthians. In some of the most clear language, the Gospel of John provocatively describes the rebirth of Jesus's followers as "not by the bloods or by the will of the flesh or by the will of a man/husband, but they were begotten by God" (John 1:13).[8]

What has often been left largely unexplored, however, is the resonance between language of birth/rebirth and families in the NT and ancient embryological and parturitive theories. Borrowing, reflecting, and subverting aspects of these anthropologies, a number of NT writings seek to establish allegiance to God as the ultimate *paterfamilias* (male head of household). In so doing, they downplay the significance of biological motherhood for women, while simultaneously opening up avenues for unconventional "mothers" to appear, such as Paul. This chapter will provide an overview of common theories of conception, generation, and childbirth that underlie and reinforce the collapsing of the categories of motherhood and womanhood outlined in Chapter 2. With this foundation in place, I will then turn to explore primarily the presentation of Mary in the Gospels and Acts to demonstrate how ancient embryological and parturitive theories shed light on the presentations of Mary, her child, Jesus, and the believing communities who are identified as the children of God. Either impregnated by God's holy Spirit (*pneuma*) in Matthew and Luke, or simply acting as the mother to his incarnate rationality or "Word" (*logos*), Jesus's mother is the conduit for God's greatest revelation on earth. Her role as mother, however, is unique. A one-time event that is unevenly narrated by NT writings, Mary's pregnancy and birth give way to a focus on the communities begotten by and through Jesus. Mothers and motherhood may be part of the narrative, but they are only a part, and one that is significantly changed by the unique conception and birth of God's Son.

Is the Mother a Parent? Ancient Theories of Conception, Generation, and Childbirth

Theories of conception, generation, and childbirth are expressed by a number of medical and philosophical authors in the ancient Mediterranean world.[9] This survey will focus again on the dominating works of Hippocratics and Aristotle due to their persistence in the writings of several Roman physicians and rabbinic authors whose anatomical and physiological constructions aided our understanding of assumptions concerning the female body and nature in the previous chapter. With their priority on reproduction as the fitting telos for the deficiency that is the female, they once again encapsulate womanhood largely in terms of interactions with a man/husband and the necessary regulation of her uterus for the production of a fetus and, ultimately, a fully formed (male) child. Yet, the emphasis on motherhood in these texts did not necessarily equate to an acknowledgment of female *parentage* in the ancient world, since a woman was not always understood to be an active agent—but rather a passive and receptive one. The assumption of male superiority again seeps through various theories of conception, generation, and childbirth among ancient authors. Turid Karlsen Seim notes that the "generative relations between men" on which ancient Mediterranean society was constructed necessitated a dominant place for fathers in conception as well; as they were the generative figures in society, so too should they function as the generative figures in reproduction. "The irony is," Seim explains, "that whereas motherhood manifests itself bodily and unmistakably, fatherhood is not visible and evident in the same compelling manner; it is in fact fragile and vulnerable."[10] Thus, medical theories provide insight into what a father's body cannot manifest. In this way, these authors draw back the curtain to peer into the female body during intercourse, conception, pregnancy, and beyond in order to detail the roles the male and female play in reproduction and, therefore, reaffirm male superiority over female deficiency and disorder.

Seeds, Bloods, and Spirit: Ancient Embryologies

While ancients agree on the need for a woman in reproduction, authors do not agree on what exactly she contributes to the process, aside from insulating and nourishing the growing fetus in her uterus. At one extreme, the female contribution is reduced to incubation alone. She receives the male seed and nourishes it until the fetus grows too large for her to support, thus prompting birth. All that is required for life is held within the seed; the mother simply provides food and a safe place to grow. Perhaps the most famous articulation of this idea comes from outside medical literature in the third part of Aeschylus's *Oresteia, The Eumenides*. Having commissioned Orestes to commit matricide as retribution for Clytemnestra's killing of Agamemnon, her first husband and the father of Orestes, Apollo appears as a witness before the judge, Athena. In this scene, Apollo does not deny Orestes's killing of Clytemnestra. Instead, he declares Orestes to be righteous because he completed this execution while the vengeful Furies, goddesses who punish those guilty of matricide, rage against him (*Eum.* 307–28).

Apollo agrees that the murder of a parent is a grave offence, yet, the killing of Clytemnestra (or of any mother) does not qualify as the murder of a parent since, for Apollo, the mother is not a parent; she is an incubator. He explains to Athena:

> The mother is no parent of that which is called her child,
> but only nurse of the new-planted seed that grows.
> The parent ("begetter") is he who mounts.
> A stranger is she who preserves the seed,
> if no god interfere. *(Eum.* 658–61*)*[11]

As a "stranger," Clytemnestra has no claim on Orestes.

Moreover, it is *her* murder of Agamemnon that demands the retribution Orestes committed at Apollo's behest (*Cho.* 270–305; *Eum.* 64–84). As Apollo's agent, Orestes meted out true justice and restores the proper order—that is, masculinity and male rule in Agamemnon's household and the kingdom of Argos. Athena, the judge and final arbiter of Orestes's fate, is presented as an example of Apollo's theory since she is the child of Zeus alone. Conveniently ignoring Zeus's swallowing of the pregnant goddess Metis, Apollo credits Athena's wisdom to the fact that she "never fostered in the dark of the womb" (*Eum.* 664–65).[12] Instead, she was birthed from Zeus's head, one traditional location for the production of semen.[13] In spite of her rather deceptive female form, then, Athena is a bodily manifestation of Zeus's order; the virgin goddess *is* masculine. Athena quickly agrees with Apollo, affirming her disposition to the side of all things "male." She settles the dispute by deciding in favor of Orestes and placating the Furies with new honors: the Furies become the *Eumenides* ("Gracious Goddesses"; *Eum.* 795–1045). With this new title and pacifying honors, the Furies leave their anger aside and turn "gracious" toward Athens. They recede into the darkness and disappear, leaving the "masculine" Olympians, Apollo and Athena, to reign. With the trilogy climaxing and resolving in the Athenian courtroom under the leadership of Athena, Aeschylus declares manliness not only to be generative of initial life, but also restorative of order when feminine chaos, such as Clytemnestra and the Furies, enters.

Apollo's comments reflect assumptions and also highlight areas of contention in the two most prevalent medical theories on embryology in the ancient world: those that believed both males and females contributed semen, and those that limited such contribution to males only.[14] As we will see, while both theories are consistent with the presumed male superiority of the larger culture, they differ quite sharply with regard to their understandings of seed: of what it is constituted, who contributes it, and how it behaves in a woman's uterus. Not surprisingly, where our theorists land in their constructions depends in large part upon where they started—whether it is in the experience of patient interaction for the Hippocratics, in the philosophical principles believed operative for [hu]mankind that are integrated into reproduction by Aristotle, or in various combinations thereof in the writings of Soranus and Galen.

The Hippocratics asserted that both men and women produced seeds that combined to create a fetus in the woman's womb.[15] Standing behind this theory was the fact that children resemble their father *and* mother, as well as various ancestors. To explain this reality, the Hippocratics assert that both partners contribute to the constituent parts that make up a child: they both contribute seed. Seed, argue the Hippocratics, is made throughout the entire human body and ejaculated during the pleasure of intercourse by men and women. The Hippocratic author of *On Generation* writes: "I assert that seed is secreted from the whole (*pan*) body, from the solid parts and the soft parts, and from all its moisture: blood, bile, water, and phlegm, for this is the number of kinds of substances a person naturally contains in himself" (3.475; cf. *Nat. puer.* 1.486).[16] Since the seed generates fully formed from throughout the whole (*pan*) body, this theory was later named "pangenesis." Having been warmed during sex, seed liquefies and passes through "vessels and cords" in the body, travelling to the testicles and penis in men and into the uterus in women (*Gen.* 1.470). That men ejaculate was not difficult to prove, but the Hippocratics also assert female ejaculation, arguing: "And women, too, ejaculate from their body, sometimes into their uterus—the uterus then becomes moist—and sometimes externally, if the uterus gapes open more than it should" (*Gen.* 4.475). When both sets of seed are retained by a woman, she conceives: "For the uterus, on receiving the seed and closing, holds it inside itself, inasmuch as a mouth contracts in response to moisture, and then what came from the man and what came from the woman are mixed together" (*Gen.* 5.477).

Thus far, the pangenetic theory contrasts quite sharply from Apollo's embryology described above, since it assigns a parallel place to women in the act of generation. Her pleasure, like that of the man, is required for ejaculation of her seed, which must mix with the man's to produce offspring.[17] For the Hippocratics, once the seed is secured in the woman's womb, a battle ensues between the stronger seed and the weaker seed contributed by *each* partner. While the stronger seed is necessarily "masculine," this stronger seed comes from both parents so that "in a man there are both female semen and male semen, and the same in a woman" (*Gen.* 6.478). This battle of seeds is decided not by strength, but by amount.

> The matter is like this: if stronger semen comes from both parents, a male is engendered, if weaker, a female. Whichever sex [of seed] exceeds in amount is engendered: for if weaker semen is much greater in amount than stronger semen, the stronger is overcome, and being mixed with the weaker is brought around to become female. But if stronger semen is much

> greater in amount, the weaker is overcome and brought around to become a male. (*Gen.* 6.478)

It is clear from this summary that "the stronger"—that is, the masculine—is preferred in all cases, resulting in a male child with correspondingly masculine/strong features. These features, however, may resemble either the father or mother, again depending on who supplies more of the seed corresponding to each body part (*Gen.* 8.481). Thus, "it is not possible for a child to look like its mother in all its features and like its father in none, nor the opposite of this, nor to look like neither parent in anything; rather there is a necessity to look like both parents in something, if sperm passes into the child from both of their bodies" (8.481). The mother, according to pangenesis, *is* a parent. While she is not the penetrator, she does contribute generative seed to the fetus as well as nourishment in the form of blood and "cold breath" or "spirit" (*pneuma psychron, Nat. puer.* 1.486). Moreover, she can contribute positive characteristics so long as her seed is strong; so long as her contribution is "masculine."

The importance of the *pneuma*, or "spirit," in this process should not be overlooked. Citing Hippocratic writings, Troy Martin argues that "ancient medical texts place *pneuma* in the category of nutrition (*trophē*)," and even as the "most important" nutrient for life. He writes, "for a person without food can live a few months and without water a few days but without *pneuma* only a few minutes."[18] For the Hippocratics, the separation and settling of the *pneuma* is a crucial component to generation. Annette Weissenrieder turns to the Hippocratic *Nature of a Child*, which states, "As the flesh grows *it is formed by the pneuma*. Each thing in it goes to its corresponding element—the dense to the dense, the rare to the rare, and the fluid to the fluid. Each settles in its appropriate place, corresponding to that which from whence it came and to which is akin."[19] The Hippocratics, therefore, offer a mechanistic view of generation; it is a process that occurs with the mixing of seeds as aided by the *pneuma* and nourishment of blood that results in the formation of the fetus. There is no rationality, or *logos*, imparted to guide the construction other than the embattlement of seeds described above.

While Hippocratic pangenesis *does* contrast with Apollo's minimalist perspective by giving space for female participation in generation, it nevertheless complies with the overwhelming assumption of masculine superiority. For the Hippocratic authors as for Aeschylus, masculinity is equated with strength, with order, and with perfection. In an ideal situation, the Hippocratics declare, the masculine seed (whether from the male or female body) dominates, resulting in a perfectly ordered/masculine child. A weak child, the weakest overall being female, is a disappointment—a demonstration that things did not proceed according to the ideal: the weak overwhelmed the strong (*Gen.* 6.478). In addition to suffering from an abundance of weak/feminine semen, the production of a weak child is blamed on the mother's womb. One that gapes too much allows semen and nourishing blood to leak out, and one that is too constrictive prevents the proper growth of the fetus in some or all of its parts. Using the analogy of a cucumber in a "jar" or "cup," the Hippocratic author of *On Generation* argues just as the "cucumber will grow like the cup in volume and form" so too will a fetus grow to fill the shape of its mother's "container," her uterus (9.483). In this way, it is the woman's womb (and indirectly, at least, the woman) that is blamed for a weak child produced by a "strong robust father and mother" (9.483). Overall, weakness is still equated with femininity, resulting from the unfortunate muting of the masculine, strong seed either through an abundance of weakness or the limitations of a female uterus. While the Hippocratics clearly articulate a woman's contribution to the generation of the fetus within her, they persist with their affirmation of masculine dominance in the production of the ideal child.

Aristotle disagrees with the Hippocratics and with the idea of pangenesis in general, offering a theory much more in line with that of Apollo. Aristotle has two contentions with Hippocratic pangenesis: first, is the assertion that both men *and* women contribute seed; second, that the formation of a fetus is mechanistic. For Aristotle, as for Galen after him, conception and generation are emphatically teleological, ordered toward a purpose. Recalling the discussion in Chapter 2, Aristotle argues that women cannot produce seed precisely as a result of their femaleness, which he defines as *the inability to create semen* (*Gen. an.* 4.1.765b8–15)! For Aristotle, then, pangenesis is a nonstarter; it results from a complete failure to comprehend what it is to be male and female.[20] Instead, females retain menstrual blood, the imperfect, material residue that signifies their failure to concoct blood completely into generative seed. The male alone, by very definition of his maleness, has enough heat to transform blood to its most perfect/complete state: that is, into generative seed (*sperma*). While "analogous" to semen, therefore, female menstrual blood is emphatically *not* semen.[21] It is the combination of these two—female matter and male animation—that results in a fetus. In Aristotle's words, "The chief principles of generation are the male and the female; the male possessing the principle of movement and generation [i.e., sperm], the female as possessing that of matter [i.e., menstrual blood]" (1.2.716a4–7).[22]

Later dubbed epigenesis, Aristotle's theory of generation does not depend on female pleasure and ejaculation in intercourse, but only on the existence of some menstrual blood in the uterus that is to be shaped by an injection of generative, male seed, produced as a result of male pleasure.[23] The shaping of female matter is a process, slowly building constituent parts, rather than the simple collection of fully formed (if yet miniature) seed-body parts from throughout the body as it was for the Hippocratics. Like the Hippocratics, however, Aristotle assigns a crucial role to the *pneuma* necessary for life, but he locates this *pneuma* in the male contribution alone. Aristotle argues that the "hot, white, thick" nature of semen is a result of its carrying the *pneuma* of animation—the movement and the order necessary for life (*Gen. an.* 2.2.735b33–35). The "air," "breath," or "spirit" that is *pneuma* is innate to semen precisely because of its extreme heat; the frothiness a signal of its potency. Bringing animate qualities—that is, *pneuma* and the heat it requires—the male seed orders, or gives rationality (*logos*) to the material blood supplied by the female, shaping and giving purpose to the otherwise inarticulate mass within the female and ordering it so that it becomes a complete fetus. He writes: "[W]hen the semen has entered the uterus it 'sets' the residue produced by the female and imparts to it the same movement with which it is itself endowed" (*Gen. an.* 2.3.737a20–22). It is male semen that injects the "sentient Soul," which initiates the ordering of female matter until it is complete, causing the potentiality of life to be actualized.[24]

In this way, "the male always completes the business of generation"; he perfects the otherwise imperfect, enabling the telos of Nature to be realized (2.4.741b4–7). In the ideal scenario, the masculine seed shapes a child that mirrors itself in both physical and psychological features; a son both looks and behaves like his virtuous father. For Aristotle, such a son was the best material to continue shaping through education so that he would persist in the pursuit of masculinity throughout his life. Children who failed to measure up to this ideal are all, in a sense, "deformed" males—whether female, effeminate, weak, or even monstrous—since they did not reach the true perfection of the human being that is the generic, able-bodied male (4.6.775a5–23). Culpability for such deformities range from a fetus's own movements in the confined uterine space, weak seed from a father (particularly if he was not ideally "masculine" himself), as well as insufficient matter or nourishment from the mother and a faulty womb.[25]

The mother, as in Apollo's verse, supplies nourishment to this developing fetus by means of her residual menstrual blood, which continues to flow into the now closed womb, as she provides room and warmth for growth. In fact, like Apollo, Aristotle uses an agricultural metaphor to describe the mother's provision of nourishment: "Now since the embryo is already an animal *potentially*, though an imperfect one, it must obtain its nourishment from elsewhere; and that is why it makes use of the uterus, i.e., of the mother, just as a plant makes use of the earth, in order to get its nourishment, until such time as it is sufficiently perfected to be a *potentially* locomotive animal" (2.4.740a25–30). Notice Aristotle's continued emphasis of female passivity: the fetus needs nourishment and so "makes use of the uterus, i.e., of the mother" whose naturally cold body retains the extra blood necessary for the fetus's growth. Since Aristotle did not believe the uterus actively drew residual blood into itself, his image here is of a fetus drawing in the naturally pooling blood around it; this is a precursor of the later suckling that will happen at the breast. Aristotle makes his connection between the womb and breasts explicit, writing: "The umbilicus consists of blood-vessels (veins) in a sheath. . .. Through this the embryo gets its nourishment, i.e., blood; the uterus being the terminus of many blood-vessels. . .. Nature lays in a store of the blood-like nourishment [that is, menstrual blood] in this part of the uterus, *as it were into breasts*."[26] Once the fetus reaches its completed, or perfected, form, it emerges, usually sometime between the seventh and ninth month.[27]

According to Aristotle, then, while the uterus/mother is necessary for the fetal body, she has no active role to play in conception, generation, or even childbirth. Life comes from the man—the parent, the begetter—and it is as a result of his ordering semen that the *fetus begins to act*; first to collect food inside the uterus and then to batter its way out when the forming is complete, only to search for a greater supply of nourishment from actual breasts. The operative nature of Aristotle's etiological construction of humanity is clear in this theory—inability versus ability (pre)determines his understanding of conception and generation.

As they did with other areas of medicine, Roman physicians combined aspects of Hippocratic and Aristotelian thought, along with the advances made through anatomical research from the Hellenistic era, to form their own opinions on conception and generation. Focusing again on Soranus and Galen offers a glimpse of the spectrum. Like the Hippocratics, both Soranus and Galen ascribed to a two-seed theory of conception. As a methodist, Soranus focuses on the importance of balance for conception and generation, taking a mechanistic view more in line with the Hippocratics. Soranus theorizes that blood and *pneuma* are brought to the developing fetus, who will resemble both parents due to the convergence of both seeds in its development. Instead of focusing on the male role in this process, Soranus details the regimen required for a pregnant woman to aid what he sees as a mechanical process. A proper regimen, therefore, results in the proper formation of a fetus both physically and psychologically.

In contrast, Galen adheres to Aristotle's teleological view and, although emphasizing a two-seed theory, he offers a version of conception and generation that elevates the male contribution in very Aristotelian ways. Like Aristotle, Galen considers all contributions from the male to be superior to what a female can supply due to the greater innate heat (i.e., *pneuma*) of the male. He also agrees with Aristotle in considering semen to be composed of spirit. Galen writes, "The semen itself is a *pneuma* like foam, so that if it ever is emitted into the outer air, there soon appears to be much less of it than when it was first emitted; . . . the semen is thick, viscous, and full of vital *pneuma*" (*UP* 14.9 [2.315]). While females also produce semen, it is "scantier, colder and wetter" and, as a result, it cannot generate life on its own (14.6 [2.301]). Female semen coats the uterus to allow male semen to adhere (*Sem.* 1.7; 2.4.12–36) and then provides nourishment throughout pregnancy (*UP* 15.4 [2.347]). Thus, while both sets of semen are "*pnuema* and a foam" it is the male semen that provides the governing motion of life, which the female semen then supports. Galen explains, "[N]o woman has ever been observed to conceive either mola [i.e., a tumor] or anything else of the sort without the aid of a man, . . . Hence it is better to suppose that the male semen represents the principle of motion and that the female contributes something toward the generation of the animal" (*UP* 14.7 [2.304]).[28]

A Necessary Sacrifice: Childbirth, Combat, and Blood-letting

In spite of the pronounced differences between one and two-seed theories, they have a number of striking similarities that came to operate as dominant assumptions concerning conception, generation, childbirth, and even nursing in the ancient Greco-Roman world. Indeed, the similarities between epigenesis and pangenesis enabled later Roman physicians to combine and alternately highlight Aristotelian and Hippocratic elements when it suited their arguments and constructions. Of the similarities, the persistent presupposition of male/masculine superiority noted above and discussed in detail in Chapter 2 is perhaps the most apparent. As Yurie Hong notes, this assumption often results in a competitive and even combative stance between male/masculine and female/feminine elements involved in the creation of a child. Focusing on the Hippocratic corpus, Hong uncovers a particularly antagonistic relationship posited between mother and fetus in *On Generation* and *On the Nature of the Child*. She argues,

> [T]he narrative of conflict implied in the competition of maternal and paternal seed shifts and broadens then to describe the relationship between not only mother and child, but implicitly mother and unborn son. The inseminating penis ("the father") and the product of insemination, that is, the fetus ("son"), are aligned against the maternal body.[29]

With their focus on the fetus, these writings relegate the maternal body to at least a secondary, and potentially an oppositional, status; one that is necessary, but almost unfortunately so, for reproduction.[30] While Hong focuses her attention on Hippocratic embryologies, her observation extends into Aristotelian fields. Like the Hippocratics, Aristotle repeatedly underscores the uselessness, and even potential danger, of menstrual blood without the generative shaping supplied by male seed. Even though neither Aristotle nor Galen picture a battle in the same way the Hippocratics do—with feminine and masculine seeds supplied by both partners lined up in various conflicts for dominance—they do reinforce the need for male/masculine control to give purpose to the female/feminine mass. For Aristotle and Galen, it is only when the female contribution is ordered by what is inherently masculine that it can have meaning. Once again the penis (and the fetus) temper the female, this time by providing the life-generating *pneuma* she innately lacks.

Combined with male seed, then, these embryological theories outline specific purposes for menstrual blood. When a woman is pregnant, menstrual blood is no longer excessive and necessitating evacuation; nor is it extra residue demonstrating her failure of heat. Rather, it is the material building blocks from which the child is formed as well as part of the nourishment consumed by the growing fetus inside her. The consistent identity of menstrual blood as fetal nourishment again reflects the understanding that blood was the "main intermediate stage in the transformation of food to flesh" discussed in Chapter 2.[31] Confined in the mother's womb, the newly conceived fetus consumes the extra blood within the female body through the umbilicus, whether actively drawn or passively flowing to the uterus. Again, *pneuma* is mentioned alongside blood as a nourishing element, required for the life and growth of the fetus.

> [T]he fetus in the belly continually sucks with its lips from the uterus of the mother and draws nourishment (*trophēn*) and breath (*pneuma*) to its heart inside, . . . If anyone asks you how you know that the fetus draws and suck in the uterus, you may reply as follows. Both humans and animals have faeces in their intestines at the time of birth, and immediately at birth pass stools. . . .. Nor would a baby know how to suck from the breast immediately at birth, if it did not also suck in the uterus. (*Carn.* 6.594)

Echoing this Hippocratic perspective, Soranus describes a "sanguineous as well as a pneumatic substance" that is "conveyed to the embryo for its nourishment" (*Gyn.* 1.17.57). Likewise, in his *On the Usefulness of Parts* Galen describes the fetus consuming a woman's extra blood as "nutriment" along with *pneuma* during pregnancy (14.8 [2.300]; 15.4 [2.347]). Evidence for this process was the cessation of menstruation during pregnancy; since the fetus consumed the menstrual blood, there was no need for it to exit the body. Moreover, a healthy pregnancy prevented such an exit by closing the "mouth" of the womb until childbirth.[32] Only a faulty womb let this nourishment escape by "gaping open," as mentioned above.

While the womb provided for such needs early on, eventually the fetus is limited by a woman's uterus and by an insufficient supply of menstrual blood for nourishment.[33] Childbirth, then, is prompted by the child, who must now break free from the maternal body. As Hong notes, the combative stance between mother and unborn child persists even through childbirth, when the child violently forces its way from the womb.

> [Birth] comes about when the infant tears some of the internal membranes with its hands and feet by moving and thrashing about. And when one is torn, the power of the remaining ones is weakened. And when the membranes are torn, the fetus is freed from its bond and goes out in a rush; for no longer is there any strength once the membranes fail and have been carried away, nor does the womb have the power to restrain the child. (Hippocrates, *Nat. puer.* 19.532)[34]

Even the arguably more maternally disposed *Diseases of Women* emphasizes the active role of the child over the passive mother, explaining: "the uterus becomes more open since the child is advancing through it and causing violence and pain [to the mother]."[35] Thus, Nancy Demand concludes that even though ancient medical authors acknowledge the existence of contractions, they retained an assumption of female passivity, so that "the pain and contractions of the woman are responses to the violent efforts of the infant" rather than the active, muscle-response of a woman's uterus that works with the infant in birth.[36] Indeed, so saturated with female passivity was the Roman world that Galen fails to note muscles in the female body in his anatomical discussions. Rather than an organ wrapped in muscle as male organs are, the uterus is supported by "sinewy" ligaments that link it to the abdomen (*UP* 14.3 [2.287–88]). Reviewing Galen's various discussions of female genitalia, Rebecca Flemming concludes: "the female genitalia and womb are left apparently muscleless." They may have "attachments, suspensions, interweavings, entwinements, and fusions . . . but few have any pretentions to muscularity."[37] Figured as a confining "cup" with membranes for bonds, the uterus and the maternal body as a whole, must be overcome by an infant for successful birth—even as the mother, herself, must survive the onslaught of her own child's "thrashings."

Given this context, Medea's famous comparison of childbirth and battle in Euripides's tragedy named for her becomes stark indeed. In her tirade on the unfortunate state of women, who suffer because "the outcome of our life's striving hangs on whether we take a bad or a good husband," she concludes:

> Men say that we live a life free from danger at home while *they* fight with the spear. How wrong they are! I would rather stand three times with a shield in battle than give birth once.[38]

This war-like description of childbirth also resonates with the following funerary inscription from the second century CE written from the perspective of the buried: "The unstoppable Fury of the newborn infant took me, bitter, from my happy life with a fatal hemorrhage. I did not bring the child into the light by my labor pains, but it lies hidden in its mother's womb among the dead."[39] These two examples stretch from Classical Greece to Imperial Rome, but reveal a consistent fear and peril associated with childbirth.

If she and her child did survive parturition—and many, of course, did not—a woman's uterine mouth was effectively reopened by her battering child. The new mother would then experience two outlets for any menstrual blood left unused by the fetus: (1) lochial bleeding and (2) lactation.[40] The lochial flow was considered evidence of the widening of a woman's passages as a result of childbirth, purging her body from below of all residual excess moisture, and pointing toward her healthier future as a fully realized *gynē*. Indeed, attention to the amount and consistency of lochial flows is similar to discussions of regular menstrual discharges; variations from expected norms were indicative of illness. Like her menstrual flows, a woman's lochial flux pointed to her own health as well as the health of the population, since it was on her ability to produce offspring that societies depended, in spite of their obsessions with masculinity.

With this fact in mind, it is perhaps less surprising that a woman's flows were described in the same terms as blood from sacrificial victims in Classical Greek literature: both the *hiereion* destined for human consumption and the *neosphakton* whose throat was freshly cut.[41] Menstrual blood, abnormal fluxes, and sanguinous fluids of childbirth are noted for non-coagulating and, therefore, *neosphakton*-like qualities.[42] With a particularly vivid simile, the *Nature of the Child* explains that when the "blood in a woman is stirred up" during parturition the child "passes out, and with the fetus a thick, sanguineous fluid, which becomes a path for it like water on a table" (7.502). Postpartum lochial flows, however, were compared to the blood of a *hiereion*. Like a healthy *hiereion*, a woman's flux was most auspicious when it was heavy and quickly coagulating in regular menstruation and in her post-birth "cleansing." Thus, following the vivid image above, our author continues describes the amount, duration, and quality of the lochia. He concludes: "The blood flows like that of a sacrificial animal (*hiereiou*), if the woman is healthy and going to stay healthy, and it congeals quickly; if not, the cleaning occurs in a smaller amount, has a more troubled consistency, and does not congeal quickly" (7.502). In a manner surprisingly similar to the legal codes of Leviticus and rabbinic literature, this cathartic period was longer in the case of a daughter's birth than a son's: requiring forty-two days as opposed to only thirty due to a daughter's later "congealing" inside her mother's womb (*Nat. puer.* 7.504–6). Leviticus 12 requires thirty-three days for a son and sixty-six for a daughter, while rabbinic texts on female fluxes establish periods of forty and eighty days respectively. These rabbinic texts also explicitly tie the lengths of cathartic purification to the days required for "forming" either a male or female fetus in the womb.[43] As an imperfect child, the female's birth is not only more troublesome, but also leaves behind more residue that must be purged from the mother's body due to her later and incomplete formation.

Helen King notes additional vocabulary that reinforces this connection between the blood of sacrificial victims and of women, particularly around the collection of their blood.[44] The *amnion* (lamb) sacrificed for the gods is also a term used to describe the cup that collected the blood that flowed from the victim.[45] This is also the term that is consistently used to describe the placenta as a cup or sac that collected blood for a growing fetus inside a woman's womb, sometimes spelled *amneios*.[46] Such associations linger in modern medical language of "amniotic fluid," which surrounds and cushions the fetus. In this way, a woman's body is the locus of regular bleeding and blood collection for the sake of mankind's well-being. Her blood flows heavily and regularly, like that of a sacrificial victim, with monthly purges, in her defloration, in her supply of nourishment for a growing fetus, as well as with her lochial cleansings after birth.[47] Flemming's summary of Galen's interpretation of the role of women here becomes particularly apt: Child-bearing "is the main explanation of why woman is, and is as she is, it being for the best in the sense that humanity thus comes as close to immortality as possible; a sacrifice was required and woman is it, continues to live and make it."[48] She is the *amnion* (lamb) par excellence.

Summary

Reviewing the wealth of literature on conception, generation, and childbirth demonstrates the sustained attention such topics received as part of the preoccupation with the female and her reproductive body in the ancient world. Explaining her difference from the male norm, Aristotle and Galen justify Nature's creation of the female in spite of her deficiency on the basis of her necessity for reproduction—man's access point for immortality. Again reinforced in all these texts is an assumption of male superiority, even to the extreme that the mother is little more than the container and conveyer of male seed, the masculine generative and ordering force, whether through umbilicus or breast. Even in the Hippocratic models the feminine is set in battle against the masculine, in spite of the fact that a woman is believed to contribute some of these "masculine" traits. As a woman, she is still the physical manifestation of a disappointment: weaker (feminine) seed overwhelmed the stronger (masculine) seed so that she was born a daughter and not a son. The masculine seed within her is given another chance, however, in her own pregnancy to drown out the feminine seeds and finally reach the ideal state in a son. Overall, these models place paternal and fetal elements in competition, if not outright combat, with the maternal as the masculine forces strive against the chaotic feminine to form rightly ordered life. In such a world, it seems Apollo's comment rings true: the mother is no parent—or, at least, she is not an active or wanted one.

To accept this bleak portrait, however, is to forget the anxieties and realities such an insistence on male superiority reveals: paternal fragility. Regardless of their emphasis on male and masculine components to reproduction, these authors *cannot* remove the female and feminine from the equation for conception, gestation, bearing, or nursing. They cannot live out Jason's dream outlined in Euripides's *Medea*: "Mortals ought to beget children from some other source, and there should be no female species. Then mankind would have no evil" (573–75). Instead, all these authors must assert a crucial—if unfortunate, but also powerful—role for women, one that leads more often to questions concerning the male role in reproduction since the female role *is* so apparent. Connected by the umbilicus and then by the breast, no additional explanation or physical ritual was needed to clarify the bond between mother and child as it was in the case of fathers.[49] Indeed, rather than downplaying the maternal connection, the next chapter will highlight how physicians and moralists often reinforce it by idealizing maternal breastfeeding in the midst of a seemingly resistant culture. The bond between mothers and children, especially sons, was expected to persist throughout life—their bond being the foundation for familial and political harmony. Mothers often remained a significant force and support for their children; chief advocates during life and first among mourners at death. In spite of Apollo's description of mothers as "strangers," then, mothers were intimate and powerful influences in their children's lives. Such access was especially significant when their husbands and sons were powerful public figures—generals, leaders, and even emperors—giving the seemingly private mother access to the public sphere. As an expected obligation of womanhood, motherhood was one avenue toward legitimacy and increased agency in Mediterranean antiquity; and it was one path that *both* women and men chose to pursue in the Roman world.[50]

Turning now to NT narratives of conception and birth, the context provided by these theories proves significant. Although the NT writings show no direct dependence on the literature outlined above, they do demonstrate general awareness of aspects of the theories articulated in them, especially with regard to the roles of blood, the *pneuma* ("spirit"), and the father's provision of *logos* (order) through his semen in Aristotelian understandings. In contrast to this general awareness from their ancient Mediterranean context, the Gospels demonstrate explicit engagement with stories of conceptions and births from Israel's Scriptures, especially the author of Luke. As Gwynn Kessler notes, in biblical contexts God's "primary partner" in procreation is the woman, whom God alternately remembers or whose womb he opens in order to provide progeny.[51] In this way, it is God who is credited with the life created inside the woman, sometimes to the exclusion of her *and* her husband's role in the process. For the audiences of the NT, the biblical background of miraculous births for matriarchs and God's promises of children as evidence of his blessing for Israel mix with Greco-Roman constructions of the origins of life to emphasize both Jesus's unique status and the transformation of those who would follow him.

Conceiving Christ and Community: Mary and Other Mothers in God's Household

The writings of the NT, and their presentations of mothers and motherhood, are saturated in this Greco-Roman context along with that of the Jewish Scriptures. These ideas of conception, generation, and childbirth undergird and reinforce not only their maternal portraits, but the very anthropologies that support the christological and communal constructions of early Jesus followers. Building narratives of Jesus's unique conception, these communities also adopted familial language to characterize their own unique reconceptions as ones having been rebegotten, reshaped, and reborn by the will of the heavenly Father, by means of his Christ, and imbued with his holy Spirit (*pneuma*). Having been reborn in this way, these new families claim a greater allegiance to their new Father, the origin of their more perfect and immortal life, than to any other earthly leader or family member donning the title *pater* or *mater*.

Various NT writings indicate their relationships with the embryological and parturitive theories discussed above. In this second portion of the chapter, I will demonstrate the significance of these theories and the anthropologies they communicate for interpreting maternal characters and metaphors, as well as the children accompanying them. I will focus on Mary, the mother of Jesus, in the Gospels and Acts, before offering a few preliminary comments on some additional maternal presentations. At home in an ancient milieu permeated by one- and two-seed theories, and the resulting emphasis on masculine domination as the ideal, these NT writings subvert the traditional narrative of the maternal telos but not without also adopting and repurposing these assumptions to put forward their own theological agendas. The Gospels and Acts resonate with aspects of embryological theories while continuing to emphasize their Jewish roots that underscore God's role as ultimate Creator who has recreated and is re-creating by means of his Son, Jesus. Combining these elements, these NT writings challenge the status quo of biological families and blood kinship and in so doing pave alternative teloi for "male and female" in Christ (Gal 3:28), but they simultaneously retain order by placing all these identities underneath the supreme rule of the heavenly *Paterfamilias* who is God alone.

Conceiving Christ: Mary and the Spirit in the Gospels and Acts

Mary, although not always explicitly named, appears in all four canonical Gospels (as well as few extra-canonical ones) and the Book of Acts.[52] Despite her consistent appearances, however, her characterization differs greatly in each account. Mark devotes the least amount of attention to her, only mentioning her as a point of contrast alongside Jesus's additional biological siblings to the family whom Jesus says consists of "whoever should do the will of God" (3:35). John offers a bit more space to her by bracketing Jesus's ministry with her ambiguous presence first at the Wedding of Cana in 2:1–11 and then again at his death in 19:25–27. Yet, like Mark, the exchange in John 2 is not without some negative overtones, as Jesus rebuffs his mother before consenting to her request concerning the wine since his "hour" has not come (2:4). At least part of the results of the unnamed mother's appearances in John, therefore, is the subordination of Jesus's allegiance to her far beneath that to his Father—the one whose will Jesus manifests as the incarnate *Logos* (translated as "Word"; John 1:14; 2:1–25; 10:30).

Matthew and Luke take different paths in their own characterizations of Mary. Although both record a version of Mark's story concerning Jesus's real family as those who do God's will (or the will of "my Father who is in heaven" in Matt 12:50), they offer more information on Jesus's biological mother, whom they identify as "Mary" (Matt 1:16; Luke 1:27). Nevertheless, even these stories choose remarkably distinct ways of narrating this same Mary. Matthew depicts her as little more than a vessel inhabited by a child "from the holy Spirit" (*pneumatos hagiou*, 1:18; compare 1:20) who must rely on repeated divine interventions to save her and her child from a number of foes ranging from the "righteous" Joseph to the wicked King Herod (1:19; 2:3, 16). Luke, in contrast, gives Mary the most robust characterization by fashioning an extensive speech for her in the opening chapter of his story, only to silence her and nearly banish her from Jesus's story after his childhood is completed. She only surfaces one more time in Luke's story. As a silent participant in the gathering of believers in Jerusalem in Acts 1, she awaits another visitation of the Spirit. While the holy Spirit may have again granted her a chance to speak prophetically in Acts as it had before in the Gospel, Luke's audience is never explicitly told of such a fact (Acts 1:14).

In all these stories Mary is an intriguing character, sometimes as a direct result of her sparse appearances and stifled words. Mark's version of Mary is recognized as part of his general tendency to distance traditional families and kinship ties. For example, when Jesus travels to Nazareth in Mark 6, he is "unable" to perform "works of power" there as a result of the community's lack of faith. The community focuses on his identity as "the carpenter, the son of Mary and brother of James and Joseph and Simon," and who also has "sisters" in town, and, therefore, cannot decipher his anointing with the "holy Spirit" that marks him as God's Son (Mark 1:9–11; 6:3). Again, it seems, his family and kin fail to act as his *real* family; they fail "to do the will of God" (3:35). Although Stephen Ahearne-Kroll argues that Mark does not require disciples to abandon their families for the sake of Jesus's message, he does conclude that "it looms as the possible consequence of choosing to follow Jesus."[53] Indeed, it is one outcome that Jesus himself seems to suffer as a consequence of his obedience to God's will. While "women" may gather to see him crucified and then to anoint his corpse, his mother is not among them (15:40; 16:1).[54] As he hangs on the cross, he is called a "god's son" by the centurion, all while firmly separated from the woman, brothers, and sisters who surfaced previously (15:39).

The role of Jesus's mother in John, in contrast, is the center of some debate. Scholars generally recognize her as being distanced from Jesus in the Gospel, but disagree on the overall degree of that distancing and her final role in the narrative. She is absent from Jesus's origin story in the Prologue (1:1–18) and is then pushed aside by Jesus in John 2, but she is present at his death in John 19, demonstrating at least some continued relationship to her son that Mark lacks. As a limited and unnamed character in these stories of Jesus, the mother is often given symbolic roles as a catalyst for Jesus or even the beginnings of the Church.[55]

Luke and Matthew again provide additional possibilities for Mary, each with an easily discernable birth narrative for Jesus that at least mentions Mary as an important participant. Yet, Mary's vastly different roles in each, and sudden disappearances afterward, lead to different interpretive possibilities again. Does Mary's character matter to Matthew—or is she simply another, possibly righteous, woman caught up in events leading to sexual deviance but nevertheless used by God like the other women in Jesus's genealogy?[56] Beverly Roberts Gaventa suggests that Matthew's repeated use of the phrase "the child and his mother" demonstrates that "the two belong together" so that they represent a singular vulnerability that must be protected by God in order to fulfill scripture (and, therefore, God's plan).[57] Luke is held up, then, as the Gospel that is most concerned with Mary as demonstrated by her narrated activities, such as travelling to see Elizabeth, and her spoken words in Luke 1:39–55. Nevertheless, debates remain over Mary's agency in all this action. Does she choose to follow God's will in an active sense, or does she submit, thereby passively repeating the womanly ideals of her era?[58] Even in Luke's Gospel, the most explicit and complete in her characterization, Mary's role is not without complicating factors.

Mary, Jesus, and Ancient Embryologies

In spite of the significant work on Mary's character and her relationship with Jesus, very few interpreters delve into the possible significance of ancient understandings of conception, generation, and childbirth for interpreting either Mary or her child, Jesus. Adele Reinhartz and Turid Karlsen Seim represent two exceptions to this general trend, both having investigated John's Prologue in light of Aristotle's epigenetic theory.[59] For Reinhartz and Seim, the epigenetic language of the Fourth Gospel reinforces Jesus's unique sonship and relationship with God as his

Father in ways that explain the later distancing of his human mother. As a result of their thought-provoking work, additional studies on John's use of procreative language in the context of ancient embryological theories have emerged from Gitte Buch-Hansen, Clare Rothschild, and, most recently, Annette Weissenrieder.[60] I will return to these studies in more detail below, but am suggesting now that they demonstrate the interpretive possibilities that paying attention to ancient medical and philosophical anthropological constructions can create when reading NT texts.

In particular, reading in light of these theories exposes a relationship between Jesus, Mary, and the "spirit" (*pneuma*) in ways that resonate with the Greco-Roman medical literature explored above. Outside of the birth narratives in Matthew and Luke, Jesus's anointing with "the Spirit" (*to pneuma*, Mark 1:10; John 1:32–34), the "Spirit of God" (*pneuma tou theou*, Matt 3:16), or "the holy Spirit" (*to pneuma to hagion*, Luke 3:22) is noted in each canonical account, always in association with his baptism by John the Baptist. Significantly, each of these scenes ends with an exclamation of Jesus's divine sonship or election, either confessed by a heavenly voice or by John the Baptist himself.[61] If part of the background to the confession of the heavenly voice in the Synoptics is rightly tied to Ps 2:7, then this moment is at least implicitly associated with Jesus's conception. After the Spirit descends on Jesus, the voice explains, "You are my Son, the beloved, with you I am well pleased" (Mark 1:11; compare Matt 3:17; Luke 3:22). The opening line of this phrase is similar to Ps 2:7, which describes God's election of the king in terms of begetting: "You are my son, today I have begotten (*gegennēka*) you" (LXX). The confession in the Synoptics also contains similarities to a description of Isaac as Abraham's "beloved son" in Gen 22:2 and God's election of Jacob/Israel in Isa 42:1. In Isaiah 42, Jacob/Israel is called God's "servant" or "child" (*pais*), and is given God's "Spirit" (*pneuma*) as a sign of his ability to administrate God's justice (*krisis*). Later in his Gospel, Matthew quotes Isa 42:1–4 as an explanation of Jesus's identity and mission (Matt 12:17–21; see also 17:5). Regardless of ability to align the baptismal scenes with these exact OT contexts, however, the message of the Spirit's descent remains clear: it is God's *pnuema* that animates Jesus. Moreover, since this *pneuma* originates directly from God, rather than from an earthly father or mother, it marks Jesus as God's Son who will enact his will on earth either in the spreading of God's kingdom or giving eternal life.

Although Mark is satisfied with the identification of Jesus as God's Son that comes at his baptism, Matthew and Luke extend this association in their narrations of his conception. Clarifying any possibility that Jesus's forming could be the result of other, potentially illegitimate spirits, both Matthew and Luke explain that a "holy Spirit" is involved with Mary's pregnancy. In Matthew, the audience is not given any detail on when or how this happened. Rather, the narrator describes Mary's pregnancy after the fact, explaining that she "was found with child from a holy Spirit" (1:18). Luke, however, emphasizes Mary's virginal status in the entire affair, having Gabriel inform the *parthenos* who has "not known a man" that her pregnancy will happen in the future: "A holy Spirit will come upon you and a power of the Most High will overshadow you" (1:35). The holy Spirit's role differs in the Gospel of John, where its appearances are focused in the promise of rebirth (or birth "from above") for Jesus's followers rather than involved in Jesus's own conception (John 3:1–21; 20:22). And although Mark does not describe any direct connection between Jesus's mother and the "holy Spirit," her singular scene in the Gospel does appear immediately following a debate centering on which "spirit" inhabits Jesus (Mark 3:20–35).

Recalling the significance of the "spirit," or *pneuma*, in the generative theories above, the concern over which spirit inhabits and enlivens Jesus and his followers in the Gospels makes sense. All the generative theories give place to *pneuma* in providing the animation and some nourishment to a developing fetus. For Aristotle, the *pneuma* is a part of the unique contribution from male semen that initiates life in the matter provided by the woman (*Gen. an.* 2.2.735b33–35). Galen mixes Aristotelian ideas with his two-seed theory that allows for *pneuma* to be provided by both the male and female, though the male's provision is of greater heat and, therefore, potency, thus supplying the necessary "motion" for life.

Although not uniform, aspects of these theories resonate with presentations of conception and generation from the OT and additional Jewish sources. In contrast to the Greco-Roman theorists, OT writings do not regularly outline detailed generative theories, but rather emphasize God's role as the one who "knits" and forms the fetus within a woman (Job 1:20–21; Psalm 139:13–16). Kessler, therefore, rightly emphasizes that scholars should not force rabbinic texts to conform to the Greco-Roman debates over one or two-seeds in conception and generation. Instead, she argues that procreation is always God's work. "Stated differently," she explains, "the dominant theory of procreation evident from biblical [that is, "Old Testament"] sources could be called a 'no seed' theory of coming into being" since the creation of the embryo is God's work alone in the same way that the creation of the cosmos is God's work alone. It is with this embryo that women "become pregnant and give birth."[62]

Yet, Kessler also notes that later Second Temple Jewish sources *do* convey familiarity with Aristotelian ideas by describing the male's "virile" and causative seed, which shapes the nourishing female blood.[63] Moreover, when *b. Nid.* 31a does mention "semen" or "parts," it retains the emphasis on God's provision of the life-giving *pneuma*.

> There are three partners in [making a] man, the Holy One Blessed be he, his father, and his mother. The father supplies the semen of white substance out of which are formed the child's bones, sinews, nails, the brain

> in his head and the white in his eye; his mother supplies the semen of red substance out of which is formed his skin, flesh [i.e., muscle and organs], hair, blood and the black of his eye; *and the Holy One, blessed be He, gives him the spirit and the breath*, beauty of features, eyesight, the power of hearing and the ability to speak and to walk, understanding and discernment. When his time to depart from the world approaches the Holy One, blessed be He, takes away his share and leaves the shares of his father and his mother with them. (emphasis added)

Ecclesiastes likewise associates the activities of the spirit with the formation of a fetus, suggesting that the "path of the spirit" (*hodos tou pneumatos*) is just as mysterious as the ways in which bones are formed in a pregnant woman (11:5 LXX). While unfathomable, Ecclesiastes asserts that it is God "who makes all things," thus firmly establishing God's life-giving role in giving the spirit and causing fetal growth. Like their Greek and Roman counterparts, therefore, biblical texts in both the Old and New Testaments, as well as later Jewish interpreters, also locate life and animation in the bestowal of "spirit" even if their precise appeal to generative theories varies.[64] Where these texts differ from the larger Greco-Roman writings is in the identification of the source of this animation—God alone rather than the male human—although some Greek and Roman authors also imply a supernatural element.[65]

Jesus's conception and birth as a living, and therefore *animated* child, thus necessitates his inhalation and inspiration of some sort of *pneuma*. While biblical and other Jewish authors ultimately credit God as the supplier of all *pneuma* in living beings, the emphasis in Matthew and Luke on Mary's conception by means of a "holy Spirit" indicates some awareness of other possible contributions of spirits in generative theories. As we saw in the generative theories outlined above, the type of *pneuma* supplied impacted the type of child formed. By claiming Jesus's conception by means of a "holy Spirit," both Matthew and Luke both mitigate the potential for scandal surrounding Mary's unconventional pregnancy. Confronted by an "angel of the Lord" in a dream, Joseph is prevented from divorcing Mary in Matthew's Gospel (1:20–25), and he never even utters a syllable of protest in Luke's. Although Joseph remains paired with Mary, he does not have a close association with Jesus in either account. Instead, it is the pairing of Jesus and "his mother" that recurs, even when Joseph shuttles the duo to safety in Matthew's story (2:13–23).[66] As a result, Mary's connection to God through her holy impregnation is further reinforced. Already the Gospel audiences know that God is Jesus's true Father, who has provided the specific, holy *pnuema* responsible for his life. In this way, Jesus's exceptional conception explains his close connection to God, which results in his controversial and yet superior teaching and his unprecedented miracles (e.g., Matt 9:33–35; 12:6, 41–42; Luke 2:46–47; 4:16–30).

For Matthew and Luke, this connection even explains Jesus's death and resurrection. Shaped and animated by God's *pneuma*, Jesus alone knows how to fulfill God's will, even though that fulfillment takes him to a cross (Luke 24:44–46).

Turning to look at Luke's narrative more closely, we find that the Gospel is more interested in mothers at the outset of its version of events than is Matthew. Including the story of Elizabeth alongside that of Mary, Luke traces not only Jesus's conception to a divine *pneuma*, but credits God's *pneuma* for the conception and birth of John the Baptist as well. Luke's greater attention to mothers exposes more engagement with ancient physiological and generative theories, although not enough to identify clearly *which* theory Luke prefers. Instead, like other biblical and Jewish authors noted above, Luke's emphasis throughout is on God's ability to create life in spite of all obstacles. Imitating the stories of the barren matriarchs from Israel's past in the lives of Elizabeth and Mary, Luke demonstrates God's life-giving prerogative, as well as his special provision for Israel. As Gabriel tells Mary, "nothing is impossible for God" (1:37; compare Gen 18:14).

In this way, Luke's account of Elizabeth's and Mary's pregnancies conforms to what Kessler observes as "the dominant theory of procreation in the Hebrew Bible": namely, "that God grants pregnancy, or, in biblical parlance, God opens, or closes, women's wombs."[67] In the case of Elizabeth's pregnancy this reading certainly rings true when she says that the "Lord has done thusly" for her by "looking in order to remove" her disgrace (1:25). Her neighbors also credit the Lord's role after Elizabeth gives birth to John in Luke 2:58. Thus, even though Elizabeth (and Zechariah) suffered disgrace due to her inability to conceive, the Lord shows mercy in finally granting pregnancy. Moreover, for Luke, this delayed conception is part of God's larger, providential plan to usher Jesus into the world. Where Luke's retelling of Elizabeth's pregnancy—and later Mary's—differs from the biblical norm, however, is in the specific emphasis on God's "holy Spirit" in both processes. Again, the role of the Spirit (*pneuma*) in these pregnancies encourages at least the possibility of hearing them in light of the general embryological theories outlined above even if the Gospel does not indicate a specific generative theory.

Read in the context of contemporaneous generative theories, Luke's conception narratives are given additional depth. Elizabeth, the one designated as "barren" or "sterile" (1:7), seems unable to contribute her assigned portion to the process of conception and generation—whether that be seed or nourishment in the form of menstrual blood. The description of Zechariah alongside Elizabeth as "being advanced in their days" (1:7) could also imply that he, too, was now beyond the ability to provide seed for new life (1:18). Thus, while John is the son of Elizabeth and Zechariah, begotten from their sexual union (1:13, 23–24), he is also quite clearly formed from surplus divine involvement. Indeed, Luke describes God's involvement in his conception and forming in 1:15 when Gabriel reports to Zechariah that John will be "filled with a holy

Spirit even in his mother's womb." Not only does this Spirit cause John's creation, but it indicates his future greatness as a prophet; John has been animated and inspired by God's holy Spirit that alone caused his existence in his mother's womb.

John's spiritual filling in utero is demonstrated in the exchange between the pregnant Elizabeth and Mary in Luke 1:39–55. Filled in her womb with the Spirit-formed John, Elizabeth, too, is "filled with a holy Spirit" when she gives a "loud shout" and proclaims both the greatness of Mary's child and her own blessed status (1:41–45). One wonders if in the background of Luke's scene is the anatomical and physiological constructions of the female body described in Chapter 2 of this study.[68] Linked from mouth/nostrils through to her uterus and vagina, Elizabeth's body contains a pathway (*hodos*) for blood as well as for this holy Spirit to travel. Bubbling up from her womb, then, the divine Spirit pours out from her mouth to utter prophetic words to her relative, Mary.[69]

Like Elizabeth, Mary's conception of Jesus is dependent on a holy Spirit's involvement. Yet, Mary's pregnancy reverses the emphasis of Elizabeth's. While Elizabeth's conception and generation explicitly requires God to provide the female contributions and, perhaps, implicitly the male as well, Mary's pregnancy explicitly requires male contributions. It could also require female, but only if the audience understood her prenuptial state as being a result of her being premenarche. Unlike Elizabeth's pregnancy, there is *no possibility* of male semen within Mary's womb. Instead, in language that reminds readers of other divine births of Greco-Roman fame, she will be "overshadowed" by a "power of the Most High" (1:35). Charles Talbert cites Plutarch, who argues that miraculous children, such as Plato and Numa, can be conceived without male semen. They are formed instead by "another power of God" and "a spirit of a god" without need for intercourse *and* resulting in "more divine offspring" (*Mor.* 9.114–19; *Numa* 4.3).[70] God's provision of the assumed superior and more critical male semen along with a holy Spirit, therefore, results in a more miraculous conception as well as a more divine child. As Gaventa writes:

> The pregnancy of Elizabeth is at least improbable, . . . or even "impossible," just as are the pregnancies of Sarah and Rachel and Hannah. A reader with even the vaguest notions of Israel's history would recognize . . . this familiar theme. [But] Mary, who is neither old nor barren nor well known for her goodness, will bear a child. If the other conceptions are to be thought of as something like miracles of healing, this one is virtually a miracle of creation.[71]

It is no wonder that, again, it is during pregnancy that Mary utters her prophetic proclamation in Luke 1:46–55, which serves as the only lengthy speech she gives in all of Luke-Acts. Again, the Spirit seems to well up within her from her womb to inspire a comprehending speech. This suggestion contrasts with the emphasis of N. Clayton Croy and Alice E. Connor that it is Mary's virginity that enables her to act as a prophet.[72] Certainly Mary is presented as a virgin, here, but Elizabeth is emphatically not—yet both women prophesy. As Dale Martin and others note, ancients regularly connected sex and prophecy in Greco-Roman texts that describe the inspiration of female prophetesses by male deities.[73] Martin's observations resonate with my own and are explained by ancient anatomical and physiological constructions of female bodies. Acting as a conduit for either male semen as a woman/wife, or for divine spirit as a prophetess, women well up with inspiration to communicate on behalf of the masculine: providing either a child or a prophetic word. Thus, it is not surprising that both virginal and elderly women were presented as prophets in literature from Second Temple Judaism and Greco-Roman contexts, literature that Croy and Connor survey.[74] Indeed, Luke appears cognizant of this tradition by employing Elizabeth and later, Anna, as prophets instead of solely employing virgins for this activity (cf. Acts 16:16; 21:9). Whether virginal or elderly (i.e., past menopause), both types of women have open wombs to be filled by a divine Spirit rather than being occupied with procreative responsibilities for their husbands. Filled with a holy Spirit, these women speak forth spirited speech to all who will listen. Instead of being bothered by any sexual overtones of Mary's (and Elizabeth's) inspiration, it seems that Luke is at home in such a world and uses these assumptions in order to emphasize both John and Jesus's divine connections.[75]

Lending further support to this reading is the change that occurs in Mary's character after Jesus's birth. Rather than prophetic speech, after Jesus's birth she is largely silent and conveys increasing misunderstanding and confusion during his childhood as she "ponders" and "keeps all things" in her heart (1:29; 2:19, 51). With Jesus's birth, it seems, the divine Spirit has left her; she has completed her gestational work. In fact, Mary seems to take on more of the traits of other characters in Luke's Gospel the farther away from her pregnancy she is mentioned, although she remains favorably disposed to Jesus in Luke 2. Thus, while Mary's contemplation of Jesus's behavior "in her heart" is often cited by scholars as further indicating her special status, it is actually quite similar to other Lukan characters who repeatedly consider Jesus's actions in their own hearts.[76] As the seemingly preferred seat of emotion and thought for Luke (6:45; 12:34; 16:15), Mary's heart, like those of other characters, is a prime location for wrestling with the identity of Jesus and his often unusual actions (5:22; 9:47; 24:25, 32, 38).

Like other characters, then, the emphasis for Mary's positive characterization—if it indeed can be considered wholly positive—is dependent on her obedience. A certain ambiguity of her character is introduced not only by her confusion after Jesus's birth in Luke 2, but again in Luke 8:19–21 and 11:27–28. Chapter 8 contains

Luke's version of Mark 3:20–35.[77] Rather than the clearly negative characterization of Jesus's family in Mark 3, where they came "to restrain him" because "they were saying, 'He is out of his mind'" (v. 21), in Luke Jesus's family arrives without a motivation (Luke 8:19). Without the negativity of Mark, Jesus's "mother and brothers" are simply set in contrast with the new "mother and brothers" of Jesus who "hear and do the word of God" (Luke 8:18).

When Mary surfaces again in Luke 11:27 the reference is oblique, found in the comments of a "certain woman from the crowd" who seems to fulfill Elizabeth's prophecy from 1:41–45 by saying, "Blessed is the womb that bore you and breasts at which you nursed!" Jesus responds with words that echo his comments from Luke 8:18 when he says, "Blessed instead are those who heard the word of God (*ton logon tou theou*) and obey." In other words, for Luke, Mary is indeed blessed, but not because she fulfilled her obligation as a woman to become a mother. Instead, she is rightly called blessed because of her willingness to hear and obey the "word" (*logos*) spoken to her—and thus implanted within her—as a part of God's plan rather than the cultural narrative of a maternal telos for all women.[78] Entering in her *hodos* by means of Mary's ears, this Spirited word impregnates her and forms the perfect son whom she then bears and nurses. Nevertheless, Mary's blessedness is not primarily a result of her maternity, it is a result of her obedience to this divine word, regardless of the fact that literal pregnancy results. In the same way, neither should the "certain woman" of Luke 11 look for the fulfillment or justification of her existence in being a mother, even of one as great as Jesus. Rather, the blessed designation passes to all who demonstrate obedience; regardless of their gendered identity, or biological and ethnic relationships, they all become part of Jesus's family (Acts 10–11).

John's Gospel communicates a similar theme, though it locates spirit (*pneuma*) in a different act of procreation: the second begetting and birthing of Jesus's followers (3:1–9; 20:22). In contrast, Mary's procreative role is left unnarrated, only indicated by her narrative epitaph "the mother of Jesus" that functions in the place of a proper name (2:1; 19:25–27). In this way, the role of Jesus's mother in John is similar to her role in Mark. John's Gospel, however, includes more potentially positive aspects to Jesus's brief scenes with his mother. In John 2:1–12, for example, Jesus and his mother engage in an abrupt conversation at a wedding in Cana. As a result of their interaction, Jesus provides a miraculous provision of (apparently outstanding) wine for the celebration. Later designated as Jesus's "first sign," this transformation of water to wine manifests Jesus's "glory" to his disciples with the result that they "believe" in him (2:11). As a result, Jesus's mother is often credited with acting as the catalyst, and perhaps as the first believer, who initiates his public ministry in John's Gospel.[79] Although she is mentioned again in John 6, the only other time the mother appears in the Gospel is at the close of Jesus's life, alongside other women and the Beloved Disciple as Jesus hangs upon the cross in chapter 19. John, therefore, is the only Gospel to include Jesus's mother explicitly at his crucifixion, thereby allowing her to fulfill the expected mother's role as mourner and allowing Jesus to care both for her and his disciples in his earthly absence.[80]

Yet, even if there are positive aspects of the mother's character in John, these aspects are never left unmitigated by the narrative. While her presence is implied as necessary for Jesus's existence, it is by no means his primary connection or point of loyalty; in John, Jesus's allegiance is to his Father alone. A closer look at the wedding scene and events that follow in John 2 illustrates this point. While Jesus does acquiesce to his mother at the wedding, and in so doing reveals his glory to the disciples, Jesus's exchange with his mother in John 2 is hardly a warm encounter. After Jesus's mother notifies him of the lack of wine at the wedding, he responds with the sharp phrase *ti emoi kai soi, gynē*—a phrase that is roughly rendered, "what is between you and me, woman?" (2:4). He follows this question by explaining, "My hour (*hōra*) has not yet come." What would seem to be "between" them is the fact that she is his mother, but Jesus does not explicitly acknowledge a maternal-filial relationship here. Although interpreters often try to mitigate the abrasiveness of Jesus's words, *ti emoi kai soi* is often used with negative overtones when it appears elsewhere in biblical and extra-biblical works.[81] In the Synoptic accounts, for example, the demons use this phrase when addressing Jesus as he exorcises them from their hosts (Mark 1:24; Matt 8:29; Luke 4:34). The phrase to his mother in John 2 lacks such straightforward vehemence, but nevertheless encouraged even early interpreters of the Gospel to understand it as a form of rebuke.[82] Regardless of his eventual consent to resolve the shortage in wine, Jesus emphasizes that his actions are not the result of having loyalty to his mother. Instead, it is Jesus's enigmatic "hour" that determines when and how he will act.

As the Gospel progresses, the audience learns that this "hour" is nothing less than Jesus's crucifixion; the moment of "glory" where Jesus finally finishes his Father's work (12:20–36; 13:1; 17:1). Indeed, wine and his "hour" surface again in the only other interaction between Jesus and his mother in the Gospel. In John 19:25–27, Jesus's mother gathers with other women and the Beloved Disciple to witness Jesus's death. In this second, and similarly ambiguous exchange with his mother, Jesus persists in calling his mother "woman" (*gynē*) and tells her to "look" at her son. Gaventa notes that this ambiguous command could instruct her to look either at himself or at the Beloved Disciple, in whose care Jesus now places his mother.[83] The narrator informs the Gospel audience that "from this hour" the Beloved Disciple took her into his own home (19:27). The "hour" has now come, and it results in a formal shift of kinship ties for Jesus's mother. She is no longer in her former household, which included other sons of her own (2:12; 7:1–9), but in the household of the Beloved Disciple. Her transition seems to indicate the beginning of a new familial network based on Jesus's word rather than blood ties (see John 1:12–13). After resolving his mother's care, Jesus moves on to the business of completion. He declares his thirst "in order that he might finish (*teleiōthē*) the scripture," and, after receiving a final drink of wine he remarks, "It has been finished (*tetelestai*)" (19:29–30). At this point, he "gave up the Spirit (*to pneuma*)" that had animated him and dies (19:30). This death, however, is not the end of Jesus's existence, but merely one point marking Jesus's return to his *Father* (17:1–26; 20:17).

Reinforcing this interpretation is the contrasting behavior Jesus displays in the scene that immediately follows the wedding narrative in John 2:13–25. In contrast to his reticence to fulfill his mother's request in 2:1–12, Jesus abounds with enthusiasm in 2:13–25 to defend his "Father's house," the temple. Crafting his own whip, he clears the temple of merchants and their wares that were sold to enable the sacrifices of Passover (2:13–16). His zealousness collides with the zeal of the religious leaders, who question the origin of Jesus's authority that might justify his shocking behavior (2:18). When Jesus responds by characterizing his own body as the "temple" (*naon*)—the residence of God's glory—the leaders are left confused and the ground is laid for further conflicts that will center on Jesus's unique relationship with the God whom he identifies as his own Father (5:16–47; 8:12–59).

At the very least, then, Jesus distances himself from his biological mother in John 2 and elsewhere in the Gospel. He calls her "woman," responds to her with a sharp phrase, and instructs her that his primary loyalty is to his "hour"—a word the Gospel continually associates with his crucifixion (7:30; 8:20; 12:23, 27; 13:1; 17:1). Thus, it is fitting that Jesus's mother disappears from the remainder of his ministry, which is all done in service to the Father and the coming hour of his crucifixion and return to the Father. She appears for the final time to discover the appointed use of wine at Jesus's "hour" of death. In this scene, too, her maternal relationship to Jesus is downplayed. In fact, it is reassigned to another household made up not of those connected through blood, but by obedience to Jesus. Again calling his mother "woman," Jesus places her on the same plain as other female characters whom he addresses in John (4:21; 19:26; 20:13, 15); she has no special status by virtue of her motherhood alone, but must also become a child of God by means of Jesus's completion of the Father's will (1:12–13).[84]

Reinhartz and Seim likewise note the distancing of Jesus's biological mother in John by her marked *absence* from the Prologue, where the incarnation of God's *Logos* (translated as "Word") is narrated with special emphasis on his relationship to God, the Father (1:14–18).[85] Noting resonances between the Prologue's language and Aristotle's generative theory in particular, both Reinhartz and Seim suggest that the Gospel of John pictures the incarnation of God's *Logos*—his generative and ordering power—without explicit need for a physical mother. Rather, God's *Logos* "becomes flesh" as the man, Jesus. As a result, Jesus is the perfect offspring of the God-Father, who is himself the ultimate masculine being. In Jesus's flesh, the glory of this Father dwells (1:14–16). It is for this reason that he can be called a *monogenēs*, a unique and only-child, who perfectly reflects his Father's being as though from a father alone (1:16; see also 3:16–18).[86] Thus, as Colleen Conway has recently concluded, "Jesus and God are not simply metaphorically related as father and son" in John's Gospel. "Instead, their relationship is the result of *ideal masculine generation*."[87] In other words, for John, the *Logos* becomes flesh in Jesus who is "necessarily" God's ideal, ontological Son.[88] Jesus may, incidentally, have a mother, but she is supremely secondary to his Father. Indeed, like all others who encounter Jesus, she too must accept him as God's *Logos* made flesh so that she can become a child of God rather than primarily his mother (1:12–13; 19:25–27).

The Prologue's story of incarnation, therefore, sets the pattern of being "begotten" as a child of God as promised in 1:12–13.[89] In contrast to their initial, physical begetting and birth, these verses promise that the children of God are begotten "not by the bloods or by the will of the flesh or by the will of a man/husband," but rather by God alone (1:13). In language that is strikingly similar to Aristotelian and later Galenic understandings of semen as concocted blood, this verse integrates ancient generative theories to contrast them with God's plan of rebirth for believers. Unlike their first begetting, where these "children" were conceived by a mixture of bloods and then formed by the will, and perhaps *logos*, of a man, they will now experience a second and superior begetting by God, whose *Logos* is reported to "become flesh" in the very next verse (1:14). Effecting God's re-creative will, Jesus encapsulates God's glory, receives his *pneuma* (1:29–34), and makes possible the new birth of those that recognize him as the incarnate *Logos* (3:1–21). In this way, the entire story of John's Gospel is a birth narrative, but not one about Jesus's birth. Rather, it describes God's re-creation in terms of procreation. Jesus is his inseminating *Logos* who shares words and life to all who receive him, and it is by means of his flowing blood, water, and spirit that they are born again (7:38; 19:34; 20:22). While perhaps a graphic image for contemporary readers, the conception and birth analogy resonates with biblical descriptions of God's prerogative as life-giver in procreation. Just as God created the cosmos by means of his word (*Logos*) in Genesis, so too does he create life for all embryos. In John's Gospel, he "speaks" again with the same life-making word made flesh in Jesus (John 1:1–5). In this act of speaking, God creates the miracle of a second birth.

Summary

Reading through the presentations of Mary and the conception narratives in the Gospels and Acts, therefore, reveals a consistent distancing of Jesus from his mother that is either established at the outset of the narrative (Mark; John), or that develops over the course of the stories (Matthew; Luke-Acts). Such is the case even when various events surrounding Jesus's birth *are* narrated, and Mary is explicitly involved and named in Matthew and Luke. Indeed, this reality reinforces the fact that the Gospels are biographical in nature, focused on the presentation of Jesus rather than other characters. Even when Matthew and Luke provide birth stories, or John provides a Prologue on Jesus's origins, they do so in conformity with other ancient biographies from their milieu, which include the commonplace of origins as an important factor in describing or justifying a subject's greatness.[90] While Mary may (or may not) feature in these events, it is the nature of her conception and the material that she provides to form and birth Jesus that matter—not a developed presentation of her character.

Thus, Matthew and Luke's focus on a holy Spirit's involvement in Jesus's conception is not only "spiritual," but profoundly corporeal since ancients understood the spirit to be crucial to the formation of a child in utero. As a holy Spirit provided by God *him*self, this Spirit is divinely ordained and divinely ordering to create a uniquely holy child. In this way, Matthew and Luke transform Jesus's potentially troubling origins into a point of praise, conforming to epideictic norms in their encomiastic renderings of Jesus's life story. John, too, transforms Jesus's origins, which the Gospel indicates are potentially problematic in various confrontations with crowds and opponents (7:37–52; 8:41–58; 9:29–34).[91] Going a step further than both Matthew and Luke, John includes *no mother* in Jesus's origin story. Instead, he is the result of ideal masculine generation as the embodiment of God's *Logos*—the ordering and life-giving principle not simply from a man's sperm, but from God himself, whose *Logos* generates, orders, and sustains the entire cosmos (1:1–5). As a result, Jesus himself replicates that life-giving order in his controversial ministry: he has life in himself just as God alone does and it is by means of him that God (re)begets those who recognize Jesus as the *Logos* with the result that they are now God's own children, regardless of their literal paternity (1:12–13; 5:26). These newly birthed children now form a new family based on their recognition of Jesus rather than on the bloods of their first birth. As in the Synoptics, it is recognition and belief that manifest themselves in the form of obedience that marks the family, or household, of God. The goal of believers, therefore, is to become children within this household rather than to create, sustain, or remain in their former ones.

Rebirthing the Community: The Mothers in God's Household

With Jesus's mother (and biological family) distanced in the Gospels and Acts, the focus for familial relationships is on those who exist in God's household, made up of members who are obedient to the heavenly *Paterfamilias* above all others. Yet, mothers *do* remain in this household (Mark 3:34–35; Matt 12:49–50; Luke 8:21). Even if distanced, Mary's maternal role is at least acknowledged, if not narrated, in each of these stories. Moreover, Jesus repeatedly responds to the concerns of mothers, restoring a number of biological families through his healings, exorcisms, and resurrections of children (e.g., Mark 5:35–43; 7:24–30; Luke 7:11–17). While perhaps not focused entirely on biological families, then, Jesus is certainly not deaf to them nor to the mothers who birth and nourish them.

Nevertheless, Jesus's need for a mother for his own existence and his concern for existing mothers in his ministry does not necessarily indicate a prioritizing of biological families in his message. Rather, in the face of Jesus's healing ministry, he repeatedly issues statements warning his disciples about their potential to lose biological family ties by responding to his call. Indeed, these stories emphasize the need to follow God's will above all else, regardless of the cost. In Matthew's Sermon on the Mount, for example, Jesus recounts the need to follow "the will of my Father in heaven" in order to enter the kingdom of heaven and compares the heavenly Father's careful provision for the disciples with other parents (7:7–10, 21–23). Emphasizing God's paternal superiority, Jesus explains, "If you then, who are evil, know how to give good gifts to your children, how much more will your Father in heaven give good things to those who ask him!" (7:11, NRSV). In each of the Synoptic accounts, Jesus issues antifamilial sayings that describe his division of biological bonds (Matt 10:16–39; Luke 12:51–53; Mark 13:9–13); he issues warnings to pregnant and nursing women in his apocalyptic discourses (Mark 13:7; Matt 24:19; Luke 21:23); and reports that those who are resurrected will "neither marry nor are given in marriage." Because they "cannot die anymore" they have no need for marriages, which lead to procreation; instead, "they are like angels and are *sons of God, being sons of the resurrection*" (Luke 20:34–36; compare Mark 12:18–27; Matt 22:23–33). In each of these passages, blood-kinship and normal households are not grounds for blessing, but rather are potential obstacles to following God's will—either because of strife of familial bonds, the difficulty of pregnancy and breastfeeding, or the fact that marriage is no longer necessary. Throughout Jesus's teaching in the Gospels, he indicates that in God's reign there is no need for *biological* mothers or fathers, just as there is no need for blood siblings or households; since there is no longer death, there is no need for procreative life meant to sustain and secure a legacy.

The overall distancing of biological families and traditional kinship bonds, however, does not remove familial language from the Gospels and Acts. Instead, like other marginal groups, early Jesus followers relocated such language to describe the members and relationships that existed in their own movement.[92] In this new family formed by belief in Jesus and obedience to God's will, God is the Father, thereby removing the need for all other fathers within the group who could challenge his superiority. Mothers, however, occupy a more liminal place. Blickenstaff suggests that they remain in the household of God since they do not threaten God's authority in the same way as fathers; they are assumed inferior and submissive. Nevertheless, she also insists that for these women, too, the primary goal remains becoming a "child" rather than a reproductive adult.[93] God's identity as Father, therefore, creates space for new understandings of mothers and motherhood even as it displaces other fathers. Since God is Father, it begs the question of the Mother's identity. By downplaying the significance of literal motherhood as the ideal telos for women, these stories open up alternative avenues for women and for constructions of motherhood within the household of God.

In contrast to the dominant narrative of motherhood for women in Mediterranean antiquity, the Gospels and Acts emphasize obedience to the Father's will as the primary goal of all people—regardless of gender. While such obedience could result in motherhood as it did for Mary, the type of motherhood still challenged contemporary assumptions: priority is given to the will of a heavenly Father and his legacy, rather than the legacy of a husband and father on earth. Thus, instead of promoting sons for prominence in traditional kinship networks and social settings, mothers are encouraged to follow God's will regardless of the outcome for themselves or for their children.

Thus, the mother of the sons of Zebedee in Matt 20:20–23 is a negative exemplar when she comes to Jesus requesting a favor on behalf of her sons: "Say that these two sons of mine shall sit, one on your right and one on your left, in your kingdom" (20:21). Although the mother's behavior resonates with traditional maternal concerns for the advancement of one's sons (and, therefore, for one's household), it is undermined in Matthew not only by Jesus's repeated emphasis on the ideal of servitude to all in 20:24–28, but also by the sheer ignorance of her request. "You do not know what you are asking," Jesus responds, "Are you able to drink the cup that I am about to drink?" (20:22); neither the mother nor her sons realize that her request is for these two to die in humiliation. Those on the right and left of Jesus are none other than the two criminals, who mock Jesus as they are crucified with him (27:38, 44). Although James and John answer Jesus with an affirmative, "We are able," Jesus responds again emphasizing that it is his Father's will that is central, rather than any maternal requests or filial hopes of advancement: "You will indeed drink my cup, but to sit at my right hand and at my left, this is not mine to grant, but it is for those for whom it has been prepared by my Father" (20:23, NRSV).

Jesus's exchanges with his own mother in John 2 and 19 likewise push back against the agenda of a mother promoting her son. Approaching Jesus to act at the wedding in Cana, his mother provides him with a chance to save the day in a public manner and receive glory from those around him. Jesus, however, does not need to acquire "glory" in this manner. He *is* the enfleshed glory of his heavenly Father—no greater glory could be given to him by people. He does not need to be given glory by mortals, rather they need to recognize the glory that is already present in him as the *Logos* to receive life. Later in the Gospel, Jesus will repeatedly emphasize this point (2:23–25; 5:41–47; 8:54; 11:40; 17:1–26). Thus, even though he does act in John 2, only the servants (*diakonois*)—those who are on the fringes of the wedding celebration—witness what he has done. Moreover, in 2:11, Jesus's miracle is said not to gain him glory, but rather to "reveal" it, with the result that his disciples believe.

As in Matthew 20, the mother in John 2 does not know what she is asking from, or for, her son. Although she may see an opportunity for public glory, it is not this sort of glory that Jesus desires or manifests. There will be an hour for wine and glory, but that comes on the cross in John 19. Pierced and naked, Jesus's greatest moment of glory comes by his suffering the death sentence given only to slaves and non-citizens. It is fitting, therefore, that the servants witness his miracle in John 2; he will be reduced to a similar social status when he hangs upon the cross. The Gospel asserts, however, that it is in this ultimate irony—the shameful killing of God's life-giving *Logos*—that Jesus completes the Father's will and initiates his true homecoming. In contrast to promoting sons and finding security through their social establishment, therefore, the mothers of God's household (as well as all those in the Gospel audiences) are encouraged to find security in the heavenly Father. Conforming to God's will, these mothers resemble more closely the mothers of Maccabean tradition who prioritize the Law above all other social expectations.[94] Like these mothers before them, they, too, are called upon to be "masculine" even in the very act of performing the feminine role of mothering (2 Macc 6:10; 7; 4 Macc 8–18; esp. 16:6–23). In other words, they are to surrender bravely even their children's lives out of their own allegiance to the God who is Father of them all.

Reshaping maternal expectations in this way also opens up avenues for alternative characters to take on maternal traits and metaphors in the Gospel texts, particularly Jesus. Since the mothers in these stories are primarily children in God's household, Jesus can step in to secure their birth and act in consort with the heavenly Father. In Luke and Matthew, for example, Jesus borrows maternal imagery from the prophets to describe his own longing for Jerusalem. Lamenting for Jerusalem and foretelling his own fate, Jesus utters the words associated with God's own longing from Israel's Scriptures: "Jerusalem, Jerusalem the city that kills the prophets and stones those who are sent to it! How often have I desired to gather your children together as a hen gathers her brood under her wings, and you were not willing!" (Luke 13:34, NRSV; Matt 23:37).[95] It is John's Gospel, however, that contains the most robust maternal imagery for Jesus.

As noted above, John's Gospel reserves explicit birth imagery for Jesus's followers rather than for Jesus himself (3:1–9). Reflecting this shift, the Gospel also underscores the Spirit's relationship with Jesus and his disciples rather than with his mother, whose conception and birth of Jesus is never recounted. Instead, it is the Spirit's abiding upon Jesus that is retold in John, along with his transmission of this Spirit to his newly begotten disciples in 20:22. Like the mothers of

Aristotelian theory, Jesus shares the Father's *Logos* and *pneuma* with the children. It is these elements that shape and give life to God's children through Jesus. By consistently following God's will, Jesus ensures the "begetting" of these children who gestate with him throughout his ministry until they are birthed through his crucifixion and resurrection. The "Spirit and water" that Jesus describes as a part of the new birth from above required for admittance into God's kingdom flow from his "womb" (*koilia*, 7:37–39; 3:1–21), and mingle with images of blood and water dripping from his pierced side upon the cross (19:34–35). Indeed, the Gospel explicitly ties the birth metaphor to Jesus's death when, during his farewell discourse to his disciples in John 16:20–22, he uses the analogy of childbirth to describe the "hour" he and his disciples are about to endure. Responding to the confusion of his disciples over his coming departure, Jesus acknowledges their fear and promises them future joy by saying,

> Very truly, I tell you, you will weep and mourn, but the world will rejoice; you will have pain, but your pain will turn into joy. When a woman is in labor, she has pain, because her hour (*hōra*) has come. But when her child is born, she no longer remembers the anguish because of the joy of having brought a human being (*egennēthē anthōpos*) into the world. So you have pain now; but I will see you again, and your hearts will rejoice, and no one will take your joy from you. (John 16:20–22, NRSV)

After his resurrection, the begetting and birthing is completed when Jesus "breathes" (*enephusēsen*) the holy Spirit upon his gathered disciples and commissions them for their mission as the children of God (20:22–23; 21:5; Gen 2:7).[96] This same Spirit will reside with the community, which conceives of itself repeatedly as God's children in the Johannine letters.[97]

Having been shaped by God's *Logos* and received God's holy *pneuma* from Jesus himself, these children are given a superior, and eternal, life directly from God through his *Logos*. They are shaped and created in the same way as the cosmos was in Genesis; their new birth is a new creation. In John, if not the remainder of the Gospels and Acts, it is Jesus's sacrifice that leads to eternal life for his followers because it is through *his* maternal sacrifice that they are born anew. With his superior blood flow and the sincere immortality it ensures, the continual sacrifice of literal maternal blood for the well-being of the community is no longer required.

Conclusions

This chapter has sought to bring new light to the presentations of Mary, in particular, and other mothers and notions of motherhood in the Gospels and Acts by incorporating observations from ancient medical texts concerning conception, generation, and childbirth. At home in contexts familiar with pangenetic and epigenetic theories about the origins of life, the Gospels and Acts reflect similar anthropological assumptions that build on the gender and physiological constructions outlined in Chapter 2. With their various versions of Jesus's origins, Matthew, Luke, and John reflect the common belief of their time that life and rationality were imparted and maintained by the *pneuma*, while John also adds special emphasis to the role of God's *Logos*. By connecting Mary to God's "holy Spirit" in Matthew and Luke, both authors sanction Jesus's unusual conception and pave the way for his exceptional life. John offers a different recounting with the presentation of Jesus as the enfleshed *Logos* on whom God's *pneuma* then rests. Nevertheless, in each account Jesus is presented as God's Son because his origins are in some way linked to God's cosmos-generating and organizing principles (*pneuma*, *Logos*).

Jesus's potentially problematic origins are, therefore, transformed into a topic of praise for Jesus—even if this cannot be recognized by all characters within the Gospels themselves. Jesus's unique origins also set the stage for his unique mission in these writings. He has come to announce God's Kingdom or to offer eternal life to all those who will demonstrate their allegiance to him and, therefore, to his Father. As a result, believers no longer need concern themselves with matters of traditional preservation, including procreation from marriages. The result is a downplaying of biological motherhood in these stories even when mothers do appear. While mothers exist in these narratives and early communities, the primary goal for all women is to become part of God's household through obedience rather than through the provision of offspring. In this way, the apocalyptic framework of Jesus's message undermines the social narrative of a maternal telos for all women. Instead, while a woman's life might include motherhood, it is not motherhood that determines her worth (Luke 11:27–28).

This difference in emphasis opens the way for a new understanding of womanhood and motherhood in the Gospels and Acts, even allowing Jesus to play a part as the mother of the community. As we move on to additional maternal images and motifs in the next chapter, the transference of maternal status continues, and the potential ambiguity of it, comes into sharper relief. Rather than focusing on literal mothers, Paul stylizes himself as a mother who bears forth her children in Galatians and who feeds her charges with milk in 1 Corinthians and 1 Thessalonians. The authors of 1 Peter and Hebrews likewise use the image of milk to encourage and chastise their audiences and, in so doing, present either themselves or Christ as a superior mother figure for these infant(ile) disciples. While such images and transference have the potential to liberate women from the predetermined social goal of motherhood, they likewise downplay the significance of literal motherhood in early believing communities. In this way, the NT writings continue to reflect the ambivalence toward mothers and motherhood found in their larger culture. If women are no longer to find their purpose in motherhood, how do they avoid being silenced like Mary by a gospel claiming to offer them, alongside men, eternal life?

4

Taste that the Lord is Good!

BREASTMILK AND CHARACTER FORMATION IN THE NEW TESTAMENT

THE PREVIOUS CHAPTER traced the distancing of mothers, especially that of Mary, in the Gospels and Acts. As a part of the larger theme of prioritizing the household of God over all other biological and kinship relationships, these narratives push mothers and other household members to the periphery while not excising them from the stories entirely. The emphasis throughout is on loyalty to the heavenly *Paterfamilias* who is God, Jesus's Father, rather than any other earthly fathers, mothers, or maternal narratives patterned for women to find their completion or to justify their existence. With the promise of an imminent eschaton, the priority of procreation is set aside. While mothers remain in God's household after Jesus's death and resurrection, including Jesus's own mother in Luke and John, their primary role is to hear, obey, and be in service to God's *Logos* rather than their own husbands.

In the final portions of Chapter 3, I suggested that one outcome of this distancing of mothers, or this destabilizing of the maternal telos, was space for alternative and unconventional mothers to appear. This chapter will explore some of these unconventional mothers in more detail, especially as they surface around the repeated use of milk imagery in various NT writings. Although perhaps most well-known from Paul's writings in 1 Corinthians and 1 Thessalonians, milk images appear also in Hebrews 5, 1 Peter 2, and are implied in the "breast/chest" imagery of the Gospel of John (*kolpos*, 1:18; 13:23). Beyond the NT, early Christian and patristic authors pick up on and develop this milk imagery in the *Odes of Solomon* and in their interpretations of Paul's language in particular.[1] I will focus my observations here on the NT writings mentioned above, but the persistence of milk language in early Christian writings demonstrates its poignancy and theological import in developing Christian traditions, which continued to reassign maternal language and activities from literal mothers to what would eventually be recognized as the "Mother Church."[2]

Milk imagery is especially poignant in these traditions, not only due to its use in Israel's Scriptures and Second Temple Jewish literature (e.g., Num 11:12; 1QH[a] 15.20–21; 17.35–36; Philo, *Migr.* 24.13), but because of the physiological understandings of breastmilk that permeated the ancient Mediterranean world.[3] As masculinized menstrual blood, breastmilk is a tempered substance; transformed by the masculine heat of male semen from a monstrous substance to the "most useful" substance for nourishment, healing, and even character formation (Pliny, *Nat.* 28.123). In what follows, I will provide an overview of ancient understandings of breastmilk, outlining the physiological theories of its origins and demonstrating its function in ancient education (*paideia, artes liberales*) in forming the characters of children. With this foundation in place, I will turn to the various NT texts mentioned above, which likewise incorporate breastmilk as a pedagogical and character forming substance. Relying on the milk of an apostle, a teacher, and even Jesus, these early believers are encouraged to be formed after the image of Christ, who was himself formed at the Father's breast (John 1:18). In this way, believers are forged by "pure, word-like milk" (1 Pet 2:2) and their ties to God's household are further cemented.

This transference of maternal imagery is, like many other maternal representations in the ancient world, ambiguous for women—containing potentially positive and negative aspects for them in developing Christianity. On the one hand, the distancing of literal motherhood as the automatic (and automatically desired) telos for all women could liberate certain women from this assumed fate. Nevertheless, the majority of women—whether elite, free, or slave—undoubtedly continued becoming mothers in believing communities out of their own desires or at least as a consequence of their status. Indeed, motherhood was a path of increased status for women in the ancient world. The downplaying of their literal roles could, therefore, potentially diminish the contributions of mothers to the community. Like Mary, these women stand on the precipice of silence. Nevertheless, by retaining and developing maternal images, even ascribing nursing to the heavenly *Pater* himself (John 1:18; *Od. Sol.* 19), the early communities rely on the corporeality of real, maternal bodies to communicate their theologies. Rather than simple ornamentation, maternal bodies *are* theology, demonstrating the vulnerability and transmission of God's message and compassion for believers. Even in the masculinization of these images, therefore, the feminine breast remains. The male nurses of NT tradition are feminized through the very act of nursing, thereby continuing the mixing of feminine and masculine elements in developing Christianity that can be traced back to the life and death of its Savior, Jesus Christ.

The Sacred Fount: Breastmilk, Paideia, *and Character Formation in Mediterranean Antiquity*

In addition to one's origins, nurture (*trophē*) was a commonplace for praise and/or blame in the ancient Mediterranean world.[4] While ancients certainly reflected on a subject's origins—their conception and generation as described in the previous chapter—their rearing and education were also important in evaluating character, including gender. For this reason, it is not surprising to find regular reflections on breastmilk, nurses, and mothers in pedagogical literature as well as in medical and philosophical texts. Material evidence also speaks to the potency of breastmilk and nursing with the famous representation of Tellus-Italia suckling children from full breasts on the *Ara Pacis*, portraits of Isis sharing her life-giving breastmilk, and stories of the young Pervo rescuing her aged father from starvation by allowing him to nurse from her.[5] Understanding the physiological constructions of breastmilk contributes to our appreciation of these motifs and images. As tempered and masculinely purposed blood, breastmilk is transformed from feminine excess to the "most useful" substance. Indeed, when from the breast of an ideal mother who has birthed a legitimate child, breastmilk continues the formation of a child's soul that began in her womb. By offering her breasts to her child, then, these mothers sustained a father's seminal patterning of his child and imbued her own positive traits in the hopes of shaping her child toward ideal man- or womanhood.

Children Are Who They Eat: Ancient Physiologies of Breastmilk

Among ancient medical and philosophical writers, breastmilk was most often understood as extra menstrual blood, heated and pressed upward by the growing fetus in utero and then ready for his/her consumption after birth. While milk collected in the breasts throughout a woman's pregnancy, it was not considered "serviceable" until the seventh or eighth month.[6] With this connection, we again see the association between food, blood, and flesh that is expressed in wider physiological constructions of the ancient world. In this light, Aristotle's comparison between the umbilicus and breasts is particularly fitting. Describing the fetus's consumption of blood during its gestation, he writes, "The umbilicus consists of blood-vessels in a sheath. . . . Through this the embryo gets its nourishment, i.e., blood; . . . Nature lays in a store of the blood-like nourishment [that is, menstrual blood] in this part of the uterus, as it were into breasts" (*Gen. an.* 2.7.746a2–4). Turning to describe breastmilk itself, he explains:

> It is clear that milk is possessed of the same nature as the secretion out of which each animal is formed . . . : the material which supplies the nourishment and the material out of which Nature forms and fashions the animal are one and the same. And this material, in the case of blooded animals, is the blood-like liquid, since milk is *concocted*, not *decomposed*, blood.[7]

In other words, breastmilk is superheated menstrual blood. Male semen is the source of this heat, providing the *pneuma* (spirit) lacking in female blood.

According to Aristotle, the heat—indicative of the injection of *pneuma* and *logos* that the masculine force of semen brings to the feminine uterus—does more than shape the menstrual blood to form the collecting mass into a developing fetus. It also makes the production of useable breastmilk in the final months of gestation, when the embryo was nearing completion in form and, as a result, not using as much maternal matter.

> When, however, the final fetations are approaching their completion, then there is more surplus residue, because less of it is being used up, and it is sweeter, since the well-concocted residue is no longer being drawn off to the same extent; it is no longer being expended upon the moulding of the embryo, but upon the small growth which it is making, as through the embryo had by now, being completed, reached a stationary point. That is why it makes its way out, . . . and that is the time when the milk becomes serviceable. (*Gen. an.* 4.8.776a31–776b4)

Pressed upward in the pathway of a woman's body, the concocted blood turned milk rests in the breasts, which fill with the whitened mixture.[8] Close to the woman's heart, the warmest part of the naturally cold female body, the milk is able to remain warm and retain its masculinely concocted state.

Aristotle's views reflect larger assumptions concerning breastmilk in both ancient Athens and Imperial Rome. These assumptions spread across the spectrum of the medical sects and one- and two-seed theorists outlined in previous chapters. The Hippocratic author of *Glands* explains:

> In women the substance of the gland [i.e., breast] is very rarified, just like the rest of their bodies, and the nourishment these glands draw to themselves they alter into milk. This passes from the uterus to the breasts as nourishment for the baby after its birth, being squeezed out by the

> omentum and cast up to the higher regions of the body when it becomes cramped by the fetus. (16.572)

Commenting on the Hippocratic connection of uterus and breast, Galen suggests that each uterine chamber was connected to a corresponding breast. He writes, "For just as two uteri ending in one neck have been made in woman, so there are two breasts, each one like a faithful servant to its own uterus" (*UP* 14.2.292).[9] And, again, "the work of the uteri is to receive the semen and perfect the fetus, that of the udders to nourish it when it has been brought forth" (*UP* 14.2.293). Continuing this connection further, he argues that if a woman's breast "withers" while she is pregnant, it indicates a miscarriage depending on which breast is impacted. If it is a male fetus, the right breast is affected; if female, the left (*UP* 14.2.293).[10] Soranus, too, cites Hippocrates as his source that "an unexpected shrinking of the breasts" can indicate an impending miscarriage (*Gyn.* 1.18.59). He also repeats Aristotle's argument that breastmilk is concocted, or cooked, blood, explaining that "raw" milk is "red-yellow [in color] . . . and not brought to perfection and therefore displays a blood-like color" (*Gyn.* 2.13.22). Rabbinic texts articulate a similar stance as these Greek and Roman writers:

> The entire nine months in which the woman does not see blood, in truth she should do so; but what does the Holy One, blessed be He, do? He directs it upward to her breasts and turns it into milk, so that the fetus may come forth and have food. (Lev. Rab. 14.3)

As in biblical and rabbinic interpretations of conception and generation, God again is credited with the creation of breastmilk in Jewish contexts, rather than male semen. Nevertheless, it remains female blood that is so transformed.

This interpretation of breastmilk reflects the anatomical construction of a pathway or *hodos* in the female body connecting her mouth and nostrils to her uterus and vagina outlined in Chapter 2. Since her food, moisture, and blood are all linked through this central avenue, it naturally follows that the concocted blood of a pregnant woman should be able to travel along this same pathway and occupy her breasts, literally filling these otherwise empty sacs with purpose. This construction of breastmilk also means that upon birth, an infant continues to consume the same food it did while inside its mother's womb; taking in the seeds (*sperma*), spirit (*pneuma*), order (*logos*), and even soul (*psychē*) of its parents as it does so.[11] Rather than suckling from the umbilicus, the child draws from the breast, an innate skill that one Hippocratic author uses to justify his interpretation that children eat and breathe in the womb:

> [T]he fetus in the belly continually sucks with its lips from the uterus of the mother and draws nourishment (*trophēn*) and breath (*pneuma*) to its

> heart inside, . . . If anyone asks you how you know that the fetus draws and suck in the uterus, you may reply as follows. Both humans and animals have faeces in their intestines at the time of birth, and immediately at birth pass stools. . . .. Nor would a baby know how to suck from the breast immediately at birth, if it did not also suck in the uterus. (*Carn.* 6.594)

Breastmilk, then, is more than just satisfactory food for a newborn. It is the same nourishment the child—and any human—received while growing and forming in the womb. It is the special semen-infused concoction that enables the creation and sustaining of new life. Not surprisingly, breastmilk is often interpreted as having additional medicinal qualities, both for the newborn child for whom it is intended *and* for anyone else in need of its ameliorating traits. Breastmilk frequently surfaces in gynecological texts as an ingredient for fertility tests, fumigations, and salves.[12] Outside strictly medical texts, breastmilk also appears as a type of cure-all. Unlike the "monstrous" nature of menstrual blood—and a menstruating woman—which kills crops (especially gourds and cucumbers!), puts pests to flight, clouds mirrors and tarnishes metal, and even causes livestock to abort or become sterile, Amy Richlin notes that breastmilk is "uniformly healthful" and "one of the most useful remedies."[13] Pliny the Elder, therefore, writes in his *Natural Histories* that "Mother's milk is the most useful thing for anybody, . . . Moreover, human milk is the most nourishing for any purpose" (28.123).[14] Having been cooked and perfected by its infusion with male semen, the female menstrual blood turns from an arbiter of death, to one of continuing and renewed life. For infants, in particular, it sustains them in their vulnerable and developing state. Indeed, by consuming the same mixture after birth that nourished them in the womb, a child continues to be shaped by the seed and spirit of his or her parents. In other words, breastmilk persists with the formative ability it had in the womb. Children are who they (continue to) eat.

From Physiology to Character Formation: Breastmilk as *Paideia*

The second-century philosopher, Favorinus of Arles makes the character-forming features of breastmilk the basis of his defense of maternal breastfeeding, a defense that deserves fuller examination here. In a well-known discourse, Aulus Gellius reproduces an exchange between the famous Favorinus, an "auditor and disciple" of his, and the disciple's mother-in-law, whose daughter had just survived a difficult labor and who was hoping to secure wet nurses (*nutrices*) to care for and to feed her infant grandson (*Noct. att.* 12.1.1–5).[15] Favorinus, however, is unmoved by the mother-in-law's concerns—instead, he is shocked at her request for nurses and uses the situation to offer his views on maternal breastfeeding in general. Rebuking the mother-in-law, he replies, "I beg you, madam, let her be *wholly and entirely the mother* of her own son! For what kind of *unnatural*, *imperfect*, and *half-motherhood* is it to bear a child and at once send it away from her? To have nourished in her womb with her own blood something which she could not see and not to feed with her own milk what she sees, now alive, now human, now calling for a mother's care?"

Rather than concern for her daughter, Favorinus accuses the mother-in-law of desiring nurses for the sake of her daughter's vanity, comparing her desire for wet nurses to women who have abortions to prevent physical disfigurement.[16] He continues:

> Or do you too perhaps think that nature gave women nipples as a kind of beauty-spot, not for the purposes of nourishing their children, but as an adornment of their breast? For it is that reason (though such a thing is of course far from your thoughts) that many of those unnatural women try to dry up and check that sacred fount of the body, the tutor of mankind, regardless of the danger of diverting and spoiling the milk, because they think it disfigures the charms of their beauty. In so doing they show the same madness as those who strive by evil devices to cause abortion of the fetus itself which they have conceived, in order that their beauty may not be spoiled by the labour of parturition. But since it is an act worthy of public detestation and general abhorrence to destroy a human being in its inception, while it is being fashioned and given life and is still in the hands of Dame Nature, how far does it differ from this to deprive a child, already perfect, of the nourishment of its own familiar and kindred blood? (12.7–9)[17]

By means of this comparison, Favorinus makes explicit the connection between breast/nipple and umbilicus—to deprive a growing child of the combined parental bloods at any stage effectively deprives the child of life. Moreover, it is a danger to the mother, whose own health depends on proper use of excess bloods in the formation of the fetus *and* in the supply of milk. When left unsuckled, this blood is dangerous and spoiling or rotting inside her breasts. Rather than a "sacred fount," the breasts become fetid, a symbol of death for both mother and child.

Favorinus's comparison relies on the understanding of breastmilk having the same function as umbilical blood in forming a child described in the medical literatures above. Furthermore, just as he assumes the bloods of Roman nobility to be superior to those of other classes when they initially come together to form a fetus, so too does he assume their bloods to continue conveying superior nourishment from a noblewoman's breast.[18] Continuing his speech, he says:

> Is the blood which is now in the breasts not the same that it was in the womb, merely because it has become white from abundant air [i.e., spirit]

> and width? Is not wisdom of nature evident also in this, that as soon as the blood, the artificer, has fashioned the whole human body within its secret precautions, when the time for birth comes, it rises into the upper parts, is ready to cherish the first beginnings of life and of light, and supplies the newborn children with the familiar and accustomed food? Therefore it is believed not without reason that, *just as the power and nature of the seed are able to form likenesses of body and mind, so the qualities and properties of the milk have the same effect*. . . . What mischief, then, is the reason for corrupting the nobility of body and mind of a newly born human being, formed from gifted seeds, by the alien and degenerate nourishment of another's milk? Especially if she whom you employ to furnish the milk is either a slave or of servile origin and, as usually happens, of a foreign and barbarous nation, if she is dishonest, ugly, unchaste and a wine-bibber; for as a rule anyone who has milk at the time is employed and no distinction is made. (12.1.12–14, 17; emphasis added)

This practice, explains Favorinus, is why "some children of chaste women turn out to be like their parents in neither body nor in mind" (12.1.19). Instead, nourished by "foreign and barbarous" milk, the children are "corrupted" and become "foreign and barbarous" themselves—the milk of the nurse(s) having overcome the nourishment received in the womb.

Favorinus's suggestion reflects the importance of nurture in Greek and Roman cultures. As noted at the outset of this section, "nurture" (*trophē*) is a commonplace in epideictic literature, which praises or blames the character of its subjects. Achilles features as a frequently cited example of this commonplace, his unique nurture by lions or tigers used to explain his violence and strength. Favorinus also makes use of Achilles as an example, making him a stranger to both his father, Peleus, and goddess mother, Thetis, by quoting Homer to credit the "gray sea" and "hard and flinty rocks" with his conception and birth since "fierce Hyrcanian tigers gave [him] suck."[19] So unlike his parents, the fierce Achilles was shaped by the tigresses' milk to have a "savage mind" and ability to slay men, even Hector. Favorinus concludes,

> [T]here is no doubt that in forming character the disposition of the nurse and the quality of the milk play a great part; for the milk, although *imbued from the beginning with the material of the father's seed, forms the infant offspring from the body and mind of the mother as well.* (12.1.20; emphasis added)[20]

According to Favorinus, then, a mother continues her role as a conduit for masculine seed by means of her milk; *this* is the other half of her role in the formation of a (hu)man; umbilicus and breast are parallel, and a "whole" mother is incomplete should she not use both.[21] Again, it is in her importance as the one who conveys the "father's seed" that she is necessary *and* precarious. The unique female ability to nurse a child is set alongside her ability to gestate and bear.

The discourse ends without explicit resolution, Aulus Gellius instead apologizing for any deficiencies in his translation of the conversation from Greek to Latin (12.1.24). Nevertheless, the scene does not end inconclusively; the mother-in-law, whose words are never directly spoken, remains silent. Favorinus appears to have won the day so completely that his discourse requires no response. The wife of his noble "auditor and disciple," having initiated her proper maternal role by birthing (with difficulty) a son, will "without a doubt, nurse the son herself" as Favorinus had initially decreed upon congratulating the father (12.1.4). In so doing, she will continue her natural role as mother and woman: conveying life-giving and character-forming seed to her child so that he can one day become a man.

The connection that Favorinus makes between breastmilk and proper formation reflects the broader understanding of education as the complete formation of a man. Thus, Favorinus describes a mother's breasts as a "sacred fount" and the "nourisher," literally the "instructor" or "educator" (*educatorem*), of humanity (12.8). Favorinus's concern is *primarily* about the formation of the son, so that he can continue to be formed to reflect his noble parents into adulthood rather than for his life be squandered by the malformation/malnourishment of strange milk. The formative qualities of milk, therefore, explain why wet nurses, mothers, and breastmilk surface as topics in pedagogical writings. While male pedagogues, professional tutors, and fathers contributed to the education of children, even very young children, their contributions toward formal education did not begin in earnest until at least the third or fourth year of life, after a child was weaned and past the most precarious period of infancy. The formation of "men," however, begins in the womb and continues in the reception of breastmilk and early child care, tasks primarily (although not exclusively) undertaken by nurses and mothers in upper-class households.[22] These women—whether mothers, grandmothers, hired or compelled nurses—were, in fact, the first educators children experienced.

In addition to providing milk and general care to keep children safe and clean, these women were also to prevent poor speech and bad habits. Thus, in instructions concerning the selection of wet nurses, authors repeatedly emphasize a nurse's ability to speak well (often Greek) and her "self-control." In Soranus's extended discussion on the topic, he describes the ideal wet nurse, writing:

> One should choose a wet nurse not younger than twenty nor older than forty years, who has already given birth twice or thrice, who is healthy, of good habitus, of large frame, and of a good color. Her breasts should be of a medium size, lax, soft and unwrinkled, the nipples neither big nor

> too small and neither too compact nor too porous and discharging milk overabundantly. She should be self-controlled, sympathetic, and not ill-tempered, a Greek, and tidy. (*Gyn.* 2.19.88)

Soranus then proceeds to explain each of these descriptors, detailing "self-control" (*sōphrona*) as abstention from sex, "lewdness," and "incontinence" of any kind and reporting that she should be a Greek "so that the infant nursed by her may become accustomed to the best speech" (*Gyn.* 2.19.88).[23] Plutarch, likewise, emphasizes that if a nurse *must* be hired, she must be Greek "in character" since "just as it is necessary, immediately after birth, to begin to mold the limbs of the children's bodies in order that these may grow straight and without deformity, so, in the same fashion, it is fitting from the beginning to regulate the characters of children" (*Lib. ed.* 5e [Babbit, LCL]).[24] Likewise, Quintilian connects good speech with good character in his argument in favor of surrounding young boys with Greek-speakers, including nurses; he writes, "First of all, make sure the nurses speak properly. . . . No doubt the more important point is their character; but they should also speak correctly. These are the first people the child will hear, theirs are the words he will try to copy and pronounce" (*Inst.* 1.1.4–5 [Russell, LCL]).

Jewish authors betray similar concerns, even though they advocate hiring a Hebrew or Jewish wet nurse, if one was needed. Indeed, rabbinic texts forbid the hiring of non-Jewish nurses.[25] In her recent analysis of this phenomenon, Cynthia Chapman argues that breastmilk is a "kinship forging substance" in ancient Near Eastern myths as well as the Hebrew Bible. Thus, Hebrew women (and a man) nurse significant persons who become foundational figures for Israel. Sarah, Jochabed, Naomi, and even Mordecai nurse Isaac, Moses, Obed, and Esther in spite of various difficulties including age, political intrigue, the presence of a foreign mother (Ruth), and biological gender (Mordecai). According to Chapman, such stories of "preposterous breastfeeding" make sense in a context where the breast is not just an organ that transmits nourishment but rather is an "organ through which ethnicity and status is transferred from the nursing mother to the suckling child."[26] As with Soranus and Plutarch, or even Quintilian, Jewish leaders likewise determined breastmilk to be formational. It is the only channel through which "kindred blood" is received outside of the womb.

Referencing wet nurses in particular, Keith Bradley suggests that these women could serve as permanent fixtures in a child's life, especially in upper-class households, becoming "the equivalent of the *educatrix* or *pedegoga*" before a child was sent to grammar school or established under the instruction of a tutor at age seven.[27] That these bonds could last is demonstrated by epigraphic and literary references, which explain why moralists of all types also encourage maternal breastfeeding to forge a lasting bond of affection between mother (father) and child. Plutarch writes,

> Mothers ought, I should say, themselves to feed their infants and nurse themselves. For they will feed them with a livelier affection and greater care, as loving them inwardly, and according to the proverb, to their finger-tips. But the good will of wet-nurses (*tithai*) and nursemaids (*trophoi*) is insincere and forced, since they love for pay. (*Lib. ed.* 5c [Babbit, LCL])

With these comments, Plutarch reflects sentiments similar to those noted by Chapman in ancient Near Eastern and Israelite narratives that breastmilk reinforces kinship bonds or creates new ones. Not only is the bond between mother and child strengthened through breastfeeding, but relationships between siblings is made strong, because "kindliness [that is, kinship] in feeding is a bond that knits kindliness together" even among "the brute beasts" (5e [Babbit, LCL]). In his praise for Cato's ability as a father, therefore, Plutarch highlights his wife's decision to nurse not only their son, but also "the infants of her slaves, so that they might come to cherish a brotherly affection for her son" (20.3).[28]

The emphasis on bonds created through breastfeeding is also highlighted in a variety of other ancient literatures. The maternal characters in these works appeal to their breasts, even baring them before adult sons, in order to illicit sympathy and effect persuasion over their actions. Hector's mother, Hecuba demonstrates the sympathetic image of a mother's breasts when she bares them before Hector in the *Iliad*. In an attempt to dissuade him from facing Achilles, Hecuba reminds her son of how her breasts comforted him when he was in pain.[29] In an imitation of Hecuba, the mother of Chaereas likewise uncovers her breasts before her son in hopes of preventing his leaving in search of his kidnapped bride, Callirhoe.[30] John David Penniman suggests that the mother of 2 Maccabees likewise imitates this trope, although this time she refers to her nursing not to prevent her youngest son from dying, but to encourage him to die as a martyr for the Law (2 Macc 7:27).[31] Highlighting the mutual affection created through nursing, Orestes hesitates to kill his mother, Clytemnestra, even though he has been commanded to do so by Apollo as punishment for her murder of Orestes's father, Agamemnon. Orestes cries, "Woe! How can I slay her?—her that nursed, that bare me?" Orestes again laments when he recalls that at the moment of her death, his mother was, "clinging, clasping my mantle, [and] bared her bosom in dying—Woe's me!"[32] As symbols of maternal love, the baring of a mother's breasts was a sympathetic sight meant to arouse pity and compliance from her children based on the relationship initiated through them.

Favorinus finishes his discourse with similar sentiments when he compares the sending of a child to the care of wet nurses to abandonment with the result that the "bond and cementing of the mind and of affection with which nature attaches parents to their children" is "obliterated." Education received from a wet nurse, rather than a mother's breasts, results in a perfunctory "affection" between *all parties* who have shared blood—mother, child, *and* father. The "natural affection" is displaced onto a stranger, literally rupturing the bloodlines of parental relationships so that their interactions are "merely courteous and conventional" (*Noct. att.* 12.23). With foreign allegiances replacing the "natural" family bonds, Favorinus insinuates later corruptions of would-be noblemen; if such men are not loyal to their parents, how then can they be loyal to their *patria* (fatherland)?

Favorinus's concern is palpable because he aims to control what is otherwise left to the feminine sphere: pregnancy, childbirth, and lactation. He hopes to secure the son's foundation so that he might not be "spoiled" before he ever has a chance to realize manhood. He, then, joins other Greek and Roman moralists and physicians by entering the conversation of maternal breastfeeding from a persistently androcentric and elite perspective: *elite* mothers should nurse their own children (especially sons) in order to form ideal leaders for the *polis* (city) and state. Rabbinic authors, too, prefer biological mothers to nurse their own children and create special accommodations for women who do so in later traditions. In addition to forbidding non-Jewish women from nursing Jewish children and claiming a husband's right to force his wife to nurse, nursing mothers are rewarded by being relieved from specific tasks or duration of work while nursing, and are encouraged to nurse a former husband's children even after a divorce by being paid to do so.[33]

At its heart, the concern for maternal breastfeeding persists in reflecting the notion that food is transformed into blood and eventually flesh—therefore, having literally a *formative* outcome on the one who consumes it. Comments on breastfeeding, then, fit within ethical writings that frequently comment on the regimen of boys and men, using poor diet as a commonplace of blame and healthy diet as one of praise.[34] Thus, Cicero complains about the general moral malaise he sees in Late Republican Rome as, at least partially, the result of wet nurses when he writes: "As soon as we are brought forth into the world and raise up at birth, straightaway we are caught up in a never-ending whorl of evil practices and the worst possible principles, so that we seem to have drunk in error virtually with our nurse's milk" (*Tusc.* 3.1.2).[35] Epictetus joins the refrain, adding that those who remain dependent on milk for too long (even if it is good milk) are stunted in their development; they never mature into full men who exercise proper control over their emotions, minds, or behavior (*Disc.* 2.16; 3.24). Consumed by fear, these fake men cry for their mothers and nurses, and refusing to be weaned they stay at home being fed rather than going out to search for truth (2.16).

Given the larger context, the charge of milk-dependence is not just one of immaturity; it is a charge of effeminacy. According to Soranus, children become "moist and delicate if fed on milk for a long time" (*Gyn.* 2.21.46). The reliance on milk for too long, then, means a child takes on *traditionally feminine qualities* (excess moisture and delicacy), making them vulnerable to vice. The Tosefta likewise condemns nursing for too long, arguing that a child who nurses for longer than two years "sucks [from] an abominable [or unclean] thing" (*t. Nid.* 2.3). Gail Labovitz suggests that this declaration demonstrates a debate over the duration of nursing in rabbinic Jewish circles since a number of other texts suggest a twenty-four month *minimum* for nursing and an awareness of nursing for up to four or five years (*m. Git.* 5.6; 7.6; *b. Git.* 75b; *t. Nid.* 2.1, 4).[36] Nevertheless, the question of purity that surfaces in these *tannaitic* traditions resonates with concerns over duration of nursing among Roman authors as well. Indeed, like Soranus, *t. Nid.* 2.3 presents its condemnation of nursing past two years as a regulation meant to care for the child and ensure its proper upbringing.

Mothers who nurse, and nurse correctly, are praised in these literary and epigraphic traditions as well.[37] Tacitus's Messalus, for example, cites the mothers of the Gracchi, Julius Caesar, and Augustus for "educating" their sons "on their laps" instead of in the hands of a "silly little Greek serving maid" (*Dial.* 28–29).[38] Their special maternal care produced "princes" for the state, guiding their education in utero and beyond: "The object of this rigorous system was that the natural disposition of every child, while still sound at the core and untainted, not warped as yet by any vicious tendencies, might at once lay hold with the heart and soul on virtuous accomplishments, and whether its bent was towards the army, or the law, or the pursuit of eloquence, might make that its sole aim and *drink up* its fullness."[39] Unlike these great men of the past, Messalus laments the laziness of current leaders, blaming parents for poor education, beginning with the employment of wet nurses and male slaves to care for children. It is from these "worthless" and "incompetent" persons that the "children receive their earliest impressions, while their minds are still pliant and unformed" (*Dial.* 29.1). Rather than the rigid discipline of past mothers, current parents imbue vicious desires "almost from the mother's womb" by handing the children over to others to educate through milk, speech, and habits, resulting in lax, loose, and lazy "men" of the Late Republic.

Underlying all of these examples is the belief that one takes on the qualities of one's nurse, whether she is the mother or a hired nurse. Far from just supplying food, the nurse supplies formative seed or seeds through her milk, shaping the child's body and well as his or her soul. Thus, the special qualities of any "man" could be traced, at least in part, to the initial nurture he received. In this way, the elite mother's hand is apparent whether her material contribution to a gestating fetus is regarded as "formative" or not. Her precariously powerful position can mold an ideal man *or* she can leave him in the hands of a nurse, with potentially tragic consequences for herself *and* for the state. Due to excess moistness, softness, and with unnatural allegiances, malnourished sons become malformed and corrupted, having the appearance and power of "men" but missing the foundational *vir*tue at their core. With such a belief, elite men railed against the well-established, and even normative, practice of hiring wet nurses, especially in the Roman world.

Summary

From this overview, the connection between physiological constructions of breastmilk and its perceived pedagogical and character-forming abilities becomes clear. With anatomical connections made between breast and uterus, the inseminated menstrual blood presumed to feed a fetus in utero was aligned with the breastmilk that flowed from breast post-parturition. In this way, mothers and wet nurses alike continued to nourish newborns and children with the same substance out of which babies were formed in the womb. For elite male authors, the identification of breastmilk with uterine sustenance means that (elite) mothers *should* nurse their own young and, in this way, ensure the continued passage of their husbands' masculine seed to the infant, along with the maternal blood that fosters kinship bonds. In so doing, mothers were to participate viscerally in the education of their children; nurturing them on the *logos* and *pneuma* first in the womb, then from their breasts, and finally in the form of proper speech and habits the young child would imitate.

Yet, this idealized image of the nursing mother contrasts with the regular employment of wet nurses throughout social strata in the ancient world. Wet nurses were employed for the sake of convenience, as Favorinus decries, but also when circumstances demanded it: a mother's death, an inability to produce milk, or even by the compulsion of a master who would not allow a new mother the freedom to suckle her child.[40] The ideology put forward by elite male authors corresponds to increased public attention to family matters during and after the reign of Augustus. In an attempt to reinforce his own masculinity after defeating the well-known Marc Antony, Augustus claimed to "restore" the traditional Roman, family values during his reign, especially with the passage of the *leges Iuliae* in 17–18 BCE and the *lex Papia Poppaea* in 9 CE. Augustus's agenda resulted in an emphasis on fatherhood as a major part of a Roman nobleman's masculine status. An unintended result, however, was the sudden public focus on maternity for ideal Roman noblewomen. A wife's fecundity, alongside her willingness to nurse her own children, therefore, became a display of a husband's masculinity: he was a real man at least in part because she was a real woman, a "complete" mother. The importance of evoking masculinity by means of one's virtuous wife, then, makes the image of a nursing mother all the more powerful in the Augustan age, whether or not such nursing was the norm in daily life.

Learning to Drink: Breastmilk and New Testament Paideia

Regardless of the reality of maternal nursing in elite households, the emphasis on this practice in the Greco-Roman world demonstrated above makes appeals to breastmilk and nursing especially significant in the NT. Like their Greco-Roman counterparts, NT authors often appeal to milk in pedagogical settings, encouraging the proper drinking of the right milk to ensure maturity, often in imitation of Jesus as God's ideal Son. The image, however, also evokes the emotional bonds of nursing, reminding audiences of the service and care provided by their teacher-mother even in the midst of struggle or rebuke. Having been nursed, or continuing to be nursed, together from the same source, these audiences are reminded of the kinship-blood-type bonds that are to exist in their communities, thus reinforcing their loyalty to not only their teacher but also to one another as members of God's household. Moreover, by drinking superior milk—milk whose insemination and production originates from the heavenly Father rather than an earthly one—these believers are encouraged to a superior forming and life.

Picturing believers drinking from the breasts of male/masculine figures, however, these images simultaneously exalt and subvert a woman's role in breastfeeding. In this way, these images continue the distancing of biological mothers and motherhood in the Gospels and Acts explored in the previous chapter, even as they depend on their unique attributes. In this section, I will explore maternal and nursing imagery from the Gospel of John, three of Paul's letters, Hebrews, and 1 Peter. In each instance, the female figure, either mother or wet nurse, is displaced by a male figure. Casting men and the masculine Divine as nursing mothers, these writings claim to provide superior milk to their charges, better than any woman could in literal breastfeeding. Nevertheless, they simultaneously rely on the corporeal constructions of women's bodies and the milk they alone can produce to communicate their theologies. Even in the writings' assumption of masculine superiority, therefore, the milk language of the NT blends masculine and feminine imagery and, in so doing, again underscores not only the inescapable overlap between corporeal constructions and theologies, but the crucial role that *female* bodies play in theologies.

At the Father's Breast: The Education of John's Jesus

In the last chapter, I discussed the generative language that is common in the Gospel and Letters of John. Playing on understandings of conception and birth from the ancient Mediterranean world, these writings characterize Jesus as the unique enfleshment of God's *Logos* and of his own ability to regenerate his followers by giving them God's Spirit (John 3:7–9; 7:37–38; 20:22). To reinforce the generative, and maternal, aspects of the Father and Jesus, Jesus's biological mother is kept at a distance throughout the narrative—both by her pronounced absence from Jesus's origin story in 1:1–18 and in the manner that Jesus addresses her in the two scenes where she does appear (2:1–12; 19:25–27). The narrator may repeatedly identify her as Jesus's mother, but Jesus himself never does, even if he does show concern for her at his death.[41] Just as the generative imagery of John focuses first on Jesus's unique relationship to his Father and then to Jesus's ability to rebirth his followers, so too is the breast imagery displaced from the mother. It is transferred first to the Father alone (1:18) and then to his ever-imitating apprentice Son, whose breast forms his "beloved" disciple (13:23). As a result, the Gospel reinforces Jesus's unique relationship and forming by his Father that results in his unique ability to birth and nourish these disciples who are "begotten" by God alone. Birthed and nursed by Jesus, who himself originates with and was nursed by the Father, the children of God are promised eternal life by John's Gospel.[42]

The interpretation offered here is admittedly implicit in the Gospel itself. The Gospel does not explicitly narrate "nursing" or "breast" in its language (e.g., *thēlazō, mastos*), but rather uses the term *kolpos* first at 1:18 and then at 13:23. Instead of the unequivocal word for "breast," then, John uses a more ambiguous term; one that *can* mean "breast" depending on context, but that can also mean "chest," "bosom," or "lap."[43] Thus, perhaps largely because of the paternal location of this *kolpos* in John 1:18, most interpreters translate the term to emphasize a general closeness between Jesus and the Father rather than an explicit location. Even if a location is offered, it is certainly not "breast," but rather "heart" or "side."[44]

Yet, the Gospel is persistent with its use of generative and birth imagery. As I explored in the previous chapter, the Gospel Prologue reflects various ancient embryological theories and then continues with birth imagery throughout the rest of the narrative. The ministry of Jesus tracks his gestation of the children "given" to him by the Father (6:37–39; 10:28–29; 17:1–26; 18:9); he nurtures them by administering the word (*logos*) given to and enfleshed by him before finally birthing these children on the cross and passing the Spirit to them at his resurrection (19:34; 20:22). Given the robust context of birth and nurture in John's Gospel, therefore, the image of Jesus being "in the Father's bosom" is certainly a provocative one—one that could conjure images of a nursing child. Indeed, exploring artistic renderings of another famous *kolpos* scene from Luke 16, this time of Lazarus in Abraham's *kolpos*, Martin O'Kane notes that interpreters of the scene understood the image as much more than a simple closeness between Abraham and Lazarus. Instead, iconographers repeatedly depict Abraham "holding a naked and vulnerable child in his bosom" rather than a fully clothed, adult man resting comfortably near his patriarch.[45]

Nursing is explicitly the context in another significant *kolpos* passage from Israel's Scriptures: namely, Num 11:12. Rebuking God for appointing him as provider for the Hebrews, Moses cries out, "I did not receive in my womb all these people, nor did I birth them, did I? Why are you saying to me, 'Receive them in your breast (*kolpon*) as a wet nurse (*tithēnos*) takes up her nursling (*thēlazonta*) to the land which you swore to their fathers'?" (LXX). The implication of Moses's words is that he did not create or gestate (i.e., "conceive" and "birth") the people of Israel, God did. As Israel's real Father and Mother, therefore, God is responsible for their nourishment just as a nurse is responsible for the nourishment and care of her nursling. Tracing the history of interpretation of Numbers 11, L. Juliana Claassens notes subsequent connections between the manna that God then provides and breastmilk (*b. Yoma* 75a; *Sifre Num.* 89; *Exod. Rab.* 1.12; *b. Soṭah* 11b). These interpretations combine the nursing imagery from Num 11 with Deut 32:13–14, which describes God's "nursing" Israel with honey, olive oil, curds, milk, fat, wheat, and wine.[46] Jacob Cherian also argues that Num 11:12 forms part of the background of the Teacher's description of nurses in the Thanksgiving Hymns (1QH[a]) of the Qumran community. In these hymns, the Teacher figures himself as a "nurse" for his community in a manner similar to God, whom he describes as the "nurse of all creation in your bosom" (1QH[a] 15.20–21; 17.36).[47] With these citations, Cherian sees an association between Moses and the Teacher in 1QH[a]. A similar connection is also made in John's Gospel, where Jesus's comparisons to Moses are also pronounced.[48] The Teacher, and later Jesus, are figured as nurses precisely because there is an established tradition of identifying God as the superior father, mother, and wet nurse who provides for all creation, and especially for the people of Israel.

Further support for noting a thematic association with breastfeeding in all three of these biblical passages—John 1:18; Luke 16:22; and Num 11:12 (LXX)—is their lexical similarity in addition to the word *kolpos*. All three passages use the phrase "at/into the breast" (*eis ton kolpon*) to describe the location of Jesus, Lazarus, or the nursling. Ruth 4:16 likewise uses this phrase in its description of Naomi's miraculous nursing of her grandson, Obed. The LXX reads, "Naomi received the child and placed him at her breast (*eis ton kolpon*), and she became a wet nurse (*tithēnon*) for him." The result of this nursing, as noted by Chapman's study above, is the guarantee of Obed's—and later, David's—legitimate Israelite origins since his kinship-blood is asserted through Naomi's Jewish breastmilk in spite of his birth from the Moabite, Ruth.[49] Thus, in Ruth 4:17 the local women react to Naomi's nursing by transferring Ruth's maternal role to her saying, "To Naomi was born a son!" Not only does the scene in Ruth contain additional lexical parallels to Num 11:12 with its uses of "receive" and "nurse," but it also communicates the maternal role assumed by the one who nurses. Just as grandmother is acknowledged as mother in Ruth, God is the Mother in Numbers as well as Father; this, too, seems to take place in John's Gospel. The extensive use of procreative language in the John's Prologue, alongside traditions of nursing with the phrase "at/into the bosom" (*eis ton kolpon*), at the very least support further consideration of nursing imagery in John 1 and 13.

Indeed, the cultural connotations of nursing and character-formation explored above resonate with the presentation of Jesus's unique relationship with the Father that are indicated by John 1:18, especially if interpreters recognize the nursing imagery it contains. John 1:18 highlights the closeness of Jesus to the Father, but also his complete reliance on him as the source of his existence and knowledge. Building on the presentation of his ideal, masculine generation discussed in the previous chapter, the image of Jesus's nursing reinforces his complete masculine generation. Like a child nurses from his mother, Jesus suckles from the Father, continuing to receive *logos* and *pneuma* from the superior, divinely masculine source. Thus, as the crowds recognize, Jesus does not need human teachers to instruct him (7:15). Instead, he receives his education (*paideia*) directly from the Divine Father; moreover, he *is* the substance of all other wisdom by which God created the cosmos as God's very *Logos* become flesh (1:14). As a result, Jesus embodies the Father's glory and effects his life-giving will by means of his words and deeds throughout the Gospel, even if this remains unrecognized by his opponents. As a result of this relationship, the love between Jesus and his Father is emphasized in Jesus's speeches, pointing to the bonds solidified in his nursing experience (3:35; 17:23–26). The love between Jesus and his Father is then shared between Jesus and his disciples who imitate him (14:21–31). Such language *never* surrounds Jesus's relationship with his biological mother.

The Gospel then builds on Jesus's nursing to describe his later nourishment of his followers. In John 6, Jesus compares himself to the manna given to Israel during their wilderness wanderings; the same food that is compared to breastmilk in Num 11, Deut 32, and later rabbinic traditions.[50] Jesus instructs his listeners to eat and drink his flesh and blood, which he describes as "true food" and "true drink" (John 6:55). By including blood, instead of just flesh alone, Jesus introduces the imagery of drinking. Furthermore, blood is the same substance turned to breastmilk by masculine seed in ancient physiological constructions. By consuming his flesh and blood, Jesus promises that his followers will receive eternal life rather than the temporary sustenance provided to Israel in the form of manna (John 6:48–58). Without such consumption, they will die, just as the Israelites did. Jesus's flesh and blood, he explains, contains the very life that comes from his Father alone. "Just as the Living Father (*ho zōn patēr*) sent me, and I live because of the Father, also the one who eats me, that one will also live because of me" (6:57). In other words, Jesus's flesh and blood communicates God's *Logos* to his charges. In so doing, it confers to them true, and eternal, life (John 1:1–5).

The startling nature of Jesus's words is not lost on the characters listening to him in the story. Instead of desiring this food and drink, they are repulsed. Consuming a man's flesh and blood was an abomination throughout the ancient

Mediterranean world.[51] Reacting to his teaching, "many" of the disciples "grumble" (*gonguzousin*) at the scandalous nature of Jesus's "word" (*logos*) and eventually abandon him (6:60–66). This grumbling reenacts Israel's "grumbling" at Moses in the scene from Num 11 above, as well as the larger wilderness tradition in Exodus, where God provides manna to nourish the Israelites. Like the crowd before them, however, many of Jesus's own disciples also refuse to receive what he has offered, even though he tells them that these words are "spirit" (*pneuma*) and "life" (*zōē*, 6:63). In John 6, therefore, the many disciples refuse the breastmilk that will be offered to them by Jesus. Even more graphically, they refuse further gestation in his "womb" that leads up to Jesus's metaphorical birthing upon the cross. When they leave his care, the disciples leave his womb. Metaphorically miscarried children, the many disciples go back "for the left-overs (*eis ta opisō*) and no longer walked about (or lived, *periepatoun*) with him" (6:66). Instead of receiving Jesus's "words of life" (*rhēmata zōēs*, 6:68), these disciples turn around and search for left-over manna even though it cannot provide eternal life, but rather rots when hoarded (Exod 16:20).

In Jesus's final meal scene, revelation and food are again conjoined, this time with a reference to *kolpos* as in John 1:18. In John 13:23, the beloved disciple is "in the bosom" (*en tō kolpō*) of Jesus in order to receive Jesus's knowledge of his betrayer (13:21–30). As the only other place *kolpos* is mentioned in John, the scene immediately recalls 1:18, and places this disciple in a unique comparison with Jesus.[52] Just as Jesus was formed by the nurture received from the Father, so too is this disciple formed by his nurture at Jesus's breast. That he alone receives such a privilege points toward his future leadership position in the Johannine community, as well as his ability to stand as a surrogate son for Jesus's biological mother in John 19:25–27. Having been formed to reflect her own son, this new son offers superior consolation for her, just as other children, portraits, or statues were to console grieving mothers in Greco-Roman sources.[53] Silent before her son, Jesus's mother appears to accept this consolation and disappears from the narrative. Moreover, just as her first son came to her without mention of her womb or breasts, so too does her second, birthed and nursed by Jesus instead.

On another level, however, this disciple's special nourishment justifies his role as the truthful witness on whose testimony the Gospel itself claims to rely (19:34–35; 21:24–25). For this reason, it is not surprising that he alone is called "beloved" and is called such for the first time at 13:23. The nursing he receives underscores his closeness to Jesus as well as his ability to reflect, and teach, Jesus's will—just as Jesus reflects and teaches that of his Father. In this way, the community is urged to "nurse" from this disciple by learning from this Gospel. As a result, they are shaped by the *logos* and *pneuma* that finds its ultimate source in the Divine Father.

Paul as Mother and Nurse: Galatians, 1 Thessalonians, and 1 Corinthians

Paul's maternity has gained attention in recent decades due, in large part, to the work of Beverly Roberts Gaventa, whose quest to rescue these images from oblivion has inspired a number of additional studies on their theological and social import.[54] I will focus my observations here on Gal 4, 1 Thess 2, and 1 Cor 3, each of which contains references either to Paul as mother (Gal 4:19–20), or to his role as a wet nurse, if not a nursing-mother (1 Thess 2:7; 1 Cor 3:1–3). In these passages we find explicit *self*-application of transparently feminine imagery to the male apostle, Paul. By appealing to such imagery, Mother Paul not only participates in the social constructions of nurses and mothers in his Roman and Jewish contexts that have been the focus of past studies,[55] but also in the anatomical and physiological constructions of maternal bodies as conveyers of life-giving *logos* and *pneuma* in the womb and at the breasts.

Paul's maternal self-description in Gal 4:19–20 comes after he has employed a number of exegetical arguments concerning the metaphorical paternity of his Galatian audience. In addition to emphasizing God as "our Father" in 1:1–5, Paul spends chapters 3–4 arguing for the Galatians' metaphorical paternity by Abraham, as long as they "believe" the gospel Paul has preached to them (3:7). Immediately after Paul's maternal self-designation, he returns to the Abraham exegesis, this time focusing on the *mothers* in this equation by contrasting the named Hagar and the unnamed Sarah to highlight the nature of their sons: the unnamed Ishmael versus the named Isaac (4:21–5:1). In addition to these mothers, variously described according to status (slave versus free) and according to a corresponding Jerusalem (Mount Sinai in Arabia, which is "present Jerusalem" versus "Jerusalem above"), is also Cybele, the Mountain Mother of the Gods, whose worship was popular in Galatia as well as the Roman Empire in general during Paul's lifetime.[56] According to Susan Elliott, Paul creates a parallel between circumcision and the practice of self-castration by the priests of Cybele, called *galli*, to argue graphically that the Galatians reveal their true mother by means of their choice concerning circumcision.[57] If they should circumcise, they are like the *galli*, and claim allegiance to a Mountain Mother—this time the "slave woman," Hagar (4:22–23). If not, they are like Isaac, children of the promise for the "barren," "free woman." Never named as "Sarah" in his allegory, the only explicit mother for the free children is "Paul" when he describes himself as suffering labor *again* to birth these believers (1:1; 4:19–20).[58] As a "mother" whose fecundity emphatically relies on God alone, Paul is a new "Sarah," whose children are begotten by God alone and, therefore, reflect Christ himself.

Paul's presentation of motherhood in Galatians resonates with the physiological constructions of maternal bodies explored in this study. In a reversal of the usual dilemma of unprovable paternity, Paul has established the identity of the Galatians' fathers at the outset of his letter and again in subsequent arguments: they are "sons of God" (3:26) and sons, or seeds, Abraham (3:7, 29).[59] Necessarily given life by God alone, the question is instead concerning the mother of these children: are they children of Hagar/Sinai (Cybele), or Paul, Jerusalem above (Sarah)? For Paul, it is their maternity that ultimately reveals their nature: slave or free, flesh or spirit. Paul's understanding that maternal contributions impact the nature of a child reflects a two-seed embryology, which argues a mother's seed is used to form a child along with paternal seed.[60] It is the maternal contributions that are shaped by God to create the child who is born and subsequently nursed. Thus, like Favorinus says above, the child is formed from the father *and* the mother (*Noct. att.* 12.1.20). Paul's recurring labor pains in 4:19–20 are for his children, the Galatians who are formed by God's begetting and shaping of Paul's "maternal" contributions, with the result that "Christ"—the ideal Son of the Father—"is formed" in them. Patterned correctly from these two sources, the Galatians batter their way out of Paul's womb as legitimate sons, "heirs of the promise," fully formed men who are free from the need of an enslaved pedagogue (3:23–4:7).[61] In order to realize *this* identity and nature, the Galatians need only recognize from whose womb they have emerged. Having God's Spirit (*pneuma*) acts as their proof, their *bulla* and toga *virilus* against those who would still call them slaves or children in need of circumcision (3:1–6; 4:6).

The nursing imagery in 1 Thessalonians and 1 Corinthians also reflects ancient physiological understandings of maternal bodies. In these passages, Paul employs constructions of breastmilk rather than generation and parturition to remind his audiences of the source of their nourishment and, therefore, their formation. In 1 Thessalonians, Paul's identification of nurses for the Thessalonian believers includes not only himself, but also his coworkers, Silvanus and Timothy, who have worked with him to found and nourish the community. Appearing in a series of metaphorical language that describes these men as "infants" (*nēpioi*),[62] "nurse" (*trophos*), "father" (*patēr*), and "orphans" (*aporphanisthentes*), Paul contrasts the authority with which these "apostles of God" could have come with the compassion and sincere concern they have for these believers (2:7–17). Invoking these familial terms from across the household structure, Paul creates blood-kinship type bonds between his group and the Thessalonians, not only shoring up their loyalty but also establishing the context for his later instructive sections in chapters 4 and 5 of the letter.[63]

The nursing imagery plays a significant role in this rhetorical strategy, beyond the affection and tenderness usually described by interpreters.[64] Certainly, the tradition of affection between a nurse and her charges—let alone her "own children"—is a common feature of ancient Mediterranean literature and epigraphical evidence noted above (1 Thess 2:7). Nevertheless, such affection and loyalty are *tied to* the formation of children by means of the breastmilk they have imbibed; the seed- and, indeed, soul-laden substance that is the first nourishment received in, and then, outside the womb. Paul reflects these physiological constructions when, in 1 Thess 2:8, he writes: "longing thusly for you we were well pleased to share with you not only the gospel of God but also our very souls (*psychas*), because you became beloved to us." More than simply a reference to the general reality that breastmilk is produced by maternal bodies, Paul's use of "soul" (*psychē*) reflects the cultural assumption that milk communicates "soul" from a mother/nurse to child. Writing on this phenomenon in Aristotle, Penniman concludes: "The power of mother's milk, consequently, is found in its unique ability to stabilize the infant, causing it to grow properly and enabling the likeness of the parent to be fashioned within the child. Breast milk carries a powerful and transformative essence through the nutritive soul of the mother into that of her child."[65] In other words, when the child consumes breastmilk, the child, "quite literally for Aristotle, ingests the stuff from which the mother's own soul is made."[66] From this ingestion, the child is patterned both by the consumption of the paternal seed in the milk, as well also from the communication of the mother's soul. Mixed with the *logos* and *pneuma* from the seed(s) discussed above, milk shapes the body, soul (or mind), and spirit of the child drinking it with the result that they resemble their nurse and demonstrate loyalty to her and her blood-kin.

Paul's use of such language in 1 Thessalonians has similar results. Having consumed the milk of these nurses, Paul reinforces the Thessalonians' imitation of himself and his coworkers already mentioned in 1:6. Because they are shaped by their superior milk, the Thessalonians can be confident that they are shaped, or "sanctified" (4:3, 4, 7), by God's Spirit and should strive to continue their proper development. With such a positive foundation in their faith-infancy, the Thessalonians have been set up to succeed in their *paideia* so that they can "live a life worthy of God" (2:12) through bodily self-control, love of another, and faith in God's loyalty (4:1–5:22). In this way, the milk imagery supports the themes of family-like bonds to Paul, his coworkers, one another, and to the entire household of God that Paul pushes in this letter. These metaphors, therefore, are not just as clever ornamentation, but create visceral and psychic clarity. Paul hits on the theme one more time when he concludes the letter with the wish that the Thessalonians' "spirit (*pneuma*) and soul (*psychē*) and body (*sōma*) be kept blamelessly whole at the coming of our Lord Jesus Christ" (5:23). For Paul, as with other ancients, these three elements cannot be severed and, in fact, come together provocatively in a mother's milk.

In 1 Corinthians many of these ideas surface again, even though the context of the letter varies significantly from 1 Thessalonians. In contrast to the general encouragement of 1 Thessalonians, 1 Corinthians is written to a community in crisis: one divided in factions and the competitions at home in masculine-seeking, agonistic contexts of the Roman Empire. Nevertheless, Paul's remedy for the Corinthians is very much the same as his words for the Thessalonians. He reminds the Corinthians of the nature of his visit to them, highlighting the contrast between his own self-presentation and that of other, more obviously masculine, itinerant speakers (1 Cor 2:1–4:21; compare 1 Thess 2:1–12). Rather than displaying "superior words or wisdom" (1 Cor 2:1), Paul performs a new masculinity, one that displays the "wisdom of God" by highlighting the paradox of Jesus's crucifixion (1:21). Relativized by God's ultimate masculinity, Paul showcases the power of God rather than his own impenetrability (2:1–5). Like Jesus, Paul appears weak, humiliated and, therefore, *feminine* so that he can be a conduit for God's glory. When Paul describes God's destruction of the "wisdom of the wise" and the "discernment of the discerning," he is in fact describing God's undermining of Roman-era performances of masculinity that seek to usurp God's unique claims (1:19).

It is, therefore, in the midst of another self-presentation as a weak and, indeed, apparently effeminate man that Paul describes himself in terms of a nurse in 1 Cor 3:1–3. Reminding the Corinthians of his first visit to them while "fleshly" infants in Christ (*nēpioi en Christō*), Paul writes: "I gave you milk (*gala*) to drink, not solid food (*brōma*), for you were not yet able [to eat]. Even now you are still not able, for you are still fleshly" (vv. 1–2). The Corinthians, according to Paul, still require the balancing and sustaining nourishment of a mother's or nurse's milk; their bodies are not firm enough, not masculine enough, to receive solid food. In other words, while the Corinthians might perceive themselves as masculine, it is according to the wrong standards. Their attraction to "wisdom of word" (*sophia logou*, 1:17), division, and other typical masculine displays in Roman society rather than to Paul reveals their sustained infancy, a diagnosis Mother Paul determines and can remedy with more character- and family-forming milk.

The effects of Paul's milk-feeding are the same as they were in 1 Thess 2:7–8: it shapes the Corinthians. The milk they have received, and are receiving, as fleshly infants is enabling their formation to be "spiritual" (*pneumatikois*, 1 Cor 3:1). In this way, Paul's nursing metaphor fits with those that follow in 1 Cor 3; just like a farmer and a builder, a nurse shapes the final form of her charges (3:5–17). Drinking in the Spirit of God through Paul, the Corinthians have the "mind (*noun*) of Christ" and should, therefore, be unified (2:16; 10:1–4; 12:13). In reminding the Corinthians of the source of their nourishment, Paul reminds them of the foundation of their formation and the educational path it should lay before them (4:14–21). Moreover, he exalts his authority over them, even while downplaying his masculinity according to Roman standards. He is the source of their milk, God's chosen conduit for their formation. The infant Corinthians, therefore, should remain loyal to him and to one another as those fed by the same breasts.

Paul's use of maternal and nursing imagery in his letters, therefore, regularly vivifies his calls for loyalty and unity. Nevertheless, they do so *because* they assume the physiological construction of maternal bodies and breastmilk as a character-forming substance that transfer parental qualities to infants. When good blood is consumed in the womb, or good milk is consumed at the breast, it forms good children. Having their initial formation in and by Paul's metaphorically maternal body, these believers have been patterned so that they should resemble him even as he resembles Christ (Gal 4:12–20; 1 Cor 2:16; 11:1; 1 Thess 2:12). Thus, these images graphically underscore Paul's calls for imitation even as they displace biological mothers and physical wet nurses. It is important to remember, therefore, that while Paul's use of maternal imagery relativizes his own masculinity, as well as Roman-era masculinity more generally, it does not do so in a way that makes room for *real* female bodies.[67] Rather, it blurs female bodies and even risks hiding them behind undeniably male ones who birth and nurse in their place—*and* who claim to bring forth and form superior offspring for the heavenly *Pater* (see Gal 4:4–7).

Moving On from the Nursery: Hebrews 5

The reference to milk and its contrast to solid food in Heb 5:11–14 comes closest to the educational parallels often cited from Epictetus and Philo, which capitalize on the place of nourishment in character-formation.[68] In these analogies, "milk" represents basic teaching or instruction, useful and necessary for "infants" in learning. "Solid food," in contrast, is more difficult teaching. Thus, Philo explains, "[S]ouls still naked like those of mere infants, must be tended and nursed by instilling first, in the place of milk, the soft food of instruction given in the school subjects, later, the harder, stronger meat, which philosophy produces."[69] Philo continues that this path of education results in a person being "reared . . . to manhood (*andrōtheisai*) and robustness to an auspicious maturity (*telos*)." Epictetus makes use of the same connection to rebuke his opponents for remaining in the nursery rather than seeking truth through philosophy (*Dis.* 2.16; 3.24). Although they pretend to be men, these hypocrites are shown to be infantile and effeminate by remaining in a passive and ignorant state: they desire to be fed rather than search for themselves.

Like Philo and Epictetus, the author of Hebrews makes use of the connection of food and education to admonish his audience to yearn for "solid food." Even though the author claims to have "much to say" on the "word" of Jesus's priesthood according to the order of Melchizedek, he must pause due to the "dull hearing" (*nōthroi gegonate tais akoais*) of his audience (5:1–11).

> For even though you ought to be teachers by this time, you again have need for us to teach you certain basics of the beginning of the words of God

> (*logion tou theou*) and you have become ones having need of milk (*galaktos*) and not solid food (*stereas trophēs*). For each one who partakes of milk (*galaktos*) is ignorant of a word (*logou*) of righteousness, for they are an infant (*nēpios*). But solid food (*sterea trophē*) is for the mature (*teleiōn*), for the ones who, on account of their stable state (*hexis*), have senses that have been trained (*gegumnasmena*) for judging both good and evil. (5:12–14)

With this brief digression, the author shames his audience with the hopes of prompting them to seek more difficult teaching about Jesus rather than remaining in the nursery.[70] The problem, according to the author of Hebrews, is that his audience is content with the "milk" that they have received. Although this "milk" is good, it nevertheless risks leaving them porous and malformed if they continue to rely on it for too long.

While past interpreters have readily acknowledged the presence of the food/education commonplace in Hebrews 5, they have not ventured beyond this basic reading to investigate how the physiological constructions of breastmilk play into this commonplace.[71] However, knowing the formative power of milk to continue shaping and stabilizing infants toward maturity makes its use in educational *topos* of Hebrews especially significant.[72] Indeed, the use of the metaphor in Hebrews reflects the physiological and soul-shaping understandings just as the previous appearances of milk from Paul's writings above. The admonishment in Heb 5:11–14, for example, is not against the consumption of milk per say, but against the consumption of milk for too long. In fact, the milk imbibed by these believers is good milk; by drinking it they have "tasted the heavenly gift" and the "goodness of the word of God" and experienced a "blessing from God" that is compared to the life-giving and nourishing rain that falls upon the earth (6:4–8). Nursed by the teachers in their community, they have been nourished by God's formative "words" (*logoi*) that should have provided the necessary foundation for their continued growth. *This* is why the audience should be teachers already! They should have been formed by the milk received to reflect those who have been teaching them up to this point (5:12; 6:12; 13:7).

Yet, like Epictetus's lolling fake-men, these believers linger too long in the nursery and, as a result, still *need* milk in order to survive. Recalling Soranus's comments noted above, he warns that children become "moist and delicate if fed on milk for a long time" (*Gyn.* 2.21.46). Thus, the reliance on milk for too long actually endangers the positive effects that milk initially provides (as in *t. Nid.* 2.3). Instead of stabilizing and firming up an infant's body and soul, it makes them permeable and soft. In other words, instead of helping a child (especially a son) toward maturity, it causes them to have traditionally feminine qualities, making them vulnerable to vice.[73] Thus, Epictetus and the author of Hebrews accuse their audiences of more than simple childishness; instead, they accuse them of effeminacy.

The difficult-to-translate *hexis* in Heb 5:14 reflects this interpretation. Although often translated "practice," "habit," or "skill," John A. L. Lee argues that its "primary meaning... is a *physical and/or mental state*."[74] While Lee's argument verges on separating the physical and mental too harshly, his overall analysis is helpful. Reviewing a number of uses of the word in ancient literature, he notes that for Aristotle, the word connotes a degree of stability in contrast to the variability of *diathesis*. While one's *diathesis* is easy to change, *hexis* is much more difficult.[75] Nevertheless, change can happen to one's *hexis*, particularly through education. Thus, Plato writes: "[I]n education a change is to be made from another *hexis* to a better one; but the physician brings about the change by means of drugs, and the teacher of wisdom by means of words" (*Theat.* 167a4.4) and in *Laws* 1.645e.5 he contrasts the *hexis* of a person's soul as a "child" versus as an adult.[76] As we have seen above, the goal of education is to shape a child into a more mature "state," one that is stable, able to discern rightly, and masculine. The use of *hexis* in Heb 5:14 fits nicely into this milieu. While the audience should have a stable *hexis*, one that is the result of "trained" senses in order to judge good from evil, they do not. Instead, they "have need" for milk; they are instable and, therefore, still susceptible to fail in the face of suffering rather than being made even more firm, or mature, by it.

The problem in Hebrews, then, is an unnatural milk-dependency that threatens to undermine the audience's standing as sons of God and brothers of Christ in God's household. Although the milk is good, a "heavenly gift," it, like the rain, must produce a mature crop: legitimate sons who resemble their brother, the ideal Son, Jesus. Having shared in the "blood and flesh" of these brothers, Jesus was "perfected" (*teleiōsai*) or brought to maturity through his suffering so that he now acts as the ideal intermediary before the Father (2:10–18; 5:9). The Hebrews, too, must be perfected through suffering; this is their "education" (*paideia*, 12:5, 7, 8, 11). In Heb 12:7–8 the author writes, "Endure for education (*paideian*). God is treating you as sons; for what son is there whom a father does not educate (*paideuei*)? But if you are without the education (*paideias*), of which all have become partakers, then you are illegitimate (*nothoi*) and not sons." Even though such "education (*paideia*) seems painful rather than joyful at the time, ... later it yields the peaceful fruit of righteousness to those having been trained (*gegumnasmenois*) by it" (12:11).

Repeating several tag words and images from 5:11–6:12, this portion of Hebrews 12 summarizes the author's exhortation: it is time to move on from the nursery! These similar themes and imagery include agriculture metaphors (6:7–8; 12:11), education (5:11–6:12; 12:3–11), maturation/perfection (5:11; 12:2), endurance, and patience (6:11–12; 12:3–11). While the agriculture theme repeats in the two chapters, the milk image is replaced by another common educational metaphor in chapter 12: namely, that of the training and running athlete. Identical words include: "training" (*gumnazō*, which only appears in 5:14 and 12:11) and "righteousness" (*dikaosunē*, 5:13; 12:11). Given these connections, one wonders if the similarity in the sound of *nōthroi* (dull, sluggish, lazy) in 5:11 and 6:12 is meant to be heard in the risk of being *nothoi* (illegitimate) in 12:8. If the audience remains *nōthroi* they will be considered *nothoi*. Inherent with this argument is the pushing of a particular masculinity on the audience as well, one that mimics Christ's. Not content to leave his charges in the nursery, the author challenges his audience with his difficult *logos* in chapters 7–10 and, thus, forces their manhood. Either they will come to imitate the ideal Son who has come before them, or they will experience their Father's wrath, disowned and left outside his newly formed household.

Longing for the Pure, Word-like Milk: 1 Peter

The final passage in our list contrasts with that of Hebrews, even as it reflects the same physiological constructions of milk in its use of the metaphor. Unlike Hebrews, 1 Peter 2:1–3 commands its audience to "long for the pure, word-like milk" (*to logikon gala*) like "newly born babes" (*artigennēta brephē*) so that they can "grow into salvation" (2:2). Having "tasted that the Lord is good" (2:3), these baby believers are to continue drinking *this* milk, and therefore, continue to be shaped by the seeds and bloods in it. In this way, the breastmilk in 1 Peter participates in the larger paraenesis of the letter, which contrasts the audience's former way of life with their new life in allegiance to God and made possible through Jesus Christ (1:13–21; 2:9–12; 4:1–6).[77] Newly begotten and born into "God's household" (*tou oikou tou theou*, 4:17), these believers are to demonstrate not only their allegiance to the Father through their demonstration of "self-control" (*sōphronēsate*, 4:7), but their very formation to reflects their new Father by means of the blood and milk of Jesus.

The context surrounding 1 Peter 2:1–3 includes a number of generative and familial metaphors that fit quite seamlessly with the reference to breastmilk in this passage. The letter begins by characterizing God as "Father" of the community who chose these believers to be his children, "sanctified by the spirit to be obedient to Jesus Christ and sprinkled by his blood" (1:2). Following this characterization, the author then repeats God's title as "Father," this time of "our Lord Jesus Christ," before describing the merciful "new begetting into a living hope" (*anagennēsas hēmas eis elpida zōsan*) provided "through the resurrection of Jesus Christ" for the audience (1:3). Having been begotten and born anew by the Father, these believers are to expect an "imperishable inheritance" (*klēronomian aphtharton*, 1:4) of salvation that contrasts "the worthless way of life" they received from their "forefathers" (1:17–21). Having received such a gift, these believers are to act as "obedient children" fitting this promise (1:14).[78] As a result of their begetting, they are to be re-formed to live as ones patterned after their new Father rather than in the "futile ways" of their former fathers: "You shall be holy, for I am holy" (1:16).[79]

While all this language generally reflects the notions of patterning and parental resemblance explained in the embryological and nursing theories outlined in the present study, 1 Peter supplies more explicit language that capitalizes on these ancient assumptions. In fact, knowing these anatomical and physiological constructions can aid in our understanding of 1 Peter, particularly its combination of seed (*spora*, 1:23), word (*logos*, *rhema*, 1:23–2:2), blood (*haima*, 1:2, 19), and milk (*gala*, 2:2) that has puzzled modern interpreters. In 1:22–2:3 the author writes of the "purification" of the "souls" of his audience by means of their "obedience." From the previous verses, one notes the implied connection between "obedience" and the new begetting of these believers: it is the mark of their new birth. First Peter 1:23, however, makes the connection explicit: "You have been begotten anew, not of perishable but of imperishable seed, through the living and remaining word of God."[80] In contrast to "flesh," this word "remains forever" and is the "good news" delivered to the believers (1:24–25).[81] In other words, their hearing and accepting the "good news" has implanted God's word in them; thus, God has sparked their new begetting through Jesus Christ. Begotten of God by means of the "imperishable seed" that contains both his word and the "precious blood" (*timiō haimati*) of Jesus, the believers are to recognize their rightful Father and have confidence in their "imperishable inheritance" (1:4).

The generative language of 1:22–25 continues into the breastmilk language of 2:1–3. Even though Karen Jobes calls the transition "abrupt and unaided," the physiological theories explored in this study reveal just how interconnected seed, word, blood, and milk are in the ancient world.[82] As Philip Tite explains, "[T]hrough the lens of ancient gynaecological views on blood (αἵματος [*haimatos*]) and milk (γάλα [*gala*]), the Petrine author's metaphorical description of the recipients' new *familia* likely evokes the 'like-to-like' image of foetal and neonate development."[83] Having been conceived and nourished by blood and word in the womb, these "newly begotten babes" are to continue drinking these elements in the milk provided at the breast. Thus, they are continually shaped by this word in order to grow into their salvation—the inheritance promised to them. While the author does not use explicitly pedagogical language as we found in 1 Corinthians or Hebrews, the connection is nevertheless clear; with this superior foundation in God's word, the obedient children are to continue growing to be obedient sons by showing loyalty to their Father, as well as loving one another as fellow nurse-mates (1:22; 2:17). Modeling the virtues and self-control of masculinity, these believers are not only to reflect the example of Jesus Christ, but of their Divine Father.

Awareness of these physiological assumptions also clarifies the complicated translation of 2:2. In this verse the breastmilk to be craved by the believers is called *to logikon adolon gala*. While interpreters have long recognized the connection of *adolon* ("without deceit," "pure") with the command for the audience to "lay aside all deceit (*dolon*)" in 2:1, there has not been such clarity around *logikon*. A number of scholars translate the phrase with something like "the milk of God's word," emphasizing the connection of 2:1 to 1:25 and playing on the idea of consuming God's instruction demonstrated elsewhere in biblical and Second Temple Jewish traditions.[84] In this way, the milk consumed is "spiritual milk" rather than literal, physical milk and corresponds to the "spiritual house" metaphor in 2:4–8 that follows. Others have focused on the "rational" and "verbal" connotations of *logikon*.[85] Lying at the heart of these translation and interpretive quandaries, however, is a lack of understanding of ancient theories concerning conception, generation, and breastmilk.[86] The milk to be sought after is full of the word—or "word-like"—because it continues to convey the "imperishable seed" involved at conception and in generation.[87] It is "pure" because of its source. These believers have the best mother and nurse, resulting in the continued conveyance of their heavenly Father's superior seed/word and, therefore, their continued formation as his children.

Tite suggests that as a result of this metaphor the author of 1 Peter "conflates maternal and paternal roles" in a manner similar to the *Odes of Solomon*, which repeatedly figure God as a nursing mother whose milk feeds and forms her/his children.[88] A closer look, however, pushes against such a reading. If, indeed, the milk and blood images are related as the context indicates, then it is through Christ that both are administered. Supporting this view is 2:3, which describes the "Lord" as *chrēstos*, meaning "good" or "benevolent." The wordplay between *chrēstos* and *Christos* ("Christ") has long been recognized; as Jobes explains, "The difference between 'the Lord is good' and the 'Lord is Christ' is but one vowel."[89] Having "tasted that the Lord is good" indicates that the believers are drinking from—and, indeed, drinking in—the Lord Christ himself. It is from Christ that they drink, just as it was through his parturitive Passion and resurrection that the believers were "newly begotten" (1:3, 23). In this way, the imagery of 1 Peter brings us back to that of the Gospel of John. Again, we find a maternal Jesus birthing and nursing his followers for their formation as children of God.[90] Like other ideal, ancient mothers, Jesus passes on the virtues of the Father first through blood, then milk, which symbolize his exemplary behavior, in order to cultivate ideal sons.

Conclusions

The above analysis demonstrates the correspondences between NT uses of breastmilk and breastfeeding imagery and assumptions surrounding milk and character formation in the ancient Mediterranean world. The similarities exist because the NT represents more than just the gendered educational presuppositions from its Greco-Roman contexts; these writings also reveal similar understandings of female anatomy and the physiology of breastmilk that lends this milk such soul- and character-shaping power. Continuing to transfer the *logos* and *pneuma* of seed and blood from the umbilicus now through her breasts, a woman who nurses conveys the very substance of life to her children and/or her charges. In so doing, she nourishes them with seeds and even her own soul. Preoccupation with the source of such a powerful substance—and its proper administration—is fitting among ancient medical and philosophical authors commenting on child-rearing, *paideia*, and the cultivation of manhood. And the iconic endorsement of mothers nursing their own sons in statues and coins communicates such ideals to those who see them, and also bolsters the family-focused image of emperors like Augustus. While the masculinities presented by NT writers differ from those of the larger Roman world, their cultivation results in similar concerns and, therefore, similar uses of breastmilk imagery to further their causes.[91] Having been begotten anew, birthed by Paul or even by Jesus, these believers must also continue to nurse at the breast of their new mothers. In this way alone can they be sure to receive proper nourishment that will continue shaping them to become proper sons of God.

The importance of breastmilk in the ancient Mediterranean world, therefore, should dispel notions of mere ornamentation for its appearances in NT texts. While breastmilk and nursing certainly can communicate ideas of affection and connection, it is not simply a metaphor of care and love between a nurse and her charge. Instead, breastmilk was understood to be transformative by its very nature; carrying the potential to either alter an infant's state from fluidity to firmness on the path to manhood, or to corrupt any potential for masculinity by rendering an infant too moist, too delicate, permeable to the vices that define the feminine, and feminized. Moreover, because of its transmission of seed, breastmilk created kinship bonds when shared among nurslings. As is clear in the writings of Favorinus and Plutarch, while a mother especially was said to nurse out of affection, the real goal of her affection was to create lasting, familial bonds between the child and both of its parents. In this way, breastmilk forges not just love, but loyalty to blood-kin that should last through adulthood. The presentation of Jesus nursing from his heavenly Father and the calls for drinking the *right* milk in 1 Peter, or for the *right* duration in Hebrews, and to remember one's nurse in 1 Thessalonians and 1 Corinthians play on these same understandings and draw on their same implications. Rather than a quaint metaphor to be dismissed, the breasts and milk present in these writings contribute significantly to the rhetoric employed and, therefore, to the theological *paideia* administered.

Nevertheless, one is unable to find a single woman's breast in the midst of all these passages. While the imagery relies on the unique ability of a female body, it displaces those same bodies, replacing them with a male apostle, teacher, Christ, or Divine Father. In this way, these writings imply a supply of superior, more masculine, breastmilk to their charges, as well as a superior manhood that results from its consumption. While women's bodies might be needed for physical birth and literal nursing, these masculine bearers and breasts offer superior births and nurture, just as Socrates describes in Plato's *Theatetus* and *Symposium*. Women bear and nourish mortal children, but men birth "immortal children" when they metaphorically give birth to virtue in philosophical *eros* (*Theat.* 148e–51; *Symp.* 201d–12c; see also *Acts of Andrew*). Thus, biological motherhood continues to be downplayed in these writings, just as it was in the Gospels and Acts.

Yet, in spite of their displacement by these masculine NT mothers, images of literal mothers' breasts are always conjured when breastmilk is consumed. As a result, there is an inescapable blending of masculine and feminine in these passages; the bodies of the masculine NT mothers are necessarily feminized by their porous ability to absorb seed (*logos*, *pneuma*) and leak milk. Indeed, all these figures stand feminized in their relationship to the Divine Father whose seed/word they communicate. Although absolutized in his own masculinity as *the* Father, even he offers his breast to his Son, giving superior and undiluted nourishment so that this Son can do the same (John 1:18; 13:23). Thus, the masculinities of these NT writings differ from those of the larger Greco-Roman world. These "sons" are shaped to follow God's perfect Son, who suffered and died pierced upon a cross before being resurrected to glory. Even in the midst of God's supreme, masculine impermeability, therefore, the feminine porousness exists to reveal and to leak in order to communicate life.

Questions remain, however, as to what such uses of feminine imagery and simultaneous displacement of biological mothers meant for actual girls, women, and mothers in early Christian communities. Paul seems to continue the message of the Gospels and Acts by discouraging marriage and procreation in 1 Cor 7, while 1 Peter 2–3 assumes Greco-Roman norms surrounding household structure and management, which included the birthing and rearing of children. If women are included in the admonishments to become "sons" of God, are they to do so as literal mothers or are they to find their telos in a different way of living? In other words, if the blurring of gender in the breastmilk imagery used in these NT passages opened the way for men to act like "women," did it also open the way for women to act like "men"—and if so, how masculine could they become? It is here that one finds the sticking point. Even in 1 Corinthians Paul pushes against women who, according to him, overreach their created location below men (11:2–16). If women are included in God's great gift of salvation, just like men, how are they to be kept "in their place"? As we move on to the next chapter we will see that early Christian communities provided no single answer to this quandary, but several, continuing their participation in the ambiguity and ambivalence shown toward women, mothers, and motherhood throughout the Greco-Roman world. In any instance, the position seems to be one of control: either through the traditional narrative of motherhood (1 Timothy; Titus) or through intact, virgin masculinity (*Acts of Thecla*). While men may be able to take on the role of mothers, women seem unable to be both mothers and men.

5

Salvation and Childbearing

DOES MOTHERHOOD MATTER?

ALTHOUGH THE PREVIOUS two chapters traced a persistent distancing of biological mothers in a number of NT works, the present chapter serves to muddy the waters a bit. While the passages explored so far either explicitly downplay literal mothers and motherhood (e.g., Luke 11:27–28) or implicitly do so by neglecting their mention in renderings of births and nursing (e.g., John 1:1–18; Gal 4:19–20), other NT passages assume and even encourage motherhood as the telos for women believers. Among the most notorious, of course, is 1 Tim 2:15 and its puzzling assertion that "the woman/wife" (*gynē*) in verse 14 "will be saved through childbearing if they should remain in faith and love and holiness with self-control." Further on in the same letter, the Pastor writes of his "desire for young widows to marry, to bear children, to manage households in order not to give the opponent an opportunity to slander us" (5:14). Similar passages in Titus, along with the assumption of motherhood that runs through the various household codes, advocate lifestyles of virtue quite similar to those of the larger Greco-Roman world (Titus 2:3–5; Col 3:18–4:3; Eph 5:21–6:9; 1 Pet 2:9–3:12). Nevertheless, outside the NT we discover additional works that discourage motherhood in favor of a life singularly devoted to Christ (e.g., *Acts of Thecla*; *Acts of Andrew*). The ambivalence of NT and early Christian communities toward mothers and motherhood, therefore, remains unresolved.

The gendered, generative, and pedagogical language used in the NT, however, provides a way forward in this conversation. As we have seen in the previous chapters, even in their distancing of biological mothers, NT authors retain the anatomical, physiological, and pedagogical paradigms of their larger Greco-Roman cultures. The goal of being more faithful followers of God is considered a process of masculinization in the NT just as it was in pedagogical literature of the era, even if the masculinities they depict differ from the Roman ideal in their exaltation of a crucified Lord. As free(d) "sons," believers are called to continue their nurture/education in order to become real "men" of God.

Yet, such a program begs a long debated question: if the goal of ideal living is to become "masculine," how should women (and, indeed, any un-men) who are believers participate in the process? Can they? Moreover, if they can participate, to what extent can they arrive at legitimate masculinity since they will always have *female bodies*, porous and leaking even if the threat of male penetration remains unrealized? For much of the ancient Mediterranean world, the answer to this question was achieved *through motherhood*, which was conflated with "being a woman." By marrying, or at least procreating, women and their problematic bodies were literally infused with masculine seed with the positive result of living children, hopefully sons, who justified their otherwise deficient existence. Controlled in a man's household, girls, virgins, women/wives, and female slaves were purposed; the masculine oversight of their *paterfamilias* preventing them from causing chaos for others and for themselves since even a woman's own health was tied to her successful pregnancies.[1] When various NT writings and even the preserved sayings of Jesus undermine this maternal narrative, however, believers must wrestle with the question of masculinization for women anew: How can female believers become masculine after God's definitive action through Jesus, his Christ? Must they become women/wives/mothers first?

This chapter will explore these questions by building on the maternal constructions outlined in previous chapters with an overview of presentations of mothers in the Augustan age. As we will see, Augustus's prioritization of family life to promote his own masculinity resulted in a simultaneous emphasis on motherhood. Not only did motherhood advertise a man's masculine purposing of his woman/wife, but it was also a legitimate path to increased agency for free(d) women who capitalized on their unique abilities to birth and nurture sons for the state. Sorting out the alternative masculinities presented in the NT and early Christian traditions also required ancient Christians to form alternative femininities in the midst of this Augustan context. Faced with this task, the NT and other early Christian writings offer different models of the seemingly impossible, but nevertheless often debated, "feminine virtue"—some of which more closely replicate the dominant maternal narrative of the Augustan age and some of which continue to undermine it.[2] Nevertheless, in their sustained wrestling with and formations of Christian gender(s), these writings betray a similar preoccupation to present salvation as masculinization for all followers of Christ, even if they disagree on whether motherhood should be a part of this process.

Molding Princes for Rome: Maternal Power in the Augustan Age

The early Imperial age during which the events of the NT occurred and the NT writings were compiled was one of transition; the result of two civil wars and the dissolution of a once republican Rome for one ruled by its singular *princeps*, the "first citizen" and emperor, who was to embody and effect masculine order for the state. Octavian, turned "Augustus," secured this status only after conquering a once popular Marc Antony, who was both a friend and ally of Julius Caesar. The adopted son of Julius Caesar, Augustus had a potentially diluted blood relationship with his esteemed (and assassinated) predecessor in contrast to Antony's bond. These challenges, therefore, complicated Augustus's pursuit and performance of masculinity. It was not good enough for him to be like any other virtuous man, he needed to be the manliest of men to justify his preeminent place in the Roman world.

Augustus's performance and crafting of a superior masculinity required other masculinities in his empire to be redefined under his own. It also required femininity to undergo similar redefinitions. Focusing on the masculinity achieved through fatherhood, Augustus highlighted the role of women/wives as mothers. As good women, mothers exhibit proper female masculinity in their submission to husbands and rearing of virtuous (i.e., manly) sons who would rule Rome as, or alongside, the emperor. That praise for such women was publicized in statues, on coins, and in literature highlights the paradoxical power of the women who could either masculinize or feminize sons, households, as well as the state and the cosmos, depending on the type of mothers they were. The age initiated by Augustus and continuing on long after his death not only assumed the normativity of motherhood as the ideal telos for free women, and the natural telos for virtually all other females, it also reinforced this normativity through legislation, material representations, and publicity of prominent matrons who appear throughout Roman history. Augustus's special emphasis on his own masculinity, therefore, underscored the importance of femininity as well; in fact, it made the performance of proper femininity by women in the imperial household a cornerstone on which the emperor's own manhood—and, therefore, that of Rome—was precariously perched.

In what follows, I will trace the rise of Roman matrons and demonstrate how motherhood offered them increased agency from late Republican Rome through the early Imperial era. Legally independent (*sui iuris*) after the deaths of their fathers, these women owned property, acted as patrons, and wielded significant power on their own as well as through their sons.[3] Yet, this power was always limited and suspect because of its permanent tie to a female body, whose indeterminate boundaries threatened to leave cravings for ever more power unchecked. Unable to become fully male, a woman—even a mother—could never be fully masculine and, therefore, never lost her potential for chaos.

From Aristotle's Athens to Augustus's Rome: The Rise of the Roman Matron

Reflecting on various types of friendships that a "good man" enjoys, Aristotle offers the analogy of family relationships, particularly the one that exists between a mother and her sons, in his *Nicomachean Ethics*. For Aristotle, maternal love acts as an ideal analogy for friendships that are unequal in terms of love since a mother loves her children more than her children love her *and* she loves them more than their father does. Moreover, maternal relationships demonstrate Aristotle's truism that one loves more what is achieved through labor, since "parenthood costs the mother more trouble (and the mother is more certain that the child is her own)."[4] Aristotle's arguments rest on the assumption that mother-love is a readily acknowledged and recognizable model for a friend's love, a universal enough aspect of his Classical Athenian world that the elite young men hearing his instruction would understand.

Thus, it is the mother who is described as the "chief" example of one who both rejoices and grieves alongside her children, and she more than anyone else desires for them to exist for their own sakes rather than for the material return which she is due from them (9.4.1166a1–5). Indeed, while a son may reciprocate such love for his mother, and even offer material provision for her, Aristotle argues that children owe their parents more than they can ever hope to repay; their initial gift of life and then nurture far outweigh any later care a child provides (8.12.1161b16–1162a10). According to Aristotle's model, the ideal mother only increases the debt owed to her by children with her constant love and utmost devotion throughout their lives. Rather than hoping for repayment, again the mother becomes a model, this time contrasting the duplicitous flatterer, since she takes delight in the act of loving rather than looking for repayment.

Aristotle's idealization of mothers and mother-love in the midst of his thoughts on friendship should not be understood to mean that he perceives any sort of equality between a mother and a son. An elite member of Classical Athens, writing to other soon-to-be elite men, Aristotle lives in a world that cloistered women, famously emphasizing that an honorable woman was a socially invisible one, her name never spoken outside the family home. In such a world, elite women married young, could not own property, and remained constantly under the guardianship of a man as her "lord": father, uncle, husband, and even eventually her son. In such a context, Aristotle's roundabout construction of the maternal ideal makes sense: a mother cannot act as an agent, but only as a conduit of and for her male guardian's will—a necessary conduit, but a conduit nonetheless. Thus, she is most assuredly a self-sacrificing model, since she has no real access to a full sense of "self" in terms of acknowledged person/manhood in her society. She cannot hope for, or rightfully desire, repayment, but only take delight in the act of loving, in the act of realizing her telos as a woman with production of (male) children for the sake of her husband. In keeping with his embryology, then, Aristotle's ideal woman/mother persists in her passive nurturing and preservation of the male seed throughout her life.

Much as his embryology was tempered with Hippocratic and later Hellenistic ideas among Roman physicians, the Athenian ideals of motherhood reflected by Aristotle also changed in the very different reality of an Imperial Roman world. While females were still expected to become mothers, the elite among them could experience increased freedom and influence as a result of their maternal role. As Suzanne Dixon notes, girls who were able to marry and become "women"—that is, freed or freeborn girls—began to marry *sine manu* ("without hand") in late Republican Rome and by the early Imperial period, marriage *sine manu* was the norm.[5] This transition in practice meant that daughters remained legally a part of their natal family throughout life, living under *pater potestas* (the "power" of their biological father) until his death instead of transitioning into the "hand" (*manu*) of their husband upon marriage. Such an arrangement meant that a woman's dowry remained her own, and therefore attached to her paternal family, since it was not absorbed into a husband's wealth at marriage.[6]

This arrangement also facilitated a father's desire for daughters to divorce and remarry according to his vacillating allegiances throughout life. While perhaps not as significant for those outside noble classes, the ability to force divorces and remarriage (even when daughters were pregnant) was a tactic used throughout the tumultuous years of civil wars, Triumvirates, proscriptions, and beyond. Remaining in the power of her father until his death, a daughter functioned with primary loyalty to her natal household, becoming another link to preserve paternal wealth and maintain paternal blood lines instead of being subsumed by (and disappearing beyond the walls of) her husband's house. Indeed, that women's paternal links were significant in the Roman world is demonstrated by the fact that maternal ancestry is cited as a means of honor in biographical accounts, epitaphs, and statues.[7]

In addition to maintaining a connection to her biological family, marriage *sine manu* had the benefit of making women legally independent upon the death of their fathers, which could happen quite early in her married life.[8] Having married and become a mother, Roman matrons had already made the transition from child to woman. A Roman matron became a woman of at least measured independence, which could vary in degree depending on her social class. Remarking on the desirability of this status change, Susan E. Hylen writes: "While [the] social reality certainly reflects the patriarchal inequalities of society, it nevertheless meant that marriage had a real impact on a woman's perceived social status, . . . While a fifteen-year-old who did not marry remained a girl in her parent's household, a fifteen-year-old who married changed social status and became a woman."[9] If she birthed living children, especially sons, and eventually outlived her husband, this status only increased.

Unlike Classical Greece, therefore, Roman women in the Augustan age were able to inherit and own property, particularly the dowries that accompanied their marriage. According to Dixon, these realities meant that women could come to have substantial wealth and, as a result, influence as patrons beyond their households and over their children who anticipated inheriting said wealth upon their mother's death.[10] Indeed, a mother's influence over children persisted even past divorces and remarriages, since mothers were expected to intestate her own children regardless of their current marital status. Preserving the paternal blood lines that passed through her, she remained connected to all her children, regardless of the fact that these children would stay with their own fathers, and under his *potestas*, in the case of divorce.[11] Dixon argues, therefore, that even though mothers were never granted legal power over their children on par with that of fathers, they exercised significant influence at least partly as a result of their economic potential.[12]

Yet, economic pragmatism is certainly not the only reason for the extended attachment between Roman matrons and their children, which is preserved in surviving literature from the early Imperial age. Especially vibrant are the relationships recorded between mothers and their elite sons, the "great men" whose lives either led Rome to glory or to tragedy depending in no small part on the education they did (or did not) receive from their mothers. While not formal tutors, mothers were responsible for conveying traditional Roman values to their sons, the *mos maiorum*. Indeed, as we have seen mothers and (or) other women caring for infants, were charged with molding a child at their most malleable state. Providing nourishment through milk, care, story-telling, proper Greek, and virtuous living, these women enabled a child to continue mimicking virtue throughout life.

Roman authors, therefore, repeatedly exult in the depiction of mothers, both ideal and otherwise, by incorporating these women into their founding myths (re)produced to reflect Augustus's ideals of Empire. In the *Aeneid*, Virgil's epic commissioned by and dedicated to Augustus, the hero and the ancestor of the Romans, Aeneas, wanders toward his destined home, Italy, and bride, Lavinia, at the behest and constant instigation of his mother, Venus. This homeland and bride are made parallel destinies for Aeneas, although both seem to pale in comparison to the comfort and passion that Carthage afford him and his men. Yet, it is in Italy alone, and by means of the girl there that he will make a woman, that Aeneas will find his destiny; it is there that he will plant his seed to form the foundation of the Roman race and state even though he carries with him the son from his first marriage, Iulus. Forcing him from Dido's arms in Carthage, Venus prods Aeneas onward, manipulating gods and goddesses to help her son as she guides him toward an unknown Italy and a persistently silent and under-described Lavinia.

While Venus is often interpreted as harsh and aloof by past scholars, Eleanor Winsor Leach argues that she consistently acts as the appropriate Roman matron in Virgil's epic. She curbs her son's misguided pursuits to compel him onward toward the greater destiny that awaits his progeny, which will be finally realized in the Augustan age. In other words, Venus behaves in a way that even Tacitus's Messalus would approve: with "severe discipline" to make him a manly/virtuous leader.[13] Like the women in Messalus's catalogue of ideal mothers, Venus uses discipline rather than a soft touch to goad her son toward his proper place as the founder of the Romans. Rather than "love" as the description of the motive for Venus's behavior, Leach emphasizes that it is "anxiety" that prompts her to act. Anxiety, then, is "an expected norm of maternal feeling," propelling Venus to remind her son to exhibit manly *pietas*—faithfulness to his family and to the gods—rather than giving in to feminine distractions like Dido.[14]

Additional Roman founding narratives are recorded and transmitted during and in the wake of Augustus's reign, among them Livy's *Histories*, Tacitus's *Annals*, Plutarch's *Lives*, and the epic retelling of the Punic Wars by Silius Italicus (*Punica*) to name but a few. In each, the depiction of feminine, and maternal, ideals plays an important part. Key moments in Rome's development hinge on the behavior of elite women within the city. Lucretia established "womanly virtue" with her post-rape suicide. In Livy's account, although innocent, she kills herself lest she "provide a precedent for unchaste women to escape what they deserve." Her death sparks the overthrow of the Tarquin dynasty, thereby removing the kings Rome so despised, and establishing the Republic (Livy, 1.58). Later in Rome's story, the murder of the young, virgin Verginia by her father is described in similar terms. Out of fear that the wicked, and last remaining oligarch of the *decemvirate* ("rule by ten men"), Appius, would rape her, Verginia's father is "forced" to kill his daughter. Her father's behavior is declared just and Livy makes Verginia's death parallel to Lucretia's own when he describes it as "no less dreadful than the rape and suicide of Lucretia." As with Lucretia's death, Verginia's demise likewise leads to a regime change when the *decemvirate* disintegrates after Appius's self-exile (Livy, 3.43–50).[15]

In addition to faithful wives and daughters, Roman historians also held faithful Roman mothers in high esteem. The story of the traitorous Roman general, Gaius Marcius Coriolanus, is recounted by both Livy and Plutarch. Coriolanus's mother, called "Veturia" by Livy and "Volumnia" by Plutarch, prevents her son from laying siege against Rome after he was spurned by the populace when they did not elect him consul. Presenting Coriolanus as an unstoppable general with very few political skills, both Plutarch and Livy assume that if permitted to attack Rome, Coriolanus would be successful in subduing it. In this moment of crisis, Livy, writes: "Men, it seemed, could not defend the city with their swords; women might better succeed with tears and entreaties" (2.40). It is in this space that his mother rallies with the other matrons to assail Coriolanus outside the city's walls with her own words.

Livy's record of Veturia's speech is a rare accounting of women's words in his histories. Filling the place normally occupied by a man, Veturia's prominence demonstrates the chaos of this narrative moment: a Roman man stands ready to destroy Rome; a Roman mother stands as the city's defender. Veturia creates a parallel between herself, as Coriolanus's biological mother, and Rome, as "the earth which bore and bred [him]" (2.40). In other words, to destroy Rome is to destroy his own mother. Plutarch's speech for "Volumnia" records a similar sentiment: "Unless I can persuade you to substitute friendship and concord for dissension and hostility, . . . then consider and be well assured that you cannot assail your country without first treading underfoot the corpse of her who bore you."[16] When her words are met with silence, she throws not only her own body, but that of Coriolanus's wife and two sons at his feet as well (*Cor.* 36.1–3). Defeated in this way, Coriolanus retreats in shame, but his mother and her allied matrons are celebrated as unlikely saviors with honors and a temple to "Women's Fortune" that includes the inscription: "Dear to the gods, O women, is your gift to me" (*Cor.* 37). Volumnia's actions, along with those of the matrons who accompanied her, are presented as nothing less than a reversal of the curse of Pandora. Instead of the deceptive gift for mankind who ushered in its destruction, these Roman women are true "gifts" who saved Rome and her men from destruction at the hands of a wayward son, Coriolanus.

Due attention must also be given to Scipio's daughter, Cornelia, who emerges as one of the most famous emblems of maternal virtue in the Augustan era. A woman of notable heritage through her father, Scipio Africanus, and her husband, Tiberius Sempronius Gracchus, Cornelia was a proud woman focused on the memorialization of her familial honor even in the wake of tragedies. Indeed, while prestigious due to her father's fame, Cornelia is chronicled as the mother of her two ill-fated sons as well, the *populares* tribunes Tiberius and Gaius Gracchi.[17] Both men were assassinated by mobs early in their careers after attempting legislation that would have redistributed the lands held by the aristocracy to landless Romans (*TG* 9.4–6). Yet, while the men were remembered as troublemakers for the Republic, they were also remembered as great men, especially for their oratory skills. Even the staunchly aristocratic Cicero praises the Gracchi brothers in his writings on oratory, explicitly crediting their education "through the conscientiousness of [their] mother Cornelia" and the Greek tutors she secured for them. Cicero and Quintilian also praise Cornelia herself for her own eloquence conveyed in published correspondences between herself and her sons (Cicero, *Brut.* 104, 211; Quintilian, *Inst.* 1.1.6). As Dixon explains, the Gracchi brothers "were among the first orators to display before the popular assembly at the capital the full flowering of an education in which natural talent had been systematically nurtured by the best of Greek and Roman training."[18]

Cornelia's crucial role in such an outcome became the center of her remembered identity. Citing a well-known legend of her husband's encounter with two serpents, an omen that forced him to choose who should die first, himself or his wife, Plutarch writes: "But she [Cornelia] did such a superb job of rearing the children and administering the estate, and was so perfectly behaved, so devoted to the children and so noble-spirited that men felt Tiberius had made the right decision in choosing to die instead of such a woman/wife" (*TG* 1.4).[19] Even after the death of her two sons, Cornelia survived into old age and retired in Misenum entertaining and philosophizing with guests, while memorializing her father and sons to preserve the family honor. Her vibrant personality, then, becomes for Plutarch the actualization of a "noble spirit" educated and therefore able to weather the storms of life without succumbing to either vice or bereavement.[20] Augustus himself capitalized on the lasting effects of Cornelia's image as the ideal matron by placing a statue of her in the portico dedicated to his sister, Octavia, whom he also figured as an ideal Roman mother.

Times of chaos, then, often became times of prominence for elite Roman matrons—the wives and mothers of the Roman men who were meant to be leading the state, but who were otherwise occupied either battling one another or an external foe. The "normal" masculine order overturned by crisis left a gap that these women (and other un-men) filled by interceding with incense and prayers before the gods, donating their jewels to the state treasury to fund wars, rescuing proscripted fathers or husbands left to be murdered by sons eager to inherit, and entering the forum or battlefield to fight with words.[21] The sudden visibility and enduring remembrance of these women intensify the tension and crises within Rome's historical retellings. Such stories emphasize the "displacement" of masculine control as well as the virtue of its women, who emerge to "restore" the balance and then properly recede behind the walls and lines of recorded text—at least these are the stories many of our Augustan era authors leave us.

Of course, such a trope is not the invention of the Augustan age, but it certainly came to occupy a much more pronounced place in and after Augustus's reign. Coming to power after a Second Triumvirate, a second wave of proscriptions, and a second civil war, Augustus casts himself as the Savior who brought peace and security to the land with his victory over the tragically feminized Marc Antony. Augustus, therefore, repeatedly employs the images of "the good woman within the good home" to perpetuate his masculine control in restoring Roman order and, in so doing, creates and perpetuates images of private Roman life, the realm of the proper matron, in contrast to public life, the realm of the proper Roman man.[22] As Kristina Milnor explains, the Augustan construction of the domesticated matron in literature, architecture, art, and coins—all very public spaces—presents *this* type of matronly virtue "simultaneously as natural, preconceived, universal and transhistorical, and also as something which requires continuous discursive policing."[23] In other words, because a matron is part of her husband's (and father's) masculine performance of control, her "private life" so-construed simultaneously occupies the center of the public gaze. It is no wonder, then, that Augustus placed a statue of Cornelia in the Porticus Octaviae, built the Porticus Liviae for his wife, Livia, who sponsored the building of an Altar to Concord in its center, and cast a fecund and barebreasted Tellus-Italia on his *Ara Pacis* along with himself surrounded by his family on the altar's reverse. Such images reinforced Augustus's construction of his masculine control and indeed his "fatherhood" of Rome (Suetonius, *Aug.* 58; Augustus, *RG* 35). Far from pushing women "back" into their husbands' homes, however, these images kept matrons in the public eye as supporters of, and as measures by which to gauge, the masculine projections of ruling elite men, including Augustus.

Debating Feminine Virtue: Praise and Polemic in the Imperial Household

Augustus, however, used more than building projects and his own domestic performance to create the "normalcy" of stable and fertile marriages. He orchestrated the passage of the *leges Iuliae* in 18 BCE and their more restrictive revision under the *lex Papia Poppaea* in 9 CE to regulate the reproductive lives of his citizens.[24] These "Julian laws" outlined ages for marriage, identified marriageable partners, and assigned punishments and rewards for men *and* women who promulgated or who threatened the proliferation of legitimate Roman children, either through celibacy or adultery. The desirability of motherhood, in particular, is made plain by the reward of freeing a woman from male guardianship upon the birth of three living children (*ius liberorum*).[25] That the honor was also symbolically bestowed upon prominent women who had not accomplished this feat, even after male guardianship was dissolved as an institution in the fourth century, demonstrates the honor of public maternal acknowledgment for Roman matrons and their families.[26] Milnor notes that these laws "became famous very quickly, soon becoming, . . . almost synonymous with Augustus's rule and the birth of the imperial system."[27] Augustus's new-old-fashioned regime earned him praise from Dionysius of Halicarnassus, who figured Augustus as the restorer of Roman law through his control of women in particular.[28]

These codes also garnered the reproach of other elite men, who chaffed at a system so invested in their private affairs. Tacitus, in particular, condemned the laws as overreaching established systems of legislation, writing in his *Annals* that "laws are most numerous when the state was most corrupt" (3.27).[29] Indeed, for as extensive as Augustus's legal program for marriage and reproduction was, Tacitus argues that its success was extremely limited; instead, this legislation "served to destroy great Roman families rather than preserve them."[30] Moreover, Milnor persuasively argues that these laws brought Roman women into the forum, effectively making the bedroom a public space by legislating the use and misuse of women's bodies. "Women had not before been a part of this picture [that is, the governance of the Republic], since they had no official role in Roman civic matters: the state was not concerned with them because they were not concerned with the state."[31] With the passage of the *leges Iuliae* and *lex Papia Poppaea*, however, women were now to be both publicly disgraced for improper sex and publicly honored for proper sex: divorced and cast off in humiliation, or released from male guardianship and granted greater autonomy with the birth of three or four living, legitimate children. In either case, Augustus's attempt to keep "the good woman within the good home" by means of legal codes effectively forced her out of that home as well—and onto a stage for public evaluation alongside, and as a key part of, the gender performances of the men with whom she was affiliated. In this way, he helped to set a new stage for battles over proper "femininity" that paralleled and contributed to the battles for masculinity that already occupied elite members of the Empire.

For Augustus, the publicity of the women of his household was manipulated both positively and negatively by contemporaries and later historians. While his troubled relationship with his daughter Julia is particularly well known, Tacitus's accounting of the mothers of the imperial household is more relevant to our discussion here. Painting a narrative of developing corruption in the imperial household, which Tacitus ties in part to the excess legal codes of Augustus's later reign, he devotes a significant amount of attention to imperial mothers. Having offered his own reflection on the importance of maternal education through Messalus in his *Dialogues*, Tacitus moves in his *Annals* to document the tragic repercussions of vicious mothers on the Roman state, Livia Augusta and Agrippina the Younger chief among them. Livia, as Augustus's own wife, brings Tacitus's critique of the Julian laws into sharp focus. Tacitus uses the *topos* of a wicked stepmother to cast both as power hungry women who usurp the bounds of their sex by promoting sons of previous marriages, Tiberius and Nero.[32] According to Tacitus, even after securing the imperial office for their sons through intrigue and murder, neither woman is willing to leave the public sphere, thus exposing her own "unnatural" lust for control. Great-grandmother and great grand-daughter, Livia and Agrippina plot similar paths for power first through imperial husbands, and then sons from a previous marriage.

Livia's son, Tiberius, is characterized as a hypocrite by Tacitus: he pretends to have masculine control while succumbing to and brewing with effeminate rage. Such character, Tacitus maintains, is in no small part the product of his mother's care. With the "old, inbred arrogance of the Claudian family" while lacking the genuine masculinity to control his "anger, hypocrisy, and secret lasciviousness," Tiberius was fueled to greater extremes with "consulates and triumphs" that were "heaped on his youthful head" (*Ann.* 1.4).[33] "Add to this tale his mother with her feminine caprice (*inpotentia*, "impotence")," writes Tacitus, "they must be slaves it appeared, to the distaff, and to a pair of striplings as well, who in the interval would oppress the state and in the upshot rend it asunder!" (*Ann.* 1.4). In contrast to Messalus's catalogue of mothers, therefore, Livia fails to prevent the continued warping of her son's inclination toward vice. She encourages his effeminate lack of control through her own lack of restraint ("impotence," 4.53; 5.1). Moreover, she uses his ignorant arrogance to propel *herself* into the imperial spotlight and becomes a "curse to the realm" (1.10). By means of an example, Tacitus records her placement of her own title before that of her son on an inscription dedicating a statue to Augustus. He explains that Tiberius interpreted this act "as a derogation from the imperial dignity" and "he had locked it in his breast with grave and veiled displeasure" to be vent at a later date (*Ann.* 3.55). Her unnaturally masculine desire for honor exposed, Livia forsakes even her relationship with Tiberius in the end, when she drives him from Rome because of her "lack of restraint." This unnatural destruction of the mother-son-bond is made permanent at Livia's death, when Tiberius refuses to return even for her funeral, forcing the young Caligula to perform the filial duties in his stead (5.1–2).[34]

Tacitus then accuses Agrippina the Younger of following in the footsteps of her great-grandmother. He charges Agrippina with Claudius's murder, arguing that she orchestrated his poisoning shortly after convincing Claudius to adopt and appoint her own son, Nero, as heir over Claudius's son, Britannicus (12.25, 61–68).[35] Like Livia before her, Agrippina, too, prematurely promoted Nero with honors throughout his life. As a result, Agrippina helped to mold another Tiberius, a ruling man without the ability to rule himself, let alone his household or Rome (12.51). Ascending as emperor at the age of seventeen, Nero may wear the toga of masculinity (*toga virilus*), but he cannot embody the ideals himself. Tacitus makes his comparison of Livia and Agrippina clear when recalling Claudius's funeral. He writes, "Divine honors were voted to Claudius, and his funeral solemnities were celebrated precisely as those of the deified Augustus, Agrippina emulating the magnificence of her great-grandmother Livia" (12.69).

Agrippina's imitation of Livia demonstrates Livia's continued popularity in spite of Tacitus's reconstruction of the first Augusta. Indeed, while Tiberius denied her posthumous honors, the senate still granted her the title *mater patriae* ("Mother of the Country") and Claudius eventually granted her the honors

Tiberius withheld in spite of Livia's contempt for him (Suetonius, *Claud.* 3.2; 11.2; Tacitus, *Ann.* 5.2).[36] Not everyone agreed with Tacitus's analysis. Yet, for Tacitus, Agrippina succeeds in not only imitating Livia, but of surpassing her jealous machinations during Nero's reign. She immediately plots out of disapproval for Nero's lovers, envious of the attention and potential persuasive power they could have over Nero. Threatening and fickle, Tacitus's Agrippina even resorts to incestuous associations with her son in hopes of retaining her power over him, and over Rome (14.2–3).

Such moves, again, serve to destroy the supposedly sacred relationship between mother and son as he removes her from the palace, feigns attachment, and eventually commits matricide. While Agrippina's wickedness is profound for Tacitus, he vents his disapproval of Nero as well, writing that although "all men yearned for the breaking of the mother's power, none credited that the hatred of the son would go the full way to murder" (14.1). Nero, in fact, issues her death warrant twice; when the first attempt to make her death appear accidental fails, he calls on his supporters to bludgeon her to death in bed. When the centurion grabs his sword for the finishing blow, Agrippina twists to have him stab her in the womb (*uterum*), crying, "Strike here!" (14.8). The death blow, thus, leaves her body marked with the source of her demise: the son of her own womb. While Livia's overreaching led to her son's impious avoidance of her funeral, Agrippina's unchecked masculine desire for power ultimately pushed her son to be the cause of hers. Nero orders the immediate burning of her corpse without honor after the deed was accomplished (14.9).[37]

The implications of Tacitus's characterizations are clear: the publicity of Roman matrons brought about by Augustus's legislation and popularization of ideal maternal images gave these women a foothold for legitimate power. Acknowledging the contributions of these women as wives and especially as mothers, who bore the sons who would rule Rome, brought them further into the public eye. As potential conduits for honor (or shame) by means of maternal ancestry and the choices made in raising their sons, mothers were perceived to have great influence over their sons' lives and, therefore, at least indirectly over the entire Empire. Augustus's honoring of his wife, Livia, his sister, Octavia, and even Cornelia Gracchus, as ideal matrons, therefore, established a pattern for other ambitious and capable women to imitate.

For Tacitus, this pattern can only bring about disastrous results since it encourages women to *act* like men without the benefit of actually *being* men. They may desire power, but they lack the self-control or restraint that only biologically male bodies perfected through masculine *paideia* can exert. In contrast, these imperial women exhibit unchecked and overly aggressive masculinity due to what Tacitus repeatedly describes as the "weakness of [their] sex" (*Ann.* 3.33–34; 12.57; 14.4). Instead of remaining in the "good home" content with raising virtuous sons, these women breach gender boundaries and in so doing, destroy their maternal bonds with their sons *and* pave the way for the destruction of the Empire by rearing vicious, effeminate rulers. Highlighting the disintegration of gendered spheres in the imperial household, Tacitus criticizes Augustus's reforms: while Augustus hoped to restore so-called traditional family structures and increase the reproduction of Roman citizens, Tacitus argues that his methods undermined these very goals. Such public acknowledgment of women, either with matronly honors or the shame of harlotry, inevitably leads to their over-masculinization. Unable to be perfectly masculine, the result is an unnatural quasi-masculine woman; a danger to any ordinary family, s/he is disastrous for the entire Empire.

Yet, Tacitus's polemical reaction also emphasizes a further reality of Augustus's reign and reforms, even if they were unevenly applied and muted by his successors. This reality is that women, especially elite matrons, were now an open topic for debate in the public sphere. Moreover, they found legitimate avenues for power and agency in this context. Indeed, as much as Tacitus rails against this feminine invasion, he maintains the female presence by means of his extensive criticisms. While not glorious renderings of Livia and Agrippina, Tacitus's characterizations nevertheless reinforce their fame and preserve their legacies. These women may live in infamy through his narrative, but they *do* live and with a vividness that Republican era women lack from existing sources. Furthermore, Tacitus's fervor demonstrates the success that both Livia and Agrippina had at negotiating spheres of power, thus prompting the vigorousness of his critique. Augustus's restorationist agenda was a key part of his own masculine performance and the female bodies and lives of the women in his household were props for him to use. The establishment of these women on the stage, however, catapulted them to further places of prominence. Having picked up the pieces from yet another Triumvirate, proscriptions, and civil war these matrons would not recede into the shadows as they may have done before. Augustus's defining and encouragement of domestic virtues brought these women into the forum and, therefore, squarely in the public eye. Female bodies adorned the Palatine as statues and friezes, but elite women were also educated patrons of the arts and participants in legal proceedings. By attempting to demonstrate his control of all things feminine, therefore, Augustus paradoxically reinforced the power of Roman matrons who pursued these social constructions of "feminine virtue." No longer simple sustainers and conduits for male seed, these women were also potential usurpers of masculine hegemony.

Summary

Augustus's family-focused agenda, therefore, reinforced the maternal telos for women desiring (and able) to pursue acknowledgement as "real" women, just as it did fatherhood for males seeking "real" manhood. While Augustus was recognized as the "Father of the Country" during his lifetime, Livia achieved her comparable status as that same Empire's "Mother" after her death and successful (if troubled) establishment of Tiberius on her husband's throne. Although powerful matrons like Livia earned the ire of authors such as Tacitus, their power and popularity both in life and long after their deaths are made plain by the attention given them. Indeed, the more elite Roman men came to acknowledge publicly the masculinizing potential of good mothers upon their sons, the more they opened themselves up to challenge by the very women/wives they had recognized needing for the survival of the Empire. As ready as their husbands to manipulate social constructions of feminine virtue to stabilize their own gendered status, elite matrons could claim motherhood to be a means not only of their own redemption from useless feminine deficiency, but as the salvation of Rome as well. These women could envision joining Volumnia at the temple to "Women's Fortune" or sitting in sculpted form like Cornelia in the forum, receiving praise for being *real women*; that is, for being Roman mothers.

Getting Saved: Multiple Traditions of the Maternal Telos in Early Christian Literature

This portrait of lauded and polemicized motherhood is further complicated in the NT and early Christian writings, which, as we have seen, do not consistently present motherhood as *the* ideal telos for all females. Nevertheless, as Anna Rebecca Solevåg has shown, these writings do spend time discussing the role of motherhood in regards to salvation.[38] Sometimes childbearing is identified as crucial (1 Tim 2:15), sometimes it is simply assumed (Eph 5:21–6:4), and other times it is seemingly inhibitive (Acts Andr. 16; 37–40). In all these instances, however, we find early Christians wrestling with what exactly it means to be a faithful woman in God's household. These struggles are simultaneous with those concerning what it meant to be a man in God's household when God occupies the place of *Paterfamilias* as shown in Chapter 3. In both instances, believers must ask whether mothers or fathers matter. It is clear, however, that early Christian communities still operated with the overarching anthropology outlined in this study: to be masculine (however construed) was to be ordered, perfect, and divine; to be feminine (again, however construed) was to be disordered, imperfect, and potentially devilish. Masculinity is reframed in accordance with various interpretations of Jesus as God's Christ, and femininity is likewise adjusted to become his opposite.[39] The crux for early believers, therefore, was not the underlying anthropology supporting the established gender hierarchy of their milieu, but rather the debates over how each gender was to be construed, and for our purposes, how motherhood figures in.

As demonstrated in Chapter 4, NT authors retain the pedagogical language of their milieu, thus repeatedly associating salvation with masculinization. Not only did this require nuancing of masculine definitions to reflect a new (and potentially problematic) ideal in Jesus Christ, it was especially challenging when related toward biological females. Without the anatomical, physiological, and psychological advantages assumed present in a male, females were leaking and susceptible to penetration for most of their lives, regardless of class. The female, therefore, was in constant danger of absorbing the wrong things, be they teachings or semen, and wrought dangerous consequences when left to herself. New Testament and early Christian authors disagree on whether curbing such permeability through virginity was enough (or even really possible), or if a man—and thus motherhood—was still required to administer needed masculinizing influences throughout her life.

In what follows, I will examine these conversations in the NT from the Pastorals, especially 1 Timothy and Titus, and the household codes (Col 3:18–4:1; Eph 5:21–6:9; 1 Pet 2:9–3:12). I will also explore several extracanonical writings that demonstrate the lingering debate over female Christians by early adherents: the *Acts of Thecla*, the *Acts of Andrew*, and the *Martyrdom of Perpetua and Felicitas*.[40] While these writings perpetuate the pattern of masculinization as salvation, they offer a variety of options for females seeking salvation. Seemingly unable to be made entirely masculine in this life, the females described in these works nevertheless experience, or are encouraged to experience, some sort of masculine transformation. At the same time, however, they embody recognizably similar constructions of feminine virtue even though such virtue is variously achieved. In these writings, therefore, mothers and motherhood retain their ambiguity. Although in some writings motherhood is assumed or apostolically endorsed, others push it aside, asserting that God alone is responsible for the masculinization/salvation of his followers—including those with problematic female bodies.

Saved Through Childbearing: The Pastoral Epistles

The most relevant passage for the present topic is 1 Tim 2:15, which forms part of the conclusion to the perennially debated passage of 2:8–3:1a. Forming the complement to the Pastor's[41] instructions for how men should behave, he follows with a description of desired behavior for women:

> Therefore, I want men/husbands (*andras*) to pray in all places by lifting up holy hands without wrath and quarrelling. Likewise, [I want] women/wives (*gynaikas*) to dress themselves in respectable clothing with modesty and self-control (*sōphrosynēs*), not with braided hair and gold or pearls

> or costly clothing, but with good works, which is fitting for a woman/wife (*gynaixin*) who proclaims piety for God. Let a woman/wife (*gynē*) learn in silence in complete submission. Even I do not permit a woman/wife (*gynaiki*) to teach or to govern a man/husband (*andros*), but to be in silence. For Adam was molded first, then Eve, and Adam was not deceived, but the woman/wife (*gynē*) after being deceived has become in transgression. But she will be saved (*sōthēsetai*) through childbearing (*dia teknogonias*) if they should remain in faith and in love and in holiness with self-control (*sōphrosynēs*). This is a faithful word (*logos*).

Reading these verses together highlights the connection between the Pastor's interpretation of the Adam and Eve narrative and his instructions for both men/husbands *and* women/wives, rather than only as the justification of his prohibitions for women. By referencing when each sex was "molded" (*eplasthē*), the Pastor justifies male superiority; and by appealing to Eve's singular deception or seduction (*exapatētheisa*), he supports his understanding that all women/wives require masculine oversight, which is made uniquely manifest in the birthing of legitimate children.

Scholars have long debated these verses, especially because of this connection between salvation and childbearing for women in verse 15. Are women saved in an alternative way than men? What about those women who cannot or choose not to have children? Why should women be forced to perform this "good work" while men are not? Moreover, such a statement makes women's salvation dependent on men's participation without any explicit holding of men to the same account. Faced with these problems, interpreters have largely focused on three words in their debates. First, should the verb *sōthēsetai* be understood to imply eschatological salvation, immediate salvation ("being kept safe"), general health ("made healthy"), or a combination of these options.[42] Second, should the preposition *dia* be interpreted temporally ("during") or instrumentally ("by means of" or "through").[43] Third, does *teknogonia* refer to the specific act of childbirth (i.e., parturition), or to the more general activity of childrearing, thus not requiring actual childbirth for all women but rather so-called maternal behavior from them.[44] Reviewing a number of these options, Solevåg writes, "It is pertinent to ask whether the aim of some of these interpretations is to elucidate the phrase [in verse 15] or explain it away."[45]

Solevåg's comment is significant because a number of these issues are resolved, even if uncomfortably, by both the context of 1 Timothy itself and its larger cultural milieu. First Timothy regularly describes salvation in eschatological terms, but interpreters only question the eschatological aspect in 2:15. Moreover, while possible, a temporal reading of *dia* is not common nor, as I will show, necessitated by the context of this verse. Finally, as Weissenrieder has demonstrated, *teknogonia* is used as a technical word for "childbirth" in medical/philosophical treatises and is considered separate from general "childrearing" in 1 Tim 5:10, which is described as *eteknotrophēsen*. While unsettling for contemporary readers, salvation of women by childbirth simply is not an uncommon idea in the ancient Mediterranean world.

Indeed, such a sentiment is quite at home in the anthropologies and gender constructions outlined in this study.[46] A woman's bearing of legitimate children for her husband is a means of purposing her deficiency and a demonstration of her own, appropriate masculinization by submitting to a man and acting as a corporeal conduit for his masculine seed. Her submission in this way brings her literal health by widening and inseminating her passages, therefore causing easier menstruation after pregnancy to expel the excess moisture her female body collects.[47] Also noting this connection, Weissenrieder points to the Hippocratic *Diseases of Young Girls*, which I discussed in Chapter 2.[48] This short document describes the dangers of prolonged virginity for young girls. Left unwidened and uninseminated, these girls desire death rather than a husband, even killing themselves due to the insanity caused by the buildup of excess menstrual blood in their bodies (*DYG* 15–37). In other Hippocratic and later Galenic works, women throughout life are said to require consistent insemination by husbands to prevent the dislocation of a womb that threatens to wander her widened passageways. Weighted down by male semen, a woman's uterus can no longer travel upward to suffocate her and cause insanity by preventing proper blood flow.

Birthing children, however, also saves a woman by preventing the perceived misuses of her body that can lead not only to her own destruction, but also the destruction of her husband, his household, and even the cosmos. Recalling the discussion in Chapter 2 again, it is the deception of Pandora—dressed in expensive clothing, gold, and adorned hair—that fools the doomed Epimetheus (Hesiod, *Op.* 2.69–82).[49] Appearing in the "image" of a virginal bride (*parthenos*), Pandora is actually a fully reproductive woman (*gynē*) who demonstrates her true bitch identity by unlawfully opening her womb-jar rather than submitting its proper use to her husband. As a result, Pandora lets loose every plague upon "mankind," leaving behind "hope" alone. This "hope" is left for men/husbands to access through their women/wives' jars in the production of legitimate heirs who safeguard their property and perpetuate mankind. Such a hope (or salvation) is only realized, however, when the woman submits to her man/husband, allowing him to open her jar and to produce his own children.

Although there is no explicit connection to the Pandora myth in 1 Tim 2:9–15, there is evidence of its influence upon the Pastor's interpretation of Adam and Eve's story as was common in the Hellenistic and Roman eras. In addition to discouraging extravagant adornment for women that is quite similar to the bridal attire that deceived Epimetheus, the Pastor hints at the sexualization of Eve's sin in his linking of speech with childbirth, her deception apart from Adam, and her greater culpability demonstrated by the lingering state of transgression for women generally ("she *has become* in transgression"; *en parabasei gegonen*, v. 14). Again recalling the anatomical construction of female bodies that pictures a pathway running through her body connecting the orifices of her head (mouth, ears, nose) to her genitalia, it is easy to see how speech and listening join mental "conceptions" with physical ones. Hearing the words of the serpent with her ears, and conversing with him with words from her own mouth, Eve "has sex" with this serpent rather than with her man/husband, Adam. In various later traditions, Eve conceives a literal child as a result of this "conversation," the murderer Cain who destroys Adam's legitimate son, Abel.[50] Once again, therefore, the improper opening of a woman's mouth/vagina/jar brings chaos to mankind.

The solution to this transgression, like that for Pandora, is the continual control of the woman by a man/husband. She should not speak or participate in dialogues with other men, but remain silent. By keeping her mouth closed, she receives only those words approved by her husband/man and, therefore, prevents improper mental conceptions that could lead to illegitimate physical ones. In other words, an open mouth implies an open vagina. By birthing children for her husband alone, a woman communicates her submission to him and her self-control with respect to other men. Allowing penetration of her mind and vagina by her husband alone, she enacts her piety and conceives what he desires as her masculine, and therefore better ordered, superior in her mind ("sound doctrine," 1:10; 6:3), in her physical comportment ("modesty"), *and* in her womb (a child). In this way, bearing children is a mark of not only her own salvation, but a mark of the continued orderliness of the believing community (5:11–14; see also Titus 2:3–5).

Such understandings also play into the moral implications surrounding childbirth in ancient Mediterranean culture. In addition to being physically unhealthy, sterile women, or women who lost children in miscarriages and stillbirths, could be evaluated as being culpable. Certainly not *all* women were blamed for such events, but the tendency of various texts to explain a good woman's sterility or death in childbirth reinforces the negative, moral implications of such events.[51] Some rabbinic passages, for example, suggest that miscarriages happen when a child is conceived through improper sex, that is, when the wife is on top rather than in the subordinate position below her husband.[52] Christopher Hutson also notes the explanations offered by a number of rabbinic texts for women who die in childbirth. According to these writings, women die in childbirth because they fail to separate themselves from their husbands during menstruation, do not offer the "dough offering" when making dough, or do not light the lamp prior to Sabbath.[53] Having failed to keep her husband's literal house in order results in the disorder (death) of the wife as well, who is often described as a type of "house" herself.[54] In this way, the connection between the woman/wife and the house is reinforced. Additional examples of the stigma of childlessness as being especially shameful for women abound in the Old and New Testaments, but is also implied by the amount of honor given to mothers discussed in the previous section. When motherhood is tied to constructions of *real* womanhood, a childless woman/wife is stuck in a liminal state of incompletion. Without birthing a living child, she has not attained her full telos. Nor can she demonstrate completely her own salvation through proper submission or her role in safeguarding the future for mankind.

Stories of painless childbirth also strengthen the moral implications surrounding birthing living children in Jewish and early Christian circles.[55] As punishment for her sin, Eve is described as "the woman" (*tē gynaiki*) and told: "Multiplying I will multiply your pains and your groanings; in pains you shall birth children and your return [will be] to your husband/man (*andra*), and he will rule over you" (Gen 3:16 LXX). Great pain in childbirth, therefore, is associated with the transgression committed by Eve—all the more so if her transgression is sexual impropriety as it is later interpreted in the Hellenistic and Roman eras. Nevertheless, this verse likewise opens up the possibility that a singularly righteous woman could birth a child without pain. Indeed, these are the traditions that develop around the births of two saviors in Jewish and Christian contexts. According to Josephus, Moses's mother, Jocabed, births him without pain to avoid detection by the Egyptians, while Mary's painless birthing of Jesus is highlighted in the *Ascension of Isaiah* and the *Protoevangelium of James*.[56] Having rightly submitted themselves to masculine forces, both superior men and God, throughout their lives, these women conceive and birth salvation in the form of male Saviors. Moreover, that they do so without pain demonstrates the virtue attached to feminine submission. So complete is their realization of their feminine inferiority that they do not need to suffer Eve's punishment.

Jocabed's and Mary's birthing salvation for their people also resonates with other depictions of salvation as birth in Jewish traditions. In Isa 54–66, for example, Jerusalem/Zion is personified first as a barren woman while suffering punishment for her sin. She is restored through marriage and then gives birth to a living son *without pain* to signify the salvation of Jerusalem by God (66:10–16). Isaiah's image of this painless birth is then connected to eschatological and later apocalyptic depictions of salvation with his description of "the new heavens and the new earth" in 66:22. Reflecting a similar connection, labor pains are a regular analogy for describing the in-breaking of God's salvation in other OT, Second Temple Jewish, and NT passages.[57] Borrowing Isaianic motifs and blending them with other ancient mythological stories, Rev 12 depicts the mysterious "woman clothed in the sun" who births a boy who "is to rule all the nations with a rod of iron" (v. 5; Isa 66:7).[58] With this birth, the woman's role is complete; her child is taken up to heaven to be reared for his own role in God's plan of salvation and she is saved from the dragon by fleeing into the wilderness "where she has a place prepared by God" for her preservation (Rev 12:6).[59]

The forcefulness of the narrative of a maternal telos for women in the ancient Mediterranean world, therefore, seems to be at least in part due to the salvific overtones it communicates. This salvation is demonstrated in the overlapping of anatomical, physiological, etiological, and ethical constructions and stories associated with women birthing children explored above. Although past interpreters of 1 Timothy have sought to separate these categories, their continual connection in the ancient Mediterranean world resists such readings. Each aspect reinforces the collapsing of womanhood with motherhood discussed throughout this study. While contemporary readers are made uncomfortable by it, 1 Timothy is quite at home in a world that aligns a woman's salvation with childbirth.

Furthermore, as Solevåg has shown, this reading supports the larger "*oikos* [household] ideology" of 1 Timothy (esp. 3:14–16).[60] Interpreting the church as God's household, 1 Timothy aligns individual and communal Christian conduct with normative Greco-Roman household structures rather than opposing them. Thus, Christian men are truly masculine in ways quite similar to other Greco-Roman men, and women demonstrate feminine virtue in ways that mimic other Greco-Roman women: they are to marry, produce children, and conform to gendered expectations. Men demonstrate masculinity by controlling both themselves and the members of their household, including their wives.[61] Women demonstrate their virtue by submitting, thereby receiving masculine deposits from their husbands and reflecting their own limited masculinity by recognizing their feminine status. Slaves and others who fall outside eligibility for these gendered roles are largely ignored in the discourse, except to reinforce their positions of subordination. Although slaves cannot seek real man- or womanhood, they, like women, attain a limited masculinization by recognizing their ultimately inferior status and not challenging it (6:1–3; see also Titus 2:9–10).[62] In other words, their submission establishes and sustains the "order" that is masculinity.

While not as explicit as 1 Timothy is in connecting a woman's salvation and childbearing, similar concerns appear in the rest of the Pastoral Epistles. In his letter to Titus, the Pastor repeats his admonishment from 1 Timothy that women should be married and have children. Mirroring language from 1 Timothy, the Pastor instructs women to show their "love" for husbands and children by being "self-controlled, chaste, good household managers, kind, submissive to their own husbands so that the word of God may not be blasphemed" (2:4–5; 1 Tim 2:9–15; 5:9–16). In 2 Timothy, the Pastor repeats his concern over proper speech from 1 Timothy, including his depiction of women's speech as problematic (1 Tim 2:9–15; 5:13). In 2 Timothy, he emphasizes the importance of "sound/healthy teachings" (*hygiainousēs didaskalias*) in contrast to the "gangrene" (*gangraina*) caused by "profane chatter" (2:16–17; 4:3). The disease is spread by false teachers "who make their way into households and captivate silly women, overwhelmed by their sins and swayed by all kinds of desires (*epithumiais*), who are always being instructed and never arrive at a knowledge of the truth" (3:6–7, NRSV). Like Eve, these "silly women" open themselves to the words of other men and are corrupted. Instead of birthing legitimate children and running orderly households, these women demonstrate a lack of self-control and potential sexual impropriety.[63] Not only are these women and false teachers threats to households, but also to the church community. The Pastor encourages Timothy to overcome them by imitating his own life and by recalling the instruction Timothy received from "infancy" (*brephous*) from his grandmother and mother, Lois and Eunice (3:10–4:5; 1:5). In this way, Eunice and Lois act as foils to the silly women from 3:6–7. Unlike those women, Lois and Eunice represent ideal womanhood, having successfully born children as well as rearing and educating Timothy so that he is able to reflect the Pastor's idea of manliness. Their implicit self-control and submission to masculine authority not only earns them honor from the Pastor, but also contributes to the salvation of the believing community, which benefits from Timothy's masculinity.

The role of mothers and motherhood in the Pastoral Epistles, therefore, is of great significance both for the salvation of marriageable females and the believing communities of which they were a part. Replicating the dominant maternal narratives of the Augustan age, the Pastorals present marriage and motherhood as the natural and desired telos for free(d) women. Married mothers benefited from the masculine oversight of manly husbands and, in this way, were at least minimally masculinized by the *logoi* administered through their instruction and seed. Moreover, these women were promised greater status in the community; Lois and Eunice join the legacy of honored matrons, standing in early Christian communities just as Cornelia Gracchi stood in the Roman forum. By controlling the temptation to become completely masculine, and therefore to teach and travel freely, good women in the Pastorals recognize the limits of their female bodies and feminine natures and stay at home. They display feminine virtue—that is, the only form of masculinity that is possible for them—through corporeal and mental submission to men.

The Mystery of Salvation: Mothers in the New Testament Household Codes

Unlike 1 Tim 2:15, the household codes in Colossians, Ephesians, and 1 Peter do not directly tie childbearing to salvation. They do, however, assume and communicate the positive results of conformity to dominant cultural norms of the household. Indeed, such conformity is presented as the way to "live a life worthy" of God's calling (Eph 4:1) and a demonstration of the "peace" and "the word of

Christ" (*ho logos tou Christou*) dwelling in the believing community (Col 3:15–16). In this way, these writings implicitly tie a harmonious household to the salvation of believers and, therefore, endorse the salvific/masculinizing function of marriage (and subsequent childbirth) for free(d) women.

The connection between an orderly household and salvation is made in Colossians with the language of clothing and the body: "You have stripped off the old human (*palaion anthrōpon*) with its practices and have clothed yourselves with the new [human], who is being renewed in knowledge according to the image of its creator" (3:9–10; Gen 1:26–27). For Colossians, this "renewed" image is none other than the unified body (*sōma*) of Christ, ruled by Christ as its head (*kephalē*, Col 1:18; 3:15). Anchored by this "head," the body is "nourished and held together by its ligaments and sinews, [and] grows with a growth that is from God" (2:19, NRSV; see also 3:14). For Colossians, believers have been transformed from beings of discord—both within themselves and with one another—to a single, perfect and mature body (3:14). This mature perfection is demonstrated on a daily level not only with self-control (3:5–17), but in the various households of believers that, in many ways, are to reflect the household structures of the ancient Mediterranean world: women/wives should be "subject" (*hypotassō*), children and slaves should obey, while men/husbands should love, refrain from exasperating their children, and should treat slaves justly (3:18–4:1).

Ephesians borrows these ideas from Colossians, but takes several of them further when the author capitalizes on the head/body analogy to establish it as a primary metaphor to depict God's plan of salvation. In Eph 1:9–10, the author explains: God "has made known to us the mystery of his will (*to mysterion tou thelēmatos autou*), according to his good pleasure that he set forth in Christ, as a plan (i.e., economy, *oikonomian*) for the fullness of seasons to gather up (i.e., bring up into a head, *anakephalioōsasthai*) all things in him, things in heaven and things on earth" (NRSV). The mixture of "mystery" and "headship" repeats throughout the rest of Ephesians, depicting salvation as a unique and cosmic unity made possible through Christ alone. Thus, Jews and Gentiles are made into one, "new human" (*kainon anthrōpon*), a single "body" (*sōma*), belonging to God's "household" (*oikeioi*), and a "holy temple" (*naon hagion*) in which God's Spirit dwells (2:11–22). Men and women are likewise made "one flesh" (Gen 2:24) through the "mystery" of marriage that, when women/wives "submit" and men/husbands "love," reflects the salvation effected by Christ's sacrifice for his "body," the church (Eph 5:22–33).

Indeed, Ephesians explicitly links men/husbands to Christ by presenting them as the "head" and women/wives as the "body/church." Just like Christ, husbands "join and knit together every ligament with which it [the body] is equipped" and "promote the body's growth in building itself up in love" (4:16, NRSV). In Eph 4, Christ's ordering and purposing headship results in the community becoming a "perfect *man*" (*andra teleion*, 4:13). In marriage, this masculinization process is completed by means of a husband's "cleansing" of his wife "so that she may be holy and without blemish" (5:26–27, NRSV). Controlling and purposing his submissive body/wife, a husband effects a "great mystery" and re-creates the primordial "man" who is "one flesh"—a restored unity that unmakes the separate woman, placing her again in her husband's side as a rib rather than a distinct individual.[64]

To be sure, neither Colossians nor Ephesians command marriage or motherhood for all females, or even for all free(d) women. They do, however, assume the positive effects of marriage for women just as they assume the perpetual existence of slavery (Col 3:22–4:1; Eph 6:5–9). Since procreation was the assumed outcome of marriage, its presence is implied in the language of submission for women/wives in both texts: their submission is to be in "all things," including their bodies (Eph 5:24; Col 3:18). Moreover, Colossians and Ephesians repeat cultural norms by tying cosmic harmony to household and marital harmony.[65] In this way, they continue to demonstrate the inescapable presentation of bodies as microcosms for theology; indeed, they capitalize on such a connection with their "head" and "body" language. While such a move may not command marriage and subsequent motherhood for free(d) women, it does assume this reality. Not only do Colossians and Ephesians justify these aspects of ideal womanhood with theology, but they exalt them as a woman's means of masculinization. By means of her virtuous submission a woman can become a man insofar as she exists as her husband's body *and* as part of the "perfect man" who is Christ's body (Eph 4:13). Nevertheless, she cannot hope to become a man on her own, not even in the limited sense of her masculine husband who is also part of Christ's body. Her hope should be for reunification within superior, masculine headship—first from her husband, and second from Christ—so that God's plan of renewed "headship" (*anakephalioōsasthai*, 1:9–10) for the entire cosmos is completed.

First Peter repeats aspects of both the codes in Colossians and Ephesians, as well as the Pastoral Epistles. As in these other letters, a woman/wife's primary virtue is in her "submission" (*hypotassō*, 1 Pet 3:1; Col 3:18; Eph 5:24; Titus 2:5). Furthermore, in 1 Peter this submission is supported theologically as pleasing to God and with the example of Sarah, who "obeyed Abraham by calling him lord" (1 Pet 3:6). Reflecting similar cultural concerns as the Pastoral Epistles, 1 Peter's instructions for wives also emphasizes the importance of modest dress and silence. As in 1 Tim 2:9–10, the women/wives of 1 Peter are not to adorn themselves with braided hair, gold, or costly clothing; rather they are to attract their husbands with evidence of their submission: a "secret heart" and the "imperishableness of a tranquil and quiet spirit, which is precious before God" (1 Pet 3:3–4).[66] Yet, while the virtuous woman/wife might look the same and demonstrate the same submissive silence as the women/wives of other household discourses, the purposes between 1 Peter and the other letters differ. Indeed, 1 Peter shifts the focus of salvation away from that of the woman/wife who needs the masculinizing force of her husband's words/seeds, to that of the husband himself.

In the previous chapter, I noted the significance of 1 Peter's identification of God's seeds as his word (1:23–25).[67] This "imperishable seed" causes the regeneration and rebirth of the believers in 1 Peter, and they continue to be shaped by this seed by drinking the "pure word-like milk" from Christ (1:23–2:3). The primary masculinizing influence in 1 Peter, therefore, is God and it is to him that all, including Christ, must submit (3:22). Christ's submission, in particular, is highlighted in 2:18–25, just prior to 1 Peter's instruction to women/wives in 3:1–6. Rather than providing warrant to resist unjust treatment, Jesus becomes an example of idealized submission; his submission unto (unjust) death is an outworking of his ultimate submission to God, his true *Paterfamilias*. In the same way, slaves, and indeed all believers, are told to "submit" to earthly rulers, masters, husbands, and elders (2:9–3:12; 5:5). Thus, even though slaves and women are feminized un-men in society, they nevertheless demonstrate authentic masculinity by submitting to God's rule. Indeed, according to 1 Peter, their masculinity is in some ways superior to that of free(d) men in society since they alone recognize their proper place beneath God and can endure any suffering out of submission to him (4:1–19).

Furthermore, 1 Peter suggests that such submission can conquer those "disobedient to the word," including the husbands of believing women/wives. Betsy J. Bauman-Martin highlights the perilous place of Christian women married to non-believing men since all occupants of a household were expected to conform to the religious preferences of the *paterfamilias*. As she explains, "[W]hen the paterfamilias converted, the entire household was obligated to convert as well, but when a wife or a slave converted alone, the order of the household was compromised."[68] In this way, a woman/wife's and slave's conversion to Christianity became a threat to the masculine rule of a stable home. Seemingly aware of this accusation, the author of 1 Peter encourages women/wives to demonstrate even greater submission in hopes of converting their husbands. The conquest of husbands is not made through verbal exchange, as though God's masculinizing word had made these women into culturally construed men. Rather God's word is to be demonstrated in a wife's submission so that these husbands "might be won over without a word by their wives' conduct" (3:1, NRSV). In this scenario, God's word is communicated via her silent transference.

Again, while 1 Peter does not explicitly prescribe motherhood for these virtuously submitting women/wives, its assumed connection to marriage in the ancient world implies the existence of mothers among these women/wives. Furthermore, the emphasis on their submission results in a picture of ideal womanhood in 1 Peter that mirrors the portraits of feminine virtue in the larger Greco-Roman culture. Having dared transgress these boundaries by becoming followers of Christ without their husbands' lead, these women/wives are not to transgress further.

Instead, they are to submit and are assumed to be "weaker vessels" than men in God's created order (3:7). Yet, for 1 Peter, their place of greater submission, like that of slaves, creates opportunities for them to imitate Christ in ways not available to the men/husbands addressed in 3:7.[69] Already in a feminized position, these women/wives act as vessels not only for their husband's seed/word, but also for the seed/word of God. In their silent acceptance, these women not only bear life in the form of their husband's children, but they also enable the rebirth of their husbands (and, thus, entire households) to experience unending life.

The NT household codes, therefore, also reflect connections between motherhood and salvation for women, even though this reading relies on the assumption of procreation that results from marriage in the ancient Mediterranean world. As in the Pastoral Epistles, these codes are built on ancient anatomical and physiological constructions of female bodies that reinforce cultural constructions of gender. Thus, in Ephesians and 1 Timothy, women/wives require the masculinizing influence of their husbands, and the Pastorals and 1 Peter reflect a consistent assumption that loose lips indicate loose legs. Yet, the household codes also differ from the Pastoral Epistles with their presentations of interdependence and mutual submission for harmony within marriage and the "body of Christ" (Eph 5:22). Indeed, even in the strongly hierarchical construction of marriage in Ephesians, complete independence is never described as a desired state for any believer; men/husbands *need* women/wives in order to be restored as "one flesh" just as Christ's head requires a body to be ruled over. And while the veneration of suffering in 1 Peter is especially dangerous, its encouragement to ancient women/wives results in an equation between them and Christ himself, thus acting as an alternative to the vision of Ephesians. Already in these few examples, therefore, we have discovered various constructions of ideal masculinity even if the femininity presented is starkly similar. For these early Christian communities, masculinity is ultimately demonstrated by Christ; but depending on whether his cosmic control or his voluntary submission is highlighted, this masculinity (and its corresponding relationship to femininity) can vary sharply.

Thecla and Her Childless Sisters: The Apocryphal Acts and Passion of Perpetua

This final selection of texts demonstrates the continuing debate over mothers, motherhood, and constructions of ideal womanhood among early Christians beyond the NT writings themselves. Rather than attempting an exhaustive analysis, the following section focuses on several characters from three especially relevant early Christian narratives dating from the mid-second to early third centuries: the *Acts of Thecla*, the *Acts of Andrew*, and the *Martyrdom of Perpetua and Felicitas*.[70] Primary attention is given to the *Acts of Thecla* since it is most approximate to the composition of the NT writings (ca. 160–190 CE). In these stories, Thecla, Maximilla, Perpetua, and Felicitas all face a choice: namely, will they marry and/or become mothers, or will they forsake this established narrative of womanhood for their new identities as Christians, regardless of the cost? The women all make the same choice: they reject marriage and children in order to become children of God. The centrality of marital renunciation as well as the enduring legacy of these writings, not to mention their sometimes ambivalent reception, make them particularly significant for the present study.[71] By either avoiding marriage entirely, or by rejecting sex once married, the elite girls and women/wives of these writings also reject motherhood for the sake of Christ, and sometimes literally reject their own children in the process.

Thecla: Saved by the Father's Word

The tale of Thecla appears in the midst of the apocryphal *Acts of Paul*; it is a late second-century story that had a popular life outside the *Acts* in which it is now contained. In this story, Thecla denounces marriage as a part of her conversion after hearing Paul deliver "God's word (*logos theou*) about self-control and resurrection" (3.5).[72] In his message, Paul emphasizes chastity for both married and unmarried believers, coupling the rejection of procreation with a rejection of worldly possessions and concerns. For Paul, one's hope should reside in God alone instead of the Empire's narrative of reproduction and accumulation (3.17). By hoping in God, believers do not need to be burdened with maintaining households and can serve God alone, secure in the life they have and will receive. Paul ends his sermon of blessings with the words, "Blessed are the bodies of virgins, for they will please God and not lose the reward for their chastity. For the Father's word (*ho logos tou patros*) will become a saving work for them (*ergon autois genēsetai sōtērias*) on the day of his son and they shall enjoy eternal rest" (3.6). Convinced and transformed by these words, Thecla commits herself to following this path of life and masculinization instead of the marriage and motherhood arranged for her by her Roman world.

It is Thecla's transformation, and sudden rejection of the Roman Imperial narrative, that causes the remaining strife in the narrative. To the horror of her own mother, Theocleia, Thecla changes from a dutiful, Roman virgin, to a lovesick follower of Paul.[73] She will not be consoled by her fiancée, Thamyris, who attempts to woo her with his words; instead, she seeks only Paul and the words that he offers. As a result, the entire household mourns for Thecla as though she were dead: "Everyone wept bitterly: Thamyris because he was losing a woman/wife (*gynaikos*), Theocleia a child, the slaves a mistress. The house was disrupted by sorrow" (3.10). When Thecla sneaks out of her house at night to bribe her way into Paul's prison, she is discovered the next morning and brought before the governor along with Paul. The governor's words likewise fail to compel Thecla, whose mother is outraged by her brash silence. Once the source of Thecla's life, Theocleia now calls for her death: "Burn the outlaw! Burn the un-bride in the middle of the theater, so that all the women/wives (*gynaikes*) who have been instructed by this fellow might learn some respect!" (3.20).

The rage that Theocleia voices vividly demonstrates what is at stake in Thecla's conversion. By ignoring the orders to marry—orders that come from not only from her mother, but from the lips of the governor who voices Iconian and Roman law—Thecla rejects the will of the Empire. She shames Thamyris, a "leading man of the city," effectively kills the line of her father's household, and threatens the well-being of the city since other young virgins could be inspired to follow her example. As Susan Calef explains: to be "not a bride" (*anymphon*, "un-bride") is to be "lawless" (*anomon*) (3.20).[74] Having situated herself outside of Roman law, Thecla is no longer under its protection, but is completely in God's care. The rest of the story, therefore, continues the battle between these two forces: God's household versus the Roman household. Thecla's body is the battleground. Her intact virginity (or "chastity," *hagnē*) declares God's victory, while Rome seeks her penetration, submission, and death.[75]

In fact, the *Acts of Thecla* sets out this competition explicitly even before Theocleia cries out for her daughter's death. Attempting to ply Thyramis with information in hopes of receiving wealth and recognition, Paul's two false disciples, Demas and Hermogenes, succinctly characterize the primary soteriological conflict in the story. On the one side is God's word as proclaimed by Paul, which, they claim "would deprive youths (*neous*) of wives and virgin girls (*parthenous*) of husbands" by claiming, "You will possess no resurrection if you do not remain chaste and do not defile the flesh" (3.12). In contrast, their gospel replicates the message of the Roman world: "We shall teach that what he [Paul] calls 'resurrection' has already taken place through the children we have" (3.14). Demas and Hermogenes's version of Paul's teaching is intentionally shaped to inflame Thyramis against Paul, who never directly condemns marriage or procreation. As we will see, there are positive married characters in the *Acts of Thecla*. Nevertheless, the best characters remain unmarried, and Thecla's salvific journey of masculinization is only possible through her rejection of Roman ideals of womanhood.

The competition between God and Rome over Thecla intensifies in Antioch, where Thecla travels with Paul after her miraculous deliverance from immolation in Iconium. Outside of any worldly household, Thecla is a woman unattached and, therefore, seemingly unprotected.[76] Living out his gospel of freedom from the world, Paul denies association with Thecla when he is questioned by Alexander, the representative of all things Roman. Alexander is the "head of the chapter of the Empire League" and his name means literally, "defender of men/husbands." Alexander approaches Paul seeking to buy Thecla with gifts and money, but Paul responds, "I do not know the woman about whom you speak; she is definitely not mine" (4.1 [26]). Although often interpreted as a harsh response from Paul, his words fit his gospel of detachment; moreover, they emphasize that he, like Thecla, belongs to God's household. It is God who protects Thecla, not Paul.[77]

Thecla's story ends after her final trial in the Antiochene arena. Having sewn herself a "man-styled garment," she reports the events to Paul. In response, he recognizes her transformation from virgin, who is under the constant threat of penetration by Rome, to a member of God's household. Previously he rejected her initial desire to be baptized for fear that she would eventually relent to marriage (or be raped) on account of her beauty. Surviving yet another attempt on her life, however, Thecla has shown herself impenetrable. Yet, it is not her own masculinity that saves her, but rather the "word of God" that she received and that marks her as a slave of God. Inseminated by this word, she is transformed into a gender-liminal state. She wears the clothing of a man, but she sewed them herself—a characteristically female task.[78] Nevertheless, this partial masculinization seems to be enough; she is now acknowledged by Paul to be a teacher and he sanctions her choice to return to Iconium with the words, "Go and teach God's word" (4.16 [41]). Yet, unlike Paul, she does not continue to travel about freely, but attempts a reconciliation with her mother before settling in Seleucia with her followers until her end, which is fittingly described as "a noble slumber" (*kalou hypnou*) rather than "death" (4.15–18 [40–43]).

Thecla's resolute behavior throughout her story demonstrates the power of her first hearing of "God's message" through Paul in 3.5–7. Her life demonstrates the truth of this word delivered through Paul, particularly the blessing on virgins quoted above: "the Father's word" becomes her "salvation" in literal rescues from physical threats, the peaceful life she eventually lives in Seleucia surrounded by her followers, and, implicitly in the "eternal rest" she will experience after death (4.18 [43]). Having heard the "Father's word," Thecla is thus inseminated and masculinized; she no longer requires the inferior masculinity offered by either Thyramis or the imperial representative, Alexander. Moreover, she does not even seem to require additional inseminating experiences from listening to Paul preach. Masculinized by the Father's word, she is able to endure tortures without Paul; his fear of her possible penetration by worldly matters is completely unrealized. It seems Paul, too, underestimates the masculinizing power of the Father's word.

The transformation of Thecla also exposes the falseness of Demas and Hermogenes's gospel of resurrection through children described above. Although in her rejection of Thyramis and Alexander Thecla is also rejecting birthing literal children, she does bring life wherever she travels. In the face of an Empire committed to killing her, Thecla herself is rescued and she brings the message of salvation to others, most notably to the house of Tryphaena, her patron and maternal substitute in Antioch (4.3–14 [28–39]). Upon reuniting with Thecla after she is saved again from death in Antioch, Tryphaena exclaims, "Now I believe that the dead arise! Now I believe that my child lives!" (4.14 [39]). Thecla's actions repeatedly betray the lie of the Empire by illustrating the eternal life that comes through accepting the Father's word about his Son. This does not mean that the *Acts of Thecla* necessarily concludes that *all* followers of Christ must be virgins and reject marriage.[79] Instead, several positive characters, including Tryphaena, are householders who have (or had) children.[80] These characters are positive examples, however, because they, like Thecla, do not look for their salvation through their households and the children meant to inherit and preserve them. Literal children require salvation themselves just as their parents. In the final lines of her story, Thecla, the one who rejects social "womanhood" to remain in perpetual childhood, never transitioning from "virgin" (*parthenos*) to "woman/wife" (*gynē*) or "mother," offers life to her mother.[81] "Theocleia, mother dear," she begins, "Can you believe that the Lord lives in heaven? If you desire possessions, the Lord will give them to you, on my behalf. If a *child*, look: here I am!" (43; emphasis added). Although Theocleia had mourned her daughter as though dead, and even attempted to have her killed, Thecla lives and is the means for her mother also to experience eternal life.

Thecla's Sisters: Maximilla, Perpetua, and Felicitas

The competition between Roman household systems and the household of God continues to be an issue into the third century, as demonstrated by the final two texts to be explored in this work: the *Acts of Andrew* and the *Martyrdom of Perpetua and Felicitas*. Each of these works merits a fuller discussion than is possible in this present work, and their presentation of women in particular has been a focus of a number of scholars. Rather than reviewing all of this literature, my appeal to these stories serves to showcase the persistence of debates over how feminine virtue was to be displayed among early Christians outside the NT. Although the Roman Imperial context continued to emphasize motherhood as the ideal telos for women, early Christians wrestled with this message. As in Thecla's story, believers questioned the need for procreation now that eternal life, or salvation, was secured by means of God's Son. As members of God's household, neither male nor female believers were required to toil with the work of preservation of legacy through possessions and children. In this soteriological context, the role of mothers and children is fluid; men can become mothers, women can become increasingly masculine, and children a potential hindrance for salvation rather than the means of its achievement.

Beginning with the *Acts of Andrew*, the virtuous matron, Maximilla, stops having sex with her husband, Aegeates, after converting to Christianity. Her explicit goal in this distance is the prevention of bearing children, whom Aegeates desires as the natural result (and, indeed, purpose) of their marriage (36).[82] After hearing Andrew's words, however, Aegeates is no longer Maximilla's lord, but is figured as her enemy, an "insolent and hostile snake" who threatens her with "boorish pollution" and "filthy intercourse" (14.7; 16.4).[83] Maximilla repeats Thecla's devotion to an apostle, not only physically distancing herself from the masculine authority of Aegeates, but also orchestrating a complex plot to keep him at bay. By disguising her slave, Euclia, as herself she successfully tricks Aegeates into having sex with a slave instead of his wife for eight months! Andrew's potent words have the power to masculinize Maximilla, making her impenetrable to her husband's verbal pleas and physical accosting. It is also Andrew's words that draw her physically near as she invites him into her own bedroom, along with other "brothers" (6; 13; 15).[84] The masculinization wrought by Andrew's words, however, does not result in her impregnation, but rather her sealing. She will not become a mother, and in so doing, she will demonstrate the superior self-control conveyed to her through these words/seeds in contrast to those of Aegeates.

Andrew's words, however, *can* impregnate—but only specific male disciples it would seem. It is Aegeates's brother, Stratocles, who upon hearing Andrew is metaphorically impregnated by him. The latent inner man within Stratocles is finally conceived and formed as a result of his hearing Andrew's *logos* and *pneuma*-rich message, which Stratocles calls "the seeds of the words of salvation" (44). Stratocles then gives birth to this inner man, guided by his husband and midwife, Andrew, who also offers to "suckle" the newborn Stratocles, thus continuing to convey the character-forming words that sparked his conception (7). Although more overtly Platonic than Paul's constructions in the passages explored in Chapter 4, the underlying anthropological and gender assumptions are the same: a male impregnated by a more masculine force than himself *can* "give birth" and "suckle."[85] Moreover, that which they birth and nurse is superior to the physical children birthed by women, who are susceptible to physical death and corruption. According to the *Acts of Andrew*, it is not women like Maximilla who need to become mothers, but rather male disciples like Stratocles, since the "children" they birth will live forever.[86]

Indeed, the consistent contrast of characters in the portions of the *Acts of Andrew* that have survived is not between Maximilla and Stratocles, but rather between the two brothers: Stratocles and Aegeates. Maximilla is a vessel caught in the middle. Aegeates, the proconsul and representative of imperial masculinity, acts out the Empire's story of salvation: he desperately desires children through Maximilla in order to secure his eternal life, the endurance of his household. Stratocles, however, acts out a superior path of salvation, impregnated and birthing his own "inner man" through the help of Andrew's insemination. In the end, Aegeates's imperial masculinity is shown effeminate as he loses control of his woman/wife, his household, and even his own body by repeatedly having sex with his wife's slave. Aegeates's desire for preservation through children eventually leads him to murder Andrew, from whom the real words/seeds of life come. Aegeates himself dies childless. Deprived of physical children through Maximilla, and failing to conceive his inner man, he kills himself in an unmanly manner by throwing himself from a cliff and passively falling to his death (64).[87]

As with the story of Thecla, however, the main battle for masculine performance centers on the body of a woman who refuses to play the part of a wife and mother. Throughout the narrative, the contest is again for an elite woman's chastity. Despite Aegeates's pleas—and the rights afforded him by his standing as a Roman proconsul—Maximilla resists, and the narrative justifies the extreme lengths she goes to in order to secure this chastity.[88] Nevertheless, unlike Thecla, Maximilla is no virgin; the question is not whether she will exist as a woman/wife, but rather, whose woman/wife she will be. Thus, when Maximilla hears Andrew's words, she does not conceive her own inner man within. Instead, the inner man within Maximilla is her "inner man/husband," Jesus himself, who acts as her masculinizing force.[89] Wedded to this man, Maximilla is to "*attain her proper kinship* through separation from those masquerading as friends but who are actual enemies" (16.6; emphasis added). Maximilla, then, proves herself a faithful woman/wife by confessing her love for this new husband to Aegeates himself. She explains, the "object of my love is not of this world and therefore imperceptible to you. Night and day it kindles and enflames me with love for it; but you can't see it, because it's difficult to see, and you cannot separate me from it, because that's impossible. So then, let me have intercourse and take my rest with it alone" (23.6–8).

The intercourse Maximilla describes does not result in physical children, but it does render her more masculine. Encouraging her again to persist in her resistance of Aegeates in spite of his threats against him, Andrew pleads, "I beg you, wise man, that your clear-sighted mind stand firm. I beg you, mind unseen, that you may be protected. I entreat you, love Jesus. Do not be overcome by the inferior. You whom I entreat as a man, assist me in my becoming perfect. Help me too, so that you may recognize your true nature" (41.1–3). Made masculine through her perpetual association with Jesus, Maximilla has no need for children, but experiences the perfection of her true nature in a "holy and quiet life" (64.4). Her persistent chastity is even presented as a reversal of Eve's sin (37); standing firm against her serpent, Aegeates, Maximilla acts as a model bride for Christ who alone brings about her salvation.[90]

The *Martyrdom of Perpetua and Felicitas* likewise undermines the significance of physical motherhood for women. The story of the martyrdom of a group of Christians on March 7, 203 in Carthage, North Africa, the accounts of Perpetua and Felicitas have a long tradition. Instead of focusing on the later developments of this narrative, however, the following interpretation will focus on the early document (ca. 211 CE), which was given the later title the *Martyrdom of Perpetua and Felicitas* (*Passio Perpetuae et Felicitatis*).[91] This short narrative contains Perpetua's written account from within the prison (chs. 3–10), followed by the account of another martyr named Saturnus (chs. 11–13), and additional narratives on Felicitas and the actual martyrdom of the saints (15.i–21.x). All of these sections are bracketed by an editorial introduction and conclusion (1–2; 21.xi). Unlike all previous documents explored in this study, therefore, there is in this story at least the potential of evidence written by an ancient woman herself concerning her own battle over how to be an ideal woman *and* a follower of Christ.[92] Of course, such evidence has been shaped to fit within a larger work; nevertheless, as Hanne Sigismund-Nielson notes, there is a decipherable voice in Perpetua's portion of the work. In this section, Perpetua fashions herself as a daughter (*filia*) of God.[93] In so doing, she detaches from her father and her infant son in order to live as God's child in his household alone.

Although the title of this work creates the expectation that Perpetua and Felicitas will share the stage, the work focuses primarily on Perpetua. She is identified at the outset with the following words: "Vibia Perpetua, who was well born (*honeste nata*), well educated (*liberaliter instituta*), honorably married (*matronaliter nupta*), and who had a father, a mother, and two brothers, one of whom was also a catechumen, and an infant son at her breast (*filium infantem ad ubera*)" (2.i–ii).[94] Perpetua's introduction is lengthy in comparison to that of her co-martyrs, including Felicitas, who seem to be slaves rather than freeborn, Roman citizens (2.i). As a Roman citizen, Perpetua lives in the midst of a social network of familial expectations outlined above, and which she has lived out up to this point in her life. She is married and has dutifully born a living son whom she nurses at her own breast rather than employing wet nurses for the task. Indeed, given the physiological and social understandings concerning breastmilk and breastfeeding reviewed in Chapter 4, the emphasis on Perpetua's nursing reinforces the bond she has with her son. She is not just a Roman wife and mother, she is an ideal woman who is living out the model of feminine virtue.

The implication from this portrait of the maternal Perpetua is that she is also an ideal Roman daughter. She has satisfied her familial obligations by marrying and birthing a son whom she personally continues to nourish and form toward manhood. If she were only to continue on this path and birth more living children, she could expect to be released from male guardianship, including that of her father (*pater potestas*), in due time. As a Roman woman from the early third century, Perpetua was most likely married *sine manu* and so remained linked to her natal household. Her dutiful performance of wifely and maternal roles should indicate her future performance of obligations to her aging parents: care for their aging bodies and burial after death. Up to this point in her life, therefore, it seems her parents—particularly her father—could count on Perpetua to live out Roman familial obligations, or *pietas*.[95] Yet, with her conversion, Perpetua's *pietas* shifts. She now identifies as God's daughter, and her obligations are to his household alone. As a result, throughout her account Perpetua's struggle is with her biological father rather than a husband; it is her father who fulfills the role of satanic tempter by appearing three times trying to regain her loyalty through pity (3.i–iii; 5.i–6.v; 9.i–iii).[96]

This parental focus also explains the unique emphasis on infants in the *Martyrdom*, first with Perpetua's infant son and, then, with Felicitas's prematurely born daughter. When Perpetua shifts her familial ties, it is not only her *pietas* toward her aging parents that she abandons; it is likewise her *pietas* toward her infant, who is much too young to fend for himself. As Sigismund-Nielson notes, *pietas* is reciprocal: "it was the duty of parents to take care of their children until they were old enough to take care of themselves," before children then turned to care for aging and dying parents.[97] That Perpetua's son literally relies on her body for continued nourishment reinforces this point. She is "tormented by anxiety for the baby" when separated from him, only relieved when he was brought to her so she could nurse him, "who by that point was starving to death" (3.vi, viii). Once she was "able to arrange for the baby to stay" with her in prison, the place becomes "a palace" since she has "no more pain and anxiety for my baby's sake" (3.ix). Perpetua's emphasis on maternal "anxiety" demonstrates her identity as a good, Roman mother. Like Venus in the *Aeneid*, Perpetua is concerned that her son grow to be a good man.

Yet, now as a part of God's household, her anxiety needs to transition. Even though she had secured care for her son by her mother and brother, who is also a catechumen, she continues to feel anxious for her son's care (3.v). She needs divine intervention to free her from this burden. It is for this reason that she counts God's weaning of her son to be a miracle. When her biological father prevents Perpetua from continuing to keep her son in prison and, therefore, to nurse him, God shows his true paternal control. Although another attempt by her father to appeal to her sense of obligation, God uses the opportunity to release Perpetua from the last traces of maternal anxiety. "It was God's will, though," writes Perpetua, "not only did the baby stop wanting my breasts but they did not become inflamed. And so I was not subjected to *anxiety for my baby* and sore breasts as well" (6.viii, emphasis added). God's provision for both Perpetua and her son demonstrates his superior fatherhood in contrast to her biological father's sustained impotence. Perpetua is no longer mother, but now daughter of God and sister to the believers, in whose care she surrenders her son.[98] In this way, the cessation of breastmilk indicates the cessation of Perpetua's parental attempts over her son's life. She enables him also to be a member of God's household and to seek nourishment from God alone. Ironically, in this surrender, she once again demonstrates that she is an ideal mother.

Felicitas, too, experiences a miraculous cessation of biological motherhood that is arguably more dramatic than that of Perpetua. Arrested while pregnant,

Felicitas experiences "the Lord's grace" (*il gratia Domini*) when she suffers through premature delivery while in prison (15.i). Since Romans did not commit pregnant women to the arena, Felicitas is fearful that her pregnancy will prevent her being martyred with her family of believers, thus forcing her to face and "to pour out her holy and innocent blood at a later time together with other, real criminals" (15.ii).[99] Her "fellow martyrs," therefore, pray for the bloodletting of parturition to begin, even though she is eight months pregnant, a time considered especially dangerous for both mother and child.[100] "[I]mmediately after the prayer [Felicitas] is beset by pains," and suffers through a difficult delivery, "as was natural in a delivery during the eighth month" (15.v). Despite the suffering, however, Felicitas and her daughter not only survive, but Felicitas has the energy to rebuff the taunts of a prison guard. The guard mocks her, saying, "If this is how you act now, what will you do when you are thrown to the beasts that you didn't care about when you decided not to sacrifice?" (15.v). Felicitas's answer aligns her parturitive suffering with her upcoming martyrdom. She explains, "Now I am the one suffering what I suffer, but then another inside me will suffer for me, since I will also be suffering for him" (15.vi). Her response makes sense in her gynecological context since ancient parturitive theories held that a mother suffers alone and even *against* her infant in childbirth, as the baby tears and thrashes free from the maternal bindings of the womb.[101] In the arena, however, the one "inside" her will suffer with her on her behalf. The infant is replaced by Christ who will work with Felicitas to deliver her into eternal life and perhaps, therefore, to reverse the curse of painful birth from Gen 3:16.

Like Perpetua, Felicitas's infant is suddenly separated from her mother. Both mothers experience "torture" at this separation. For Perpetua her maternal anxiety persists until God weans her son from her breast, while Felicitas suffers the "natural" difficulty of an eight-month delivery. Both mothers also experience a cessation of their motherhood when they stop providing physical nourishment to their babies by means of their bodies. Pregnant or lactating, Felicitas and Perpetua were providing inseminated blood to their infants. As I have shown, according to ancient theories, the very blood that shaped the bodies and souls of these infants *was* the very blood and souls of their mothers (and fathers) both in utero and at the breast. When they are miraculously freed of the burden to nourish, Perpetua and Felicitas relinquish their maternal identities. They will not be the ones to nourish (*educavit*, 15.viii) their children, they will trust this task to the God who now calls these women to eternal life by means of their physical deaths. That God can and does provide nourishment is emphasized not only in the miraculous survival of the infants despite physical separation from their mothers, but also by Perpetua's first vision, where she drinks and eats the milky cheese provided for her by the "shepherd" (4.viii–ix). Awaking from the vision still "chewing on something sweet," Perpetua understands the vision to indicate her coming martyrdom and transition to a life beyond "this world" (4.x).

In the final scenes of the story, Perpetua and Felicitas finally join the stage together; two mothers-made-daughters whose bodies demonstrate God's miraculous intervention to end their maternity. Perpetua enters the arena "with a steady gait, like a bride of Christ (*matrona Christi*) or the favourite of God (*Dei delicata*), parrying the gaze of all with the strength of her own; and Felicity too, rejoicing to have survived childbirth so that she might battle against the beasts, going from one blood-sport to the next, from midwife to gladiator, to bathe after childbirth in her second baptism" (18.ii). Once in the arena, the narrator again describes their appearance, "stripped naked and hobbled by nets, they were brought out. The people were aghast as they looked upon them, the one a beautiful girl (*puellam delicatam*), the other a woman fresh from giving birth and with dripping breasts (*partu recentem stillantibus mammis*)" (20.ii). Certainly, Sigismund-Nielson and others are right to note the horror of this scene as well as the highly sexualized language used to describe Perpetua as first the "favourite" of God and then as a "beautiful girl."[102] Yet, the descriptions also reinforce the physicality of the miracles provided by God. Perpetua's body is made firm; not only does she no longer show signs of lactating, but she looks like a virgin, one whose body has never received male seed or carried a child. Felicitas's body, in contrast, highlights her recent delivery that was God's gift for her. Permeated and leaking, Felicitas's body bleeds lochial blood and drips with milk. The two women stand together, stark contrasts in appearance, but demonstrating the same reality: God's grace for both has ended their motherhood so that, regardless of their social class and separation in the Roman world, both women now stand together as sisters, daughters of the one true God.

All three of these narratives establish the gospel of God in competition with the gospel of Rome.[103] According to Rome and, indeed, additional literature from the ancient Mediterranean world, the "good news" of life comes through the establishment and sustaining of households. The gospel of God in each of these early Christian stories, however, offers a different path of salvation. Rather than finding eternal life through the birthing and rearing of children who will safeguard and grow a household's physical wealth, these narratives proclaim a life already secured through God's Son. It is God's Son, rather than one's own, who gives eternal life to all who join the household of his *Paterfamilias*, often at the cost of abandoning literal households in the world. As the crucial conduit for either continuing or disrupting households, therefore, women and their bodies figure as battlegrounds in these early Christian narratives. By rejecting Roman households in favor of God's, each of these women accept and perpetuate God's words/seeds. In so doing, they proclaim God's superior masculinity, and masculinizing ability, to perpetuate life without physical procreation.

Conclusions

Attitudes toward mothers and motherhood in the Augustan age were complex and often ambivalent. Ideal women/wives were assumed free(d) by definition, and they exercised their virtue through marital submission to men/husbands that resulted in the production and rearing of legitimate sons for Rome. Augustus's legislative and political agenda of tying fatherhood to superior masculinity likewise reinforced the ideal of motherhood upon women seeking superior femininity: motherhood is highlighted as the physical manifestation of both a husband's manhood *and* a wife's proper submission to, and masculinization by, her husband. Such women contribute to the overall masculinization of the Empire, and can even facilitate its salvation in times of extreme threat when real men are lacking, thus acquiring greater agency. Nevertheless, this idealization of motherhood, along with the standard practice of marriage *sine manu*, caused concern among at least some elite males that mothers were overreaching their place. Indeed, women like Livia and Agrippina can be depicted as assuming a greater masculinization for themselves than was perceived possible due to their inescapable femininity. For Tacitus and many other elite Roman era males, a masculinized woman can be good, but only when still under the control of a superior, masculine male to restrain her feminine excesses.

Operating in this complex environment, NT and early Christian writers likewise wrestle with constructions of feminine virtue and ideal women, especially with the means of their masculinization and continued control. Although they include females, particularly free(d) females, in their narratives of salvation, they offer various possibilities for how such salvation is to be realized: must a girl become a woman/wife, and even a mother, in order to demonstrate her masculinized status? For 1 Timothy and Titus, at least, the answer is yes. The household codes of Colossians and Ephesians similarly assume such a process. A woman is a wife, and she is masculinized through her complete submission to her husband; a submission that allows for her mental and physical insemination and that often results in the production of children. Yet, such a portrait is problematized already by 1 Peter, whose household code both mirrors its ancient context *and* undermines it with the depiction of women/wives in defiance of husbands by following Christ instead of the household religion of a husband's choice. The extra-canonical texts explored continue to demonstrate the spectrum of possibilities for Christian girls and women/wives. Thecla, Maximilla, Perpetua, and Felicitas are examples of a girl, two women, and a slave who do not require consistent masculine insemination from a husband for their salvation. Instead, they are masculinized by hearing a male apostle's word for a time, or even by God alone, resulting in their rejection of marriage, sex, and even infant children as the evidence of their greater submission to the heavenly *Paterfamilias* and his Son.

This spectrum illustrates the various possibilities for female believers at least in the literature of early Christianity. As Hylen and others have noted, however, such options do not separate these females from their femininity; their key virtue remains submission.[104] Instead, the key difference between these works seems to be their overarching constructions of God's household: does it largely replicate those of the dominant Greco-Roman culture or does it replace them? In other words, if the ideal male believer is also a man/husband/father (as in the Pastoral Epistles), then the ideal female believer must also be a woman/wife/mother. If the ideal believer is a child, then marriage and motherhood become less of an imperative even if they were an ever present reality in actual early Christian contexts. Indeed, even the works explored above that downplay motherhood rarely condemn it. Aside from Maximilla in the *Acts of Andrew*, motherhood is a possible option for believing women in the *Acts of Thecla* and the *Martyrdom of Perpetua and Felicitas*, even if it is inferior to the exceptional examples of the narratives' heroines. The important distinction is that eternal life is not found in physical children, but in women's rebirth and regeneration by means of God's word, which requires their ultimate submission in whatever form.

Such a distinction emphasizes the liminality of girls, women/wives, and female slaves in the Roman world, including in early Christian contexts. Certainly marriage remained a possibility for many free(d) females who were undoubtedly encouraged to marry and have children not only by their larger cultural contexts, but also by their faith communities. As means of legitimatizing or controlling their femininity, and even ensuring their physical health, marriage and motherhood were potentially positive options for free(d) girls and women in the ancient Mediterranean world. Yet, grappling with their belief in Jesus's messiahship, death, and resurrection, early Christians also had to confront constructions of gender in light of their Greco-Roman contexts. Jesus's fatherless status, his ultimate rejection by both Jewish and Roman authorities, and his effeminate humiliation on the cross challenge constructions of masculinity, thereby forcing a reshaping of virtue both for male and female disciples. In these ancient contexts, NT and other early Christian authors replicate the assumption of masculine superiority and, therefore, the need for masculinization of females due to their inherently more vice-ridden state. Moreover, they also communicate continued suspicion of female believers who can never completely escape the reality of their female bodies, only becoming safe from improper penetration at their deaths.[105] Nevertheless, while 1 Timothy's emphasis on maternity as the path of salvation for women makes sense in such a context, it is by no means the *only* option advocated for these female believers. Instead, the larger emphasis is on their submission to God's masculinizing word, regardless of whether that submission results in biological motherhood, adoptive motherhood, or even a childless life. Indeed, submission to God may involve repeated, and very public, insubordination to human men, regardless of their claims over the lives of believing slaves, girls, and women. Motherhood may matter, but it is relegated to a status below a female believer's submission to her divine *Paterfamilias*.

6

Conclusions

THE BLESSEDNESS OF WOMEN

I BEGAN THIS study by reflecting on the familiar scene of Elizabeth and Mary from the Gospel of Luke; two women, inexplicably pregnant, and wrestling with the seemingly impossible status of "blessedness" as a result of their burgeoning motherhood. While this scene remains one of the most poignant between two women in the NT, if not the entire biblical corpus, the investigation throughout this book has served to complicate it a bit. Grounded in a milieu that binds up womanhood with motherhood, Elizabeth and Mary stand at the edges. Elizabeth is a post-menopausal female who, although married, never completed her transition to full "woman" (*gynē*) as a result of her failure to provide children for her husband. Even though she is described as righteous, Elizabeth never realized her culturally conditioned telos of enabling Zechariah to "be fruitful and multiply" in accordance with God's command. Mary, too, is liminal. A "virgin" (*parthenos*) in the midst of her own transition to woman/wife (*gynē*), she skips the intermediary steps of marriage and physical intercourse with her sudden, divine fecundity. Once again, a Jewish man's ability to fulfill God's procreative prerogative is jeopardized.

These two females, both transitioned into womanhood by the divine masculine rather than by their human men/husbands, are blessed, but in very unconventional ways. This scene in Luke is but one part of Luke's larger narrative that emphasizes the role of God as divine *Paterfamilias*, whose operative agenda overshadows not only the lives of female followers, but males as well. When God is the Father, the role of human parents—and the understandings of womanhood and manhood that accompany them—must be redefined.

In this Lukan narrative we already see how NT writings use and subvert assumptions about mothers and motherhood in the ancient Mediterranean world. Pregnant and prophesying by means of a holy Spirit, Elizabeth and Mary simultaneously subvert and reinforce gender expectations, and the corporeal constructions that were a part of these expectations. Both women fulfill the narrative of a maternal telos for their existence; they act as vessels for life by accepting God's words and, therefore, give meaning to their own presence (Luke 1:24–25, 38). At the same time, however, it is not their pregnancies alone that are praised, but rather their submission to God's will, which happens to facilitate pregnancy in spite of male inability or absence. Moreover, these women, whose pregnancies and birthing are so celebrated in Luke's opening chapters, are characters of transition. Their motherhood matters because of the sons they bear: one, a heralding prophet, and the other, a heralded savior. Once their roles are completed, the women all but disappear, taking with them the assumption that motherhood stands as an untouchable good for all female members of God's household. Instead, as in the other Gospels, Luke's Gospel downplays biological motherhood in the rest of the story as a part of the larger devaluation of human households as institutions of stability and immortality through production and preservation of children and wealth. Rather than claiming life is a result of striving for and within human households, Luke and the other NT Gospels claim life is secured through the faithfulness of and to Jesus as God's Christ, the ideal Son. It is now through this Son, who himself remains unmarried and childless, that God begets children into his household. And like this Son, these children are to place their primary allegiance to God as Father, regardless of, and indeed often in direct opposition to, their membership in human households (Matt 10:16–42; Luke 12:51–53; 14:26–27; Mark 10:28–31).

Although at points resisting the overarching maternal telos of the Greco-Roman era, these writings nevertheless largely retain the gender assumptions that buttressed it: namely, the core assumption that perfection is masculine. In such a context, salvation is presented as a process of masculinizing meant to reorient not only individual people, but the entire cosmos toward the Good, the life-generating masculine, in whatever form he is to be recognized. According to the Gospels and undisputed Pauline letters, Jesus is the new model of masculine Sonship, he demonstrates submission to God's will even to the point of crucifixion, and he calls on his followers to do likewise (e.g., Mark 8:34–38; Matt 16:24–26; Luke 9:23–26; John 12:24–26; 1 Cor 3:21–23). Rather than preserving life through households and children, believers are to give up their lives so that they might gain them through their submission to God's life-giving, and therefore, most masculine will.

Yet, that this ideal was not always possible—or even desired—by early Christians is likewise demonstrated in other NT writings. Thus, the NT contains household codes and the Pastoral Epistles, which create analogies between human households and God's household of the "church" rather than antagonism. As vessels of theological belief and expression, therefore, the bodies of believers, maternal and otherwise, showcase the convictions of these developing communities. By portraying believers as either persisting within human households, or dividing from them, early Christian writings simultaneously repeated assumptions from the larger Greco-Roman culture and repressed them. The debate is not whether God will masculinize, but rather, *how*. In this debate, women's bodies are especially powerful elements. Will God (continue to) rely on literal men to emulate his masculinizing work through marriage and procreation (e.g., 1 Tim 2:15; Eph 5:25–26)? Or will God disrupt the script, directly taking over the masculinizing role to transform girls, women, and even men into life-giving disciples without the need for a husband's words and seeds (*logoi*)? In the NT and other early Christian writings, at least, it seems that God does both. And motherhood, both physical and metaphorical, repeatedly surfaces as a vivid embodiment of this salvific work.

How to Become a Woman: Reviewing the Maternal Telos

Before investigating the primary texts of importance for this study, Chapter 2 outlined the overarching gender constructions of the ancient Mediterranean world to expose the entrenched association between femaleness, inferiority, and the redemption possible through motherhood. Driving this maternal narrative is the fundamental gender hierarchy assumed throughout the ancient Mediterranean world: that which is "good" or superior is assumed to be "masculine." Life, therefore, is generated by the masculine; it is gestated by the inferior, feminine. Not only does such an assumption solidify the general superiority of biologically male humans, it also prescribes particular understandings of masculinity (along with those things determined "good") in its constructions of "manhood" and its superlative, "divinity." Thus, while "perfection" is agreed upon as a good thing, its construction is aligned with so-called masculine activities: generation, physical and cultural impermeability, public agency, particular manifestations of bodily comportment and behavior, and the domination and protection of those within a man's designated sphere, to name a few. These constructions and activities, therefore, limit which biological males can participate in the competition for masculine recognition.[1] They also significantly impact the constructions of their necessary opposite: the feminine.

Indeed, the entire assumption of superiority necessitates the existence of an inferior. Masculine superiority is predicated on female inferiority. Again, as Rebecca Flemming explains, "It is not so much that the female is inferior as that the inferior is female."[2] Any falling away from perfection/masculinity is imperfection/femininity. A female is an especially significant deviance; she lacks a penis to penetrate, absorbs moisture, and leaks blood and milk through her soft flesh. A woman's inferior traits center on her *permeability* in contrast to the solid masculine. She is physically and culturally permeable, which necessitates her domination and protection by masculine superiors: rulers, fathers, guardians, masters, husbands, and even sons. Furthermore, her permeability is emphasized in stories of her origin, as either Pandora or the Hellenistic Eve who wrought destruction (death/femininity) by acting outside masculine control. The control of women is thus necessary to prevent further chaos descending upon mankind.

Central to the construction of the feminine, therefore, is also what is central to the construction of that which is "female"; her hollow and porous body results in a perpetually vulnerable state. This permeability is emphasized in the focus on her genitalia—her vagina, uterus, and breasts—that distinguish her from the male in gynecological literature. Yet, the implications of this permeability stretch far beyond the medical and philosophical writings of elite males. Their writings justify as well as reflect the larger assumption that females (and the feminine) must be purposed by the male (and masculine), for her own sake as well as his. While this purposing is realized in a variety of ways, none seems to occupy the attention of ancient writers as much as motherhood. This "proper" masculine use of woman's womb by and for her husband ensures not only her own protection, perpetuation, and physical health, it also makes possible the survival of mankind—a fact that justified the existence of the imperfection that is the female. In motherhood, her stark deviance from the masculine is explained. In this way, the unique ability of women to conceive, gestate, and birth is constructed simultaneously as her greatest purpose *and* her greatest potential for destruction. She is quintessentially ambivalent, and her depictions in culture, written and material, reflect this liminality.

In such a context, the alignment of womanhood with motherhood is quick and complete, and outliers only seem to reinforce the normative ideal.[3] If being a man requires particular behaviors that correspond to a realization of his telos, so too, does being a woman. Once again, this necessarily limits those females who can compete for such acknowledgment—although the general association of pregnancy with female health also justified the impregnation of female slaves alongside their marriageable counterparts. A man keeps chaos at bay in his own household, the state, and the cosmos, by controlling his females, including by their impregnation. Moreover, this construction affirms the agency of the man above all else. It is the man, as husband or master, who *makes* a female a woman through his penetration; she merely submits and *becomes* that which she was "naturally" meant to be.

The operating assumption of masculine superiority, therefore, has far-reaching effects. Yet, the malleability of masculinity needs also to be acknowledged. Masculine competitions existed in a variety of spheres of socio-economic, class, ethnic, and religious diversity. Indeed, Dale Martin argues that part of masculinity's permeating influence is a result of its flexibility, imprecision, and constant need for performance.[4] It was easier to define things that were un-masculine than it was to identify an ineffable masculine ideal. Certainly any number of first-century Jews, for example, would not define the Roman emperor as the most masculine representative on earth. Instead, various groups constantly shaped and reshaped their own constructions of masculinity even as emperors and other elite, Roman men asserted and reasserted their own. However, while that which is "masculine" might be reshaped to correspond to various cultural ideals, the underlying assumption that what is "good" is necessarily "masculine" does not shift. Thus, whatever (or whomever) is defined as the most Good is also the most Masculine. And his construction necessarily impacts the sliding gender scale that drifts after him toward femininity and effeminacy. It is this flexibility that fuels the redefinitions of masculinity in NT and early Christian writings. When God is *Paterfamilias*, and Christ is the ideal Son, masculine and feminine categories must again be reshaped. As a key component of these constructions, motherhood is a frequent part of the discussion.

Becoming a Woman after Christ: Mothers and Motherhood in the New Testament

While we find a mix of use and subversion of gender categories in the NT, therefore, we nevertheless discover a sustained assumption of masculine superiority corresponding to the larger, ancient Mediterranean culture. As a result, Chapters 3 through 5 also uncovered a consistent ambiguity toward mothers and motherhood that mirrors other cultural anxieties concerning the female and the feminine used to affirm masculine superiority. Although necessary for the birth of Christ, biological motherhood is not always assumed as the ideal telos for female believers after his death and resurrection. Instead, believers belong to God's household; God, as Father, is the ultimate generator and preserver of life. He can impregnate women to bring about the miraculous births of exceptional sons, but his Fatherhood also creates metaphorical motherhood as his Son and later disciples gestate, birth, and nurse new children for this Father God. Not only is physical motherhood not always the avenue for feminine purposing and redemption—though, sometimes it is—at times it is rejected entirely, even replaced by a man birthing in the woman's stead. Early Christians, therefore, reflect their cultural context both in their incorporation of the same underlying gender assumptions *and* in their ability to reshape these constructions to fit their theological and soteriological perspectives.

This reality leads NT authors and communities to retain and subvert constructions of mothers and motherhood from their contexts. The telos of all persons is salvation, or eternal life, but as a form of perfection, salvation *is* masculinization—although this masculinity now reflects interpretations of Jesus of Nazareth as God's Christ and Son. Thus, Chapter 3 demonstrates that Matthew, Luke, and John present Jesus as being conceived by the most masculine seed and a holy Spirit, which contains the divinely masculine *logos* and *pneuma* to fashion him to reflect his divine Father (Matt 1:18–25; Luke 1:26–38; John 1:1–18). While Matthew's and Luke's presentations sustain Mary's continued, even if truncated, maternal role in this process, John excises her from the narrative in order to present Jesus as the incarnation of God's life-generating and sustaining *Logos* itself, a perfect reflection of the Father's "glory" (John 1:14–16). These presentations of Jesus's origins serve to absolutize his masculinity in Matthew, Luke, and John, thereby disrupting potential polemic against him and his followers (cf. John 8:41). Although Jesus's birth may seem to indicate questionable origins, these Gospels resolve the tension by invoking divine paternity, the *only* possible paternity that can rightly usurp a husband's role. In this way, Jesus's masculinity is made stable at the outset of these stories, justifying the later rejection he faces and even his utter humiliation on the cross. As the Son of the Divine One, Jesus and his actions are presented as reflecting the will of the most Masculine, God, even when he is rejected, tortured, and killed by the so-called masculine powers on earth. Vindicated by his resurrection, Jesus's masculinity is shown to be "true" and his followers, male and female, are challenged to replicate it regardless of the consequences.

In Jesus's conception and birth, mothers and motherhood seem to change little from the dominant cultural constructions. Mary, when she does appear, is a vessel—a special vessel, but a vessel nonetheless. She is purposed in a superior way by virtue of her being chosen by God, the most Good and most Masculine. Yet, the divine interruption of Joseph's manly, procreative role points toward continued interruptions of cultural masculinity in the Gospels and Acts. Salvation may indeed persist in being masculinization, but the masculinity achieved is quite different from the masculinity of a Roman imperial society. Indeed, Jesus's apocalyptic message prioritizes God's reality over and against the Roman peace (*pax*), and promotes a sustained childhood for believers in God's household rather than a life that culminates in biological parenthood, whether maternal or paternal. Taking the procreative imagery further, again, John frames salvation as becoming "children of God." Reconceived, generated, and birthed by the divine *Logos* and enlivened by his Spirit (*pneuma*), believers experience their own masculine generation so that they might imitate Jesus even as he reflects the Father. In this way, these children are constantly oriented toward God and, therefore, eternal life (John 1:12–13; 20:30–31).

As seen in Chapter 4, traces of this agenda drift into the epistolary literature as well, with images of birth-by-apostle as well as nursing from male breasts in Paul's letters and beyond (Gal 4:19–20; 1 Thess 2:7–8; 1 Pet 2:1–3). Situated in the ancient Mediterranean world, NT writings also betray assumptions that breastmilk is the same substance out of which fetuses are formed in a woman's womb. Breastmilk, therefore, continues to communicate the body- and soul-shaping seeds that shaped the infant in a mother's womb. With their use of maternal metaphors of birth and nursing, NT writings emphasize the divine source of the *logos* and *pneuma* by which believers are reconceived, reborn, and renourished so that their souls are shaped to reflect the Divine Masculine who initiated their first, and now their new, superior begetting. The Son, apostle, and teacher take on a feminized role beneath this Masculine, supplying womb and breast for the infusion of believers with the seed that will pattern in them everlasting life (1 Pet 1:22–2:3).

The birth and education these believers receive, therefore, is focused on their masculinization regardless of the feminization of various male figures in service to God. Indeed, by recognizing their feminine (i.e., inferior) status before the Father, these males demonstrate their masculinity; they rightly submit to the One who is greater so that they might transmit greater order, greater masculinity, upon the cosmos as desired by its Creator.[5] Moreover, they supply superior nourishment for the production of superior, and more masculine, offspring. Birthed and nourished by these masculine teachers, disciples are encouraged to continue in their masculinization, either by weaning from the metaphorical breastmilk supplied by these mothers, or by remaining attached, gaining nourishment from this breast alone (1 Cor 3:1–3; Heb 5:11–14; 1 Pet 2:1–3). In either case, the disciples are to become even more like God's ideal Son who submits to God's perfect, life-giving will. In their metaphorical reenactment of the woman's role as mother, therefore, these men simultaneously exalt her unique ability and usurp it. The superior, masculine children metaphorically emerge from and are nourished by male bodies *alone*, bodies that "naturally" exhibit greater masculinity than their female counterparts and, thus, convey greater masculinity as well.

In this way, the depiction of salvation as masculinization that pervades the NT becomes increasingly more complex whenever female bodies are included. How are girls and women to be masculinized in spite their porous and leaking bodies? And if male disciples can be masculinized via feminization, what does this mean for female disciples who *already exist* in an infinitely more feminized state? In Chapter 5 I showcased the divergent answers in the NT corpus and on into additional early Christian writings. While the answer for female masculinization was motherhood in much of the ancient Mediterranean world, it is not the automatic answer in the writings that would later become the NT. In the Gospels, Acts, and many of Paul's letters, biological maternity is downplayed in favor of the unique maternity of Mary, Jesus, or Paul himself. The apocalyptic perspectives of these writings undermine God's procreative command from Genesis; since God is ending history to initiate his Kingdom, there is no need for more offspring. Instead, the offspring who already exist should recognize their status as God's children, and stop trying to become women and men according to worldly standards (Mark 3:31–35; Matt 19:10–30; Luke 20:34–35; John 1:12–13). Outside these apocalyptically charged contexts, however, other NT writings continue to idealize biological motherhood as the telos for marriageable, female believers, even if it is inferior to the maternity of Christ and his male apostles (1 Tim 2:8–3:1a). Inseminated by believing husbands, these women are masculinized by their husbands' seeds and by their right submission to a husband's masculinity just as he submits to Christ (Eph 5:26–27). Even non-believing husbands require submission, since feminine submission demonstrates divine order. Through her quiet submission, a believing woman/wife conveys God's seed and word (*logos*) and participates in not only the birth of her husband's children, but perhaps the metaphorical re-birth of her husband as well (1 Pet 3:1–6).

The problem of masculinizing female bodies persists in these writings and in other early Christian literatures. As a result, they continue to debate motherhood because of its unique place as the telos for females in the ancient Mediterranean world. Although NT and other early Christian writings agree that all followers of Jesus should desire to replicate his version of manhood, they do not know what such a telos does for the lives of female believers.[6] Must they become "women" first, or can they be masculinized by God directly, thus circumventing the need for men/husbands to inseminate and control their female bodies? In spite of the instructions from the Pastorals and the household codes, therefore, Thecla and Maximilla eschew marriage and motherhood after receiving God's words through a male apostle. Rather than seeking protection and hope in a man's household, these women find and transmit life as members of God's household. Even when Perpetua and Felicitas die as a result of their new allegiances to God as Father that usurp other fathers and lords, recorded visions emphasize their continued existence. Perpetua conveys life to her deceased brother, Dinocrates, through prayers made powerful by means of her martyrdom and enjoys the heavenly scenes alongside Saturnus and the other martyrs, presumably including Felicitas (*Perp.* 4; 7–8; 11–13). God's life-giving provision is also emphasized in the preservation of life for the two infants left in the world without their biological mothers. These infants do not require their mothers' milk or care; they are members of God's household, where sisters and brothers rear children under the Father's protection (6.viii; 15.vii).

The diverse presentations of mothers and maternal motifs in these writings thus demonstrate sustained attempts to emphasize that God's identity as the source and sustainer of life is uniquely revealed in the person and work of Jesus, his Christ and Son. Jesus's culturally disruptive masculinity requires a simultaneous reassessment of gendered roles in these writings, even if it does not dramatically challenge the underlying gender hierarchy. Nevertheless, understanding the constructions of mothers and motherhood, both philosophically and medically, in the ancient Mediterranean world enables readers to discover greater depth to the ways in which these images are employed, and reassessed, in the NT and early Christian literatures. Mary's and Elizabeth's sudden pregnancies by means of a holy

Spirit overflowing the pathways (*hodoi*) of their bodies explains their sudden prophetic pronouncements, even as their subsequent deliveries explain their sudden silences. The physiological understandings of breastmilk as a soul and character-forming substance explains its importance as an analogy for education and salvation. And Jesus's existence as the most ideal transmitter of God's words (*logoi*) establishes him as both God's ideal Son and partner as he gestates and births new children for God's household. Faithful followers, male and female, continue his disruptive masculinity by metaphorically bearing additional children, even abandoning literal mother- and fatherhood to do so. In this way, motherhood did not hold an untouchable place in early Christian circles, in spite of the implacable admonitions of 1 Timothy and Titus.

The conversation in early Christian circles reveals the constant fluidity of gender assessment in human societies; motherhood has simply never been the *only* way women have found to live or to be identified, not even in the ancient Mediterranean world, even if it does persist as one dominant narrative of ideal womanhood. Indeed, that elite male authors spend so much energy reinforcing the narrative of a maternal telos reveals that motherhood was not as stable as they might desire. Moreover, additional research by scholars such as Emily Hemelrijk traces the education and power of elite Roman women, such as Cornelia Gracchus and Livia Augusta, which this study also explored in Chapter 5.[7] B. J. Brooten and Ross Shepard Kraemer likewise highlight the leadership roles some Jewish women also played in their communities, even being conferred the title "leader of the synagogue" (*archisynagōgos*).[8] While many of these women were mothers, motherhood does not fully capture the totality of their identity, even when these women used their motherhood as part of the advancement of their own agency. Like those of the men with whom they shared their lives, the gender identities of these women were also up for debate and, thus, required constant performance and evaluation.

The disruption and reshaping of masculinity and femininity in the NT and other early Christian writings, therefore, are simply a part of the larger, and continual, assessment and performance of cultural ideals that are never as transcendent as they might seem (or that their advocates claim them to be). The new-old-fashioned family of the Augustan age needed to be propagandized and legislated because, much like the stereotypical American nuclear family of the post-World War II era, it was a minority reality at best.[9] To ignore the fluidity of and debates over gender constructions in the NT and early Christian writings, therefore, detaches maternal imagery and characters from their contexts. As a result, maternal elements are separated from ancient corporeal and philosophical assumptions that make plain the theological significance of mothers and motherhood in these writings. Instead of being contextualized, the mothers and maternal imagery of the NT and early Christian literatures are both exalted and assumed, made transhistorical and ornamental, rather than contextual and substantive. Since they are assumed stable, commentators and interpreters quickly read over them, relegating them to footnotes and brief comments, rather than to critical reflection. Reading without these contexts, therefore, NT interpreters participate with larger western society by enshrining the maternal telos even in the face of narratives that undermine it.[10]

Wading into the debates of gender identity and motherhood from the ancient Mediterranean world, however, does not endorse such facile application. While some early Christians affirmed that a woman could (and, indeed, should) be masculinized—that is, oriented toward life—through marriage and motherhood, many others emphasized that God's superior masculinization was possible by other means. Moreover, some argue that the *best* Christians will reject marriage and procreation entirely, regardless of their biological sex (1 Cor 7; *Acts of Thecla*; *Acts of Andrew*). Direct contact with God, his Son, or disciples can make these women children again. Like Perpetua, the daughter of God, they are firmly situated in God's household rather than (only) in a human father's or husband's household that may or may not bring them life. What these texts do agree on is the need to be oriented toward life, the source and continuance of which is located in God alone; what they disagree on repeatedly is how this orientation is accomplished. In this way, the multiplicity of NT and early Christian constructions of mothers and motherhood offers hope for all women—regardless of class, race, desire, or physical ability to birth living children—to experience life.

The Blessedness of Women: Some Lingering Effects of the Maternal Telos

The analysis in this book has focused primarily on the NT. Nevertheless, it exposes assumptions and constructions that are still relevant in contemporary western societies concerning womanhood and motherhood, both in and outside of "Christian" environments. Their relevance remains because many of these assumptions and constructions have informed western societies since the Roman era. Thus, while many aspects of contemporary "womanhood" and motherhood certainly differ from the first centuries of the Roman Empire, much of the embedded assumptions concerning gender hierarchies remain even if packaged differently for twenty-first century consumption.

As Rebecca Jo Plant has shown, contemporary American motherhood has undergone significant changes in the modern era. Plant traces the diminishment of Victorian era "Mother Love" in the western imagination after two world wars. No longer is motherhood conceptualized primarily as a civic responsibility and the mother the "angel of the house" whose diligent and life-long care resulted in the rearing of sons for the state. Instead, a woman is to become a mother to achieve her own personal self-actualization, but not too much. The psychologizing of motherhood in the postwar era transformed motherhood from an ideal of constant, explicit moral shaping of one's children to constant presence, and focused detachment to encourage autonomy. For this reason, the ideal mother of postwar America is to limit her intensive mothering to the first few years of her children's lives and then find additional fulfillment elsewhere, lest she be accused of "helicopter" mothering or creating "momma's boys." She can be constantly present, but never too involved, lest she be seen to seek her identity through her children and, in so doing, limit—or emasculate—their own development.[11] Nevertheless, even with this great divergence, Victorian and postwar era women in the United States have been formed with the same ideal: a *real* woman is a mother.

Reading the history of American constructions of motherhood with Roman era ideals in mind uncovers even more connections. Jodi Vandenberg-Daves notes the sudden encouragement of women's autonomy during World War I and World War II as well as in the interwar period. When peace was restored, however, she notes a "postwar backlash" that created "the century's most rigidly enforced definitions of masculinity and femininity."[12] Plant, too, highlights what she sees as a resurgence of "masculinity" in this era.[13] Rather than a resurgence, however, a more precise description might be a reframing of masculinity that highlighted male control of public spaces in the United States, rather than abroad in military settings that no longer existed after the end of these wars. The assurance of peace, therefore, is made through the (re)establishment of traditional order and hierarchies at "home," so to speak: men operate in public spheres (business, politics, etc.), while women remain in private homes. Much like Augustus's campaign after two Roman civil wars, postwar America idealized the wife-in-the-home and created legislation that perpetuated this ideal. In this baby boom time period and beyond, white middle-class women have been encouraged to bear children and remain in the home. Women who fail to meet this ideal—whether due to race, socio-economic class, or other life choices and constraints—have faced stigma and legislative repercussions.

A few examples serve to illustrate this point. In the mid-to-late twentieth century, detached "refrigerator mothers" were blamed for the spike in autistic diagnoses even as other mothers were accused of loving too much, thus stunting their children's development through "over-affection" and emotional manipulation.[14] Various theorists and political figures argued that a mother who worked outside the home was a danger to her children. J. Edgar Hoover, for example, sounds like a twentieth-century Tacitus when he writes that ambitious mothers "risked creating children who were 'driven first to perversion and then to crime.' "[15] *Real* women, that is, good mothers, should instead "accept" their feminine role: namely, their utter dependence on a man and their purpose in being a wife and mother.[16] When they accept their femininity, these women both serve their purpose and achieve personal fulfillment by bearing and raising balanced citizens—sons to lead the state, and daughters who will likewise find contentment in the middle-class wife-and-mother ideal. Poor women and women of color, however, were never afforded such opportunities of "salvation" since they could never fit into the "wife-and-mother box." The history of eugenics in America is one extreme example of legislative attempts and enacted measures that granted states the right to force sterilization of women deemed undesirable to reproduce.[17] Vandenberg-Daves and Patricia Hill Collins argue that additional social policies surrounding family leave and welfare support still work to discourage reproduction among these communities, even as they claim to uphold the broader ideal that all women become mothers.[18]

What undergirds these contradicting and impossible constructions, even in their diverse manifestations, is the persistent alignment of perfection and order with masculinity. Life and peace are found when the world is ordered, that is, when it reflects the masculine ideal. With this alignment, any deviation from order is necessarily femininity. Femininity, therefore, must be constantly controlled. In the wake of civil and world wars, a backlash against perceived feminine autonomy is not surprising. The out of control woman is more than an irritant, she is a threat to the cosmos and the precariously reinstated peace. In the second half of the twentieth century, and on into the twenty-first, therefore, American culture has persisted with a rather similar stance toward feminine control as the Augustan age, even as the majority of modern families look less and less like this ideal. In this way, the model of womanhood as motherhood remains trenchant, pitting women against women as well as women against men, and claiming a level of normativity that belies its constructed and contextualized reality.

One of the goals of this book has been to demystify this construction by digging into the presentations of mothers and motherhood in the NT and several early Christian works. In so doing, this book has taken seriously the maternal elements of these writings, continuing the work of previous scholars by examining the theological import mothers and motherhood convey in these writings. Not only has this exploration led to a greater understanding of the richness of maternal imagery in the NT and early Christian writings examined, it has also exposed the fluidity of gender assessment within them. Salvation may remain a process of masculinization, but the masculinity and the process by which it is attained, are dramatically reshaped when one claims that Jesus is God's Christ and ideal Son. Femininity, therefore, is also reshaped, no longer automatically equated with requiring physical motherhood. This unsettling of gendered ideals in these writings, although not the assumed superiority of masculinity itself, offers us an avenue for continued reflection. It shows us that the enshrined maternal telos has never been the *only* avenue for a woman's legitimacy; even early

Christians acknowledged there were alternative paths for women to receive and reproduce life.

This unseating of the maternal ideal can, therefore, encourage us to take up the more difficult challenge of uncoupling masculinity and perfection as well. Such a move would remove the assumed, and required, equation of femininity with imperfection that results in a need to legitimatize women's (or any unmanly person's) existence in the first place. Instead of being deficient in comparison with the masculine, and the male body, feminine and female bodies can be acknowledged as whole already, not requiring "masculinization" to make them complete. Indeed, in the NT and early Christian texts, men and women repeatedly misstep when they attempt to masculinize each other through traditional household structures alone. Even Ephesians and the Pastoral Epistles emphasize that it is God alone who generates and sustains life—Christian households and churches merely replicate this ideal. One's hope, therefore, is not in a household, or in securing a legacy by means of procreation; rather, it is in God alone. For these writings, striving to establish immortality and security without acknowledging God's role is not only fruitless, but ultimately leads to destruction since it is asking created beings to stand in for their Creator.

What should be acknowledged in all this, however, is that the male is no closer to the divine than the female. Her existence needs no justification, just as his existence does not merit unending praise. In this way, we are freed to see that motherhood can indeed be a blessing, but it is not a woman's *only* means of being a blessing or being blessed. The blessedness of Elizabeth and Mary is, therefore, rightly countered by Jesus's response to the woman in Luke 11:27–28. These women are blessed not because of the work their wombs and breasts have accomplished. Rather they are blessed because they have acknowledged that life is not something they can monopolize, confine, or control, either through a "righteous" marriage or in singleness. In other words, Elizabeth and Mary are "blessed" when they "hear the word of God and obey it," regardless of how that obedience is made manifest.

Notes

CHAPTER 1

1. New Testament translations are the author's unless otherwise noted. Joseph A. Fitzmyer, *The Gospel According to Luke* (AB28; Garden City, NY: Doubleday, 1981), 352; Joel B. Green, "Blessed Is She Who Believed: Mary, Curious Exemplar in Luke's Narrative," in *Blessed One: Protestant Perspectives on Mary*, ed. Beverly Roberts Gaventa and Cynthia L. Rigby (Louisville: Westminster John Knox, 2002), 15; François Bovon, *Luke 1*, trans. Christine M. Thomas, Hermeneia (Minneapolis: Fortress, 2002), 53; F. Scott Spencer, *Salty Wives, Spirited Mothers, and Savvy Widows: Capable Women of Purpose and Persistence in Luke's Gospel* (Grand Rapids: Eerdmans, 2012), 72–75. Emphasizing Mary's self-identification as a *doulē* (slave), Beverly Roberts Gaventa argues that Mary does not choose, but rather "recognizes . . . God's selection of her and the compulsion under which her role is to be played." Nevertheless, Gaventa suggests that her response in verse 38 "indicates that she consents to that service" just as later apostles will consent to theirs (*Mary: Glimpses of the Mother of Jesus*, Personalities of the New Testament [Minneapolis: Fortress, 1999], 54).
2. Gaventa, *Mary*, 71.
3. In the Synoptic Gospels Jesus describes the identity of his true mother, brothers, and sisters in Mark 3:31–35; Matt 12:4–50; and Luke 8:19–21. Johannine literature also frequently describes the community as the "children of God" and uses birth imagery (1:12–13; 3:1–21; 11:52; 1 John 2:29; 3:1, 2, 9, 10; 4:7; 5:1, 2, 4, 18; 2 John 13; 3 John 4). See also the household codes of Eph 5:21–6:9; Col 3:18–4:1; 1 Peter 2:13–3:7.
4. The limiting of this discussion to Christian traditions, especially the NT, and western societies is a result of needing to place boundaries on the scope of study as well as an indication of my own personal experience.
5. Beverly Roberts Gaventa, *Our Mother Saint Paul* (Louisville: Westminster John Knox, 2007); Susan Eastman, *Recovering Paul's Mother Tongue: Language and Theology in Galatians* (Grand Rapids: Eerdmans, 2007).

6. Jennifer A. Glancy, *Corporal Knowledge: Early Christian Bodies* (Oxford: Oxford University Press, 2010), 5.
7. Janet Martin Soskice, *The Kindness of God: Metaphor, Gender, and Religious Language* (Oxford: Oxford University Press, 2007).
8. Ibid., 5.
9. Ibid., 6.
10. Ibid., 6; emphasis added.
11. Gaventa, *Our Mother*, 12.
12. Ibid., 62.
13. Ibid., 79.
14. Gaventa and Eastman trace a variety of maternal images used in Old Testament (OT) passages and Second Temple Jewish literature. Some particularly significant passages include Num 11:12; Ps 48:6; Isa 13:6, 8; 26:17–18; 42:10–17; 45:9–11; 54:1; 66; Jer 6:24; 8:18–9:3; 13:12; Mic 4:9–10; 1QH[a] 11.6–8; *1 En.* 62.4; *2 Bar* 56.6; *4 Ezra* 4.42. See Gaventa, *Our Mother*, 32–34; Eastman, *Recovering Paul's Mother Tongue*, 63–88, 111–16.
15. Gaventa, *Our Mother*, 12–13; emphasis original.
16. Eastman, *Recovering Paul's Mother Tongue*, 7–8.
17. Ibid., 7–9; Gaventa, *Our Mother*, 13.
18. Eastman, *Recovering Paul's Mother Tongue*, 15–18.
19. Ibid., 188.
20. Eastman describes Paul's admonition to "stand firm" in Gal 5:1 as the "climatic exhortation" of his letter (Ibid., 11). The Galatians are encouraged not only by Paul's repeated willingness to "be in labor" but also the eschatological promises of God's faithfulness described by Isaiah and Jeremiah's use of barren-mother motifs (Isa 54:1; Gal 4:27).
21. Ibid., 187–88; Brigitte Kahl, "No Longer Male: Masculinity Struggles Behind Galatians 3.28?" *JSNT* 79 (2000): 45–46. While there is some truth in this claim, nuance must be added since there is Socratic precedent for men being presented as mothers (Plato, *Symp.*; *Theaet.*).
22. Tal Ilan, *Jewish Women in Greco-Roman Palestine* (Peabody, MA: Hendrickson, 1996), 105–7; Michael L. Satlow, "'Try to Be a Man': The Rabbinic Construction of Masculinity," *HTR* 89 (1996): 31–32. Satlow notes the exclusion of women from Torah study as a result of assumed lack of self-control as well as a sexualization of Torah study for men, which created competition between time for study and time with wives. Ross Shepard Kraemer comments on these interpretations, but argues that the existence of such opposition toward women's studying Torah indicates that many did so (*Unreliable Witnesses: Religion, Gender, and History in the Greco-Roman Mediterranean* [Oxford: Oxford University Press, 2011], 41–46).
23. Rebecca Flemming, *Medicine and the Making of Roman Women: Gender, Nature, and Authority from Celsus to Galen* (Oxford: Oxford University Press, 2000), 317.

24. Of course, most of the surviving literature is written by a very limited group of elite men, which certainly skews their perspective. Instead, the ideas and ideologies reflected in these texts are simply that—they aim to convey and convince their readers of certain ideologies that may, in fact, be very contrary to everyday realities (Kraemer, *Unreliable Witnesses*, 5–11; see also Elizabeth A. Clark, *History, Theory, Text: Historians and the Linguistic Turn* [Cambridge: Harvard University Press, 2004], esp. 173–78).
25. Anna Rebecca Solevåg, *Birthing Salvation: Gender and Class in Early Christian Childbearing* (BIS 121; Leiden: Brill, 2013).
26. Ibid., 23–27.
27. Solevåg traces the differing ways freeborn women are characterized versus slaves in *Acts of Andrew* and the *Martyrdom of Perpetua and Felicitas* (Ibid., 190–95, 230–35).
28. Dale B. Martin, *Sex and the Single Savior: Gender and Sexuality in Biblical Interpretation* (Louisville: Westminster John Knox, 2006), 47.
29. Rebecca Jo Plant, *Mom: The Transformation of Motherhood in Modern America* (Chicago: Chicago University Press, 2010), 13. Patricia Hill Collins traces the interrelationship between categories of race and class in motherhood in *From Black Power to Hip Hop: Racism, Nationalism, and Feminism* (Philadelphia: Temple University Press, 2006). See also Jodi Vandenberg-Daves, *Modern Motherhood: An American History* (New Brunswick: Rutgers University Press, 2014), 234–42.
30. Plant, *Mom*, 10.
31. Ibid., 116.
32. On the Victorian notion of "Mother Love," see Ibid., 1–12.
33. Ibid., 56–58.
34. Plant reviews the transformation of the concept of "silver cords" that mothers were metaphorically to weave in their children from the Victorian to postwar eras (Ibid., 86–117).
35. Ibid., 15.
36. Ibid., 117.
37. Collins, *From Black Power to Hip Hop*, 71.
38. See especially the discussions of Livia and Agrippina the Younger in Chapter 5.
39. Collins, *From Black Power to Hip Hop*, 7.
40. Of recent note is *Burwell v. Hobby Lobby Stores, Inc.*, (573 U.S. [2014]); *Whole Woman's Health v. Hellerstedt* (579 U.S. [2016]). These debates are not new to American courtrooms, which have often ruled that the state has rights to legislate for fetuses in potential opposition to pregnant women/mothers, and even forced sterilization for women deemed undesirable to reproduce (Vandenberg-Daves, *Modern Motherhood*, 237–42, 270–79; Collins, *From Black Power to Hip Hop*, 59–72).
41. Martin, *Sex and the Single Savior*, 122.
42. Lindal Buchanan, *Rhetorics of Motherhood* (Studies in Rhetorics and Feminism; Carbondale: Southern Illinois University Press, 2013), 3.

43. Ibid., 5. See also Adrienne Rich's classic analysis of motherhood as cultural "institution" versus personal "experience" in *Of Woman Born: Motherhood as Experience and Institution* (repr., New York: Norton, 1995).
44. Buchanan, *Rhetorics*, 21.
45. Ibid.
46. Heather A. K. Jacques and H. Lorraine Radtke, "Constrained by Choice: Young Women Negotiate the Discourses of Marriage and Motherhood," *Feminism and Psychology* 22 (2012): 444.
47. "Intensive mothering" is a term coined by Sharon Hays and is described as Vandenberg-Daves as, "the updated version of moral motherhood" (*Modern Motherhood*, 274).
48. Vandenberg-Daves, *Modern Motherhood*, 282.
49. Ibid., 267.
50. Jacques and Radtke, "Constrained," 453.
51. Ibid., 458.
52. Ibid., 445.
53. Jane Clare Jones, "Idealized and Industrialized Labor: Anatomy of a Feminist Controversy," *Hypatia* 27 (2012): 107.
54. Erin N. Taylor and Lora Ebert Wallace, "For Shame: Feminism, Breastfeeding Advocacy, and Maternal Guilt," *Hypatia* 27 (2012): 85. Vandenberg-Daves (*Modern Motherhood*, 276) notes the special emphasis placed on breastfeeding among white women who, according to a study by Linda Blum, "saw breastfeeding as an important measure of their success as mothers. Typically for white women, breastfeeding embodied 'natural' mothering and the value of maternal labor."
55. Taylor and Wallace, "For Shame," 85 (emphasis added).
56. See, for example, Rich, *Of Woman Born*; Collins, *From Black Power to Hip Hop*; Andrea O'Reilly, ed., *Maternal Theory: Essential Readings* (Toronto: Demeter, 2007); Plant, *Mom*; Vandenberg-Daves, *Modern Motherhood*.
57. Buchanan, *Rhetorics*, 6.
58. H. R. Jauss, *Aesthetic Experience and Literary Hermeneutics* (Minneapolis: University of Minnesota Press, 1982); Peter Rabbinowitz, "Truth in Fiction: A Reexamination of Audiences," *Critical Inquiry* 4 (1977): 121–41; idem, "Whirl without End: Audience Oriented Criticism," in G. Douglas Atkins and Laura Morrow, eds., *Contemporary Literary Theory* (Amherst: University of Massachusetts Press, 1988), 81–100; Gian Biagio Conte, *The Rhetoric of Imitation: Genre and Poetic Memory in Virgil and Other Latin Poets*, ed. Charles Segal (Ithaca, NY: Cornell University Press, 1986).
59. Charles H. Talbert, *Reading Luke-Acts in its Mediterranean Milieu*, NovTSup 107 (Leiden: Brill, 2003), 16.
60. Elizabeth A. Clark, "Antifamilial Tendencies in Ancient Christianity," *JHS* 5 (1995): 359.
61. The "Augustan age" is not precisely limited to the dates of Augustus's reign. As Kristina Milnor writes, Augustus's ideology "did not spring fully formed onto the

Roman political scene when Augustus assumed 'office' in 27 BCE, nor did it cease to be refined when he died forty-one years later" (*Gender, Domesticity, and the Age of Augustus: Inventing Private Life*, Oxford Studies in Classical Literature and Gender Theory [Oxford: Oxford University Press, 2005], 4).

CHAPTER 2

1. Pushing against this trend are the following studies, each of which will be give fuller attention in the chapters that follow. Adele Reinhartz, "'And the Word Was Begotten': Divine Epigenesis in the Gospel of John," *Sem* 85 (1999): 83–103; Turid Karlsen Seim, "Descent and Divine Paternity in the Gospel of John: Does the Mother Matter?" *NTS* 51 (2005): 361–75; eadem, "Motherhood and the Making of Fathers in Antiquity: Contextualizing Genetics in the Gospel of John," in *Women and Gender in Ancient Religions*, ed. Stephen P. Ahearne-Kroll, Paul A. Holloway, and James A. Kelhoffer, WUNT 263 (Tübingen: Mohr Siebeck, 2010), 99–123; Anna Rebecca Solevåg, *Birthing Salvation: Gender and Class in Early Christian Childbearing*, BIS 121 (Leiden: Brill, 2013), esp. 66–76.
2. Thomas W. Laqueur, *Making Sex: Body and Gender from the Greeks to Freud* (Cambridge: Harvard University Press, 1992).
3. Helen King's criticisms of Laqueur focus on his lack of thorough investigation of ancient sources which leads to his emphasis on genital anatomy over physiological constructions of the female that center on menstruation (King, *The One-Sex Body on Trial: The Classical and Early Modern Evidence*, The History of Medicine in Context [London: Ashgate, 2013], 33). See also Rebecca Flemming, *Medicine and the Making of Roman Women: Gender, Nature, and Authority from Celsus to Galen* (Oxford: Oxford University Press, 2000), 119–22. Tal Ilan comments that the rabbis and other Second Temple Jewish authors assert "the operative assumption, quite explicitly expressed, . . . is that there are basic *differences* between men and women" (*Jewish Women in Greco-Roman Palestine* [Peabody, MA: Hendrickson, 1996], 123; emphasis added).
4. For a fuller discussion, see Flemming, *Medicine*, 116.
5. Aristotle, *Gen. an.* 4.1.766a1–30; 4.6.775a5–22; Soranus, *Gyn.* 1.3.12; Rufus of Ephesus, *Onom.* 184–87; 193–98. See also Flemming, *Medicine*, 199–200. The anatomical naming that dominated the Roman era was largely influenced by the work of the Hellenistic physician and so-called "father of anatomy," Herophilus of Alexandria, whose medical school in Alexandria eventually gave rise to the later sects that dominated the Roman medical landscape.
6. This argument is a main feature in Flemming's analysis of various medical writings of the Roman world. Flemming suggests that the "medical woman" constructed by these texts *is* fragmentary, only briefly emerging "from behind a generic male façade" (*Medicine*, 227).
7. Flemming, *Medicine*, 116.

8. Julius Rocca, "Anatomy and Physiology," in *A Companion to Science, Technology, and Medicine in Ancient Greece and Rome*, ed. Georgia L. Irby, BCAW (Malden, MA: Wiley Blackwell, 2016), 1:356. The mechanism of the Hippocratics and methodists (i.e., Soranus) contrasts with Galen's Aristotelian emphasis on purpose in the creation and function of the human body and humans generally. For further discussion in the present volume, see Chapter 3 § "Seeds, Bloods, and Spirit: Ancient Embryologies."
9. Galen explains, "For women are similar to men to the extent that they too are rational animals, that is, capable of acquiring knowledge; but to the extent that the genus of men is stronger and superior in every activity and learning, and women are weaker and inferior, in this they are unlike; and again, women are opposite [to men] in so far as they are female and, on account of this, adapted for childbearing, . . . So it is correct to say that in one respect women are similar to men, in another they are opposite" (*PHP* 9.3.25–26; translated by Flemming, *Medicine*, 358).
10. Translations of Soranus are from Oswei Temkin (trans.), *Soranus' Gynecology* (Baltimore: Johns Hopkins University Press, 1956).
11. Flemming, *Medicine*, 89.
12. For an overview of ancient Roman medical sects or "schools" see Flemming, *Medicine*, 80–128; Molly Jones-Lewis, "Physicians and 'Schools,'" in Irby, *A Companion to Science, Technology, and Medicine in Ancient Greece and Rome*, 1:386–401. The main medical sects of the Roman era include, the "rationalists" (*logikoi* or "dogmatists") who remained most closely aligned with Herophilus's epistemology and argued for the continued use of dissection and vivisection to explain medical theories; the "empiricists" (*empirikoi*) founded by Herophilus's student, Philinus of Cos, who adamantly opposed dissection and instead emphasized observable experiences of patients; and the "methodists" (*methodikoi*), who combined aspects of both schools and to which Soranus of Ephesus belonged. Methodists had an underlying theory of "manifest generalities" described above, but were not entirely opposed to dissection when it proved useful (see Soranus, *Gyn.* 1.3.6–18 where he describes the uterus and vagina based on dissection). In addition to these three dominant groups were the "eclectics" (*eklektikoi*) who claimed no precise allegiance, but who borrowed freely from various traditions.
13. Flemming, *Medicine*, 121–22. Lauren Caldwell also notes the lack of consensus among writers on gynecology in the ancient Mediterranean ("Gynecology," in Irby, *A Companion to Science, Technology, and Medicine in Ancient Greece and Rome*, 1:363).
14. Flemming, *Medicine*, 180–81. As Flemming explains concerning Roman medical authors, "The notion of writing for anybody else than their fellow men, of the elite or the [medical] profession, probably never occurred to them, and their audience would have had similar expectations. It was men who mattered" (183).
15. Ibid., 119.
16. Dale B. Martin notes a pervasive "horror of the feminine" in the ancient world that leads, for example, to the accusation of effeminacy, or "softness" (*malakos*), being

one of moral failing (*Sex and the Single Savior: Gender and Sexuality in Biblical Interpretation* [Louisville: Westminster John Knox, 2006], 46–47).

17. See especially Colleen M. Conway, *Behold the Man: Jesus and Greco-Roman Masculinity* (Oxford: Oxford University Press, 2008), 36–39. Conway explains, "if masculinity is equated with perfection, unity, rationality, order, and completeness, as it was in the ancient world, God would *necessarily* be masculine, even while incorporeal and asexual. Rather than transcending gender, God is the perfect example of masculinity" (36; emphasis original). Further, when a person became more perfect through virtue—that is, more "masculine"—they approached divinity. In Aristotle's words: "men become gods by excess of virtue (*aretēs hyperbolēn*)" (*Eth. nic.* 7.1.2).
18. Jonathan Walters, "Invading the Roman Body: Manliness and Impenetrability in Roman Thought," in *Roman Sexualities*, ed. Judith P. Hallett and Marilyn B. Skinner (Princeton: Princeton University Press, 1997), 30. Walters writes: "Verbal propositions and pestering, touching, beating, and sexual penetration—all are seen as degrading invasions of the personal space of the victim of these assaults" (44). Openness to any sort of penetration created the possibility for more intimate forms of bodily invasion ultimately leading to the final insult of "having a woman's experience" (*muliebra pati*), that is, "suffering" (*pati*) the part of a woman in sex (31).
19. Ibid., 29.
20. On various phallic imagery in the Greco-Roman world see Amy Richlin, "Pliny's Brassiere," in Hallett and Skinner, *Roman Sexualities*, 215; Conway, *Behold the Man*, 22; as well as Plutarch's narrations of the "mutilation" of the Hermae in Athens, whose distinct phallic members were rudely excised on the eve before the departure of the Athenian forces during the Peloponnesian War (*Alc.* 18–22; *Nic.* 13).
21. Conway, *Behold the Man*, 21. On masculinity and control see Walters, "Invading the Roman Body," esp. 30–32; Conway, *Behold the Man*, 20–26; Jennifer A. Glancy, "Protocols of Masculinity in the Pastoral Epistles," in *New Testament Masculinities*, ed. Stephen D. Moore and Janice Capel Anderson, SemSt 45 (Atlanta: SBL, 2003), 239–41.
22. Jennifer A. Glancy, *Slavery in Early Christianity* (Minneapolis: Fortress, 2006), 24.
23. Ibid., 25.
24. Shane Butler, "Notes on a *Membrum Disiectum*," in *Women and Slaves in Greco-Roman Culture: Differential Equations*, ed. Sandra R. Joshel and Sheila Murnaghan (New York: Routledge, 1998), 248. Glancy incorporates this same narrative and analysis in *Slavery in Early Christianity*, 29.
25. *Rep.* 4.443d–e. Translation by G. M. A. Grube, *Plato: Republic*, rev. C. D. C. Reeve (Indianapolis, IN: Hackett, 1992).
26. Michael L. Satlow, "'Try to Be a Man': The Rabbinic Construction of Masculinity," *HTR* 89 (1996): 21–26. The uniformity that Satlow is highlighting is on the notion of self-control. The arguments of *how* a man was to achieve this manly ideal differed from group to group (see Brittany E. Wilson, *Unmanly Men: Refigurations of Masculinity in Luke-Acts* [Oxford: Oxford University Press, 2015], 22–24).

27. 1QS IV.2–14; 4Q186; see also the discussion of Polemo and Favorinus's self-presentations in Maud W. Gleason, *Making Men: Sophists and Self-Presentation in Ancient Rome* (Princeton: Princeton University Press, 1995), 3–54.
28. *Inst.* 12.1.3 (Russell, LCL; emphasis original). Compare Cicero, *De or.* 2.53.182–84; Aristotle, *Rhet.* 3.7.1–11. For further information on physiognomic analyses of masculinity, see Gleason, *Making Men*, 27, 58–81; Conway, *Behold the Man*, 19–20.
29. Hence, the metaphor of rulers as shepherds caring for their flocks and the appropriate name of "Alexander" for the prince and king, since he was indeed to be a defender of *men* (*alex-anēr*) and, therefore, of all those whom these men were likewise controlling/protecting.
30. Conway, *Behold the Man*, 39–40.
31. Ibid., 41–49; Suetonius, *Aug.* 58. As Rome's "father," Augustus acquired a seemingly imperishable status since filial piety was a key measure of masculinity (e.g., Virgil, *Aen.* 2.921–1045). This Roman "father" would be honored by all of his "sons," who have the charge of caring for and multiplying the patrimony he leaves behind (see Plutarch, *Cat. Maj.* 21.8).
32. Gleason, *Making Men*, xxvi. Lesley Dean-Jones, *Women's Bodies in Classical Greek Science* (Oxford: Clarendon, 2001), 41.
33. Aristotle argues that women should not be blamed for their femininity, because their passivity and "softness" (*malakos*) was a natural state (*Eth. nic.* 7.7.6). Nevertheless, their openness to excess reinforces their need for control by men and their permanent inferiority. Femininity displayed by men, however, was especially dangerous. According to Anthony Corbeill, ancients argued that effeminate behavior by men resulted in gender blurring, making such males open to the vices of both genders—male aggression and the female lack of control or passivity ("Dining Deviants in Roman Political Invective," in Hallett and Skinner, *Roman Sexualities*, 107–13). See also Holt N. Parker, "The Teratogenic Grid," in Hallett and Skinner, *Roman Sexualities*, 52–59.
34. Flemming, *Medicine*, 123.
35. For additional narratives of women's origins from the ancient Mediterranean world see: Karen L. King (ed.), *Women and Goddess Traditions in Antiquity and Today*, SAC (Minneapolis: Fortress, 1997); Joan O'Brien, "Nammu, Mami, Eve and Pandora: 'What's in a Name?'" *The Classical Journal* 79 (1983): 35–36.
36. Helen King, *Hippocrates' Woman: Reading the Female Body in Ancient Greece* (London: Routledge, 1998), 24.
37. Ibid., 27.
38. Froma I. Zeitlin, *Playing the Other: Gender and Society in Classical Greek Literature*, Women in Culture and Society (Chicago: University of Chicago Press, 1996), 65–66. Discussing the associations between sacrificial victims in Greco-Roman cultic practices and menstrual blood, King argues that the act of "cutting" is a breaking of boundaries, something only men were permitted to do. Such a suggestion resonates

with the constructions of masculinity outlined above, since a man controlled the boundaries of his own body while all un-men could not. For King, sacrificial victims and women bleed, while men cut (*Hippocrates' Woman*, 93–95). The blood drawn from women occurs regularly each month, but is also present in defloration, parturition, and often features in erotic Roman literature (e.g., *Leucippe and Clitophon*; *Chaereas and Callirhoe*; *Aethiopica*; Iphigeneia's bloody sacrifice to Artemis). See also Walters ("Invading," 31). For further discussion in the present volume, consult Chapter 3 § "A Necessary Sacrifice: Childbirth, Combat, and Blood-letting."

39. Xenophon, *Oec.* 7; [Ps.]-Aristotle, *Oec.* 1.4.1344a1–20; cf. Hesiod, *Op.* 699; *Joseph and Aseneth*. B. M. Wolkow notes that ancient authors encouraged men to marry young girls so that they could "train" their wives and form her character (*ethos*) before she could reflect another. A key problem with Pandora, according to Wolkow, is that she was given to Epimetheus with an *ethos* already—one shaped by the gods as "the mind of a bitch" (*kyneon te noon*) ("The Mind of a Bitch: Pandora's Motive and Intent in the *Erga*," *Hermes* 135 [2007]: 255–57).
40. On the relationship between the designation of a woman as a "bitch" (*kyneon*) and greediness see Ibid., 247–62; Margaret Graver, "Dog-Helen and Homeric Insult," *Classical Antiquity* 14 (1995): 41–61. See also Hesiod's description of Pandora's greed in *Theog.* 570–615.
41. Phyllis Trible, *God and the Rhetoric of Sexuality* (Philadelphia: Fortress, 1978), 98–100.
42. Robert J. V. Hiebert (trans.), *New English Translation of the Septuagint*, 2d ed. (Oxford: Oxford University Press, 2009).
43. Daniel Boyarin, *Carnal Israel: Reading Sex in Talmudic Culture*, The New Historicism 25 (Berkeley: University of California Press, 1993), 36–37.
44. The entire passage reads: "Said R. Samuel bar Nahman, 'When the Holy One, blessed be he, created the first man, he created him with two faces, then sawed him into two and make a back on one side and a back on the other.' An objection was raised, 'And he took one of his ribs' (Gen. 2:21). . . . He said to them, 'It was one of his sides, as you find written in Scripture, 'And for the second side [using the same root] of the tabernacle' (Ex. 26:20)" (trans. Jacob Neusner, *Genesis Rabbah: The Judaic Commentary to the Book of Genesis A New American Translation*, vol. 1, BJS 104 [Atlanta: Scholars Press, 1985]).
45. Boyarin identifies this ontological difference as a key divergence between Hellenistic and early imperial Roman era Judaisms (including incipient Christianity) and developing rabbinic Judaism in the first centuries CE. In a reaction against the acceptance of Platonic dualism in Hellenistic Judaisms, rabbinic Judaism emphasizes the inherent corporeality of creation and, therefore, the goodness of the material world (Gen. Rab. 8.1.2–3). For Boyarin, the corporeality of rabbinic Judaism prevents it from assuming a thoroughly misogynistic stance because it reserves a place for sexuality and women in the role of mothers (*Carnal Israel*, 31–35, 77). While Boyarin is right to note these very real differences in later, more developed

rabbinic writings and those of the "Church Fathers," the analysis to follow also indicates the ways in which these traditions overlapped in the NT era. Moreover, that there was some openness to corporeality among early Christian groups (although many were later defined as heretical by various "Church Fathers") is aptly illustrated by April D. DeConick, *Holy Misogyny: Why the Sex and Gender Conflicts in the Early Church Still Matter* (New York: Continuum, 2011).

46. Translations from F. H. Colson and George Whitaker, *Philo*, vol. 1, LCL 226 (Cambridge: Harvard University Press, 1929).
47. Translations of *Questions and Answers on Genesis* are from Yonge (1991), unless otherwise noted.
48. Elsewhere, Philo writes: "But with reference to the mind, the woman, when understood symbolically, is sense, and the man is intellect" (*QG* 1.37; see also *QG* 1.45). Satlow highlights the pervasiveness of aligning femininity with sensual weakness in Second Temple Jewish and later rabbinic writings ("Try to Be a Man," 21–23).
49. See also Ilan, *Jewish Women*, 124–25 where she catalogues the importance of the creation narrative for establishing difference between male and female among rabbinic authors. On the basis of her later creation from flesh, women "have a bad odor because they were created from flesh . . . they have higher voices because they were created from bone . . . they lie on their backs and face the man during intercourse in order to look towards the place of their creation" (Gen. Rab. 17.8). Ilan concludes, "The creation story is thus seen as the source not only for men's domination over women according to the natural order of things, but also for the biological and psychological differences between men and women" (125).
50. The reception history of the *Life of Adam and Eve* is quite complicated, owing to the fact that no complete manuscript of the text survives. The breadth of translations and recensions illustrates the popularity of the story, however, and its importance particularly in early Christian communities who are responsible for its preservation and various mutations. Gary A. Anderson and Michael E. Stone, *A Synopsis of the Books of Adam and Eve*, EJL 5 (Atlanta: Scholars Press, 1994).
51. Vita Daphna Arbel, *Forming Femininity in Antiquity: Eve, Gender, and Ideology in the Greek* Life of Adam and Eve (Oxford: Oxford University Press, 2012), 34–36; *LAE* [Latin] 18.1–21.3.
52. Arbel, *Forming Femininity*, 33–37. See also Solevåg, *Birthing Salvation*, 46.
53. Thus, one interpretation in Genesis Rabbah explains the punishment in Gen 3:16 that a woman's "desire" will be for her man even though he will rule over her in the following manner: "When a woman sits down on the birthstool, she says, 'I shall never again have sexual relations with my husband.' Then the Holy One, blessed be he, says to her, 'You will return to your lust, you will return to have lust for your husband'" (Gen. Rab. 20.7.2).
54. This statement does not mean that women did not have influence or power in the ancient Mediterranean world (see Carol Meyers, *Rediscovering Eve* [Oxford: Oxford University Press, 2013]; Suzanne Dixon, *The Roman Mother* [Norman: University

of Oklahoma Press, 1987]; cf. Plutarch, *Coriolanus*; *Themistocles*; *Alexander*; Euripides, *Hecuba*). Instead, since a woman's identity was intimately bound up with her uterus, what her uterus did (or did not) produce often defined what power she could claim and helped to demonstrate how precarious such these claims could be depending on how they was construed or perceived.

55. See also Solevåg, *Birthing Salvation*, 61.
56. Translations are from Paul Potter (trans.), *Hippocrates. Places in Man. Glands. Fleshes. Prorrhetic 1-2. Physician. Use of Liquids. Ulcers. Haemorrhoids and Fistulas*, LCL 482 (Cambridge: Harvard University Press, 1995).
57. In the *Nature of Women* patients are often encouraged to have sex with their husbands as a part of their treatments and pregnancy was an indication of a woman's return to health (2.315; 3.316; 8.324; 35.379; 43.388–89; 53.395; 67.402).
58. Charlotte Elisheva Fonrobert, *Menstrual Purity: Rabbinic and Christian Reconstructions of Gender*, Contraversions (Stanford, CA: Stanford University Press, 2000), 63; Gwynn Kessler, *Conceiving Israel: The Fetus in Rabbinic Narratives*, Divinations (Philadelphia: University of Pennsylvania Press, 2009), 66.
59. For further discussion, see Dean-Jones, *Women's Bodies*, 45–46.
60. Translations are from Paul Potter (ed. and trans.), *Hippocrates. Generation. Nature of the Child. Diseases 4. Nature of Women and Barrenness*, LCL 520 (Cambridge: Harvard University Press, 2012).
61. *Nat. mul.* 4.317; 5.318–19; 8.324; 9.325; 15.334; etc. The role that food could play in a woman's menstruation is also reflected in Soranus's *Gynecology*. Writing in the second century CE, Soranus argues against rigid expectations for the amount of blood, duration of flow, and time of flow for menses in part because he states that a physician must take into account what types of food were consumed prior to menstruation (1.4.20).
62. Flemming notes the persistence of dichotomies in the constructions of human natures and suggests that the pairings of hot/cold and dry/wet were the most common in both the Greek and Roman worlds (*Medicine*, 93).
63. Flemming writes that "[b]lood was universally conceived of as the main intermediate stage in the transformation of food to flesh" (Ibid., 98).
64. Translations are from A. L. Peck (trans.), *Aristotle. Generation of Animals*, LCL 366 (Cambridge: Harvard University Press, 1942).
65. This should not be read to imply that Aristotle believed femininity and masculinity were biologically determined. Instead, Aristotle considered gender to be flexible. Thus, a man could become feminine through castration or simply by behaving in a feminine manner (*Gen. an.* 1.2.716b.1–10). This femininity did not automatically inhibit his ability to concoct blood into semen, but it did diminish the quality of the concoction so that it was "thin and cold." In a parallel manner, "masculine women" could not produce semen, but her additional heat could impede menstruation by evaporating the excess blood (*Gen. an.* 2.7.746b20–747a24). Neither state is ideal since they prevent the production of children.

66. Flemming notes that while empiricists (*empirikoi*) remained active in the Roman era, it is the writings of methodists (*methodikoi*), and especially the rationalists (*logokoi*) and eclectics (*eklektikoi*), which have survived (*Medicine*, 185). Amongst these, Galen is the most prolific (Jones-Lewis, "Physicians," 399).
67. Flemming, *Medicine*, 361.
68. *Women's Regimen*, translated by Flemming, *Medicine*, 223 (*Ruf. ap. Orib. Coll. Med. lib. inc.* 20.1–2; *CMG* VI.2.2.109.26–28). See also Galen, *UP* 1.299.
69. Flemming, *Medicine*, 236, 317. See Galen, *HNH* 3.25.
70. The necessity of menstruation and pregnancy for female health is a common, but not universal, conclusion in the ancient Mediterranean world. Among those endorsing the need for menstruation include the Hippocratics, Aristotle, Rufus of Ephesus, Pliny the Elder, Celsus, as well as Galen. Soranus and other Roman methodist physicians, however, argue that menstruation (as well as pregnancy and lactation) rob the female body of needed nourishment (*Gyn.* 1.4.19–6.29). Indeed, Soranus recommends the use of wet nurses for his aristocratic clientele and provides extensive guidelines for their selection and routine (*Gyn.* 2.11.18–14.26).
71. *UP* 1.299–300. Translated by Margaret Tallmadge May, *Galen: On the Usefulness of the Parts of the Body*, vol. 2 (Ithaca, NY: Cornell University Press, 1968).
72. Dean-Jones, *Women's Bodies*, 69.
73. Helen King suggests that ancient authors believed the womb could traverse the female body because there was no "proper" place for such an organ in the generic, male body assumed by ancient medicine (*Hippocrates' Woman*, 36). Plato describes the womb as a wild animal, almost distinct from the woman in whose body it resides, whose wanderings cause hallucinations and literal *hysteria* (e.g., *Tim.* 91c–d). The wildness of female bodies also surfaces in "taming" metaphors for young girls who acted out in religious rituals worshipping Artemis ("playing the bear"), the goddess who would also guide their transition from child to bride, and from wife to mother (Nancy Demand, *Birth, Death, and Motherhood in Classical Greece* [Baltimore: Johns Hopkins University Press, 1994], 55–57, 102–7; King, *Hippocrates' Woman*, 76–85).
74. Aristotle, *Gen. an.* 2.7.745b29–30; Soranus, *Gyn.*1.3.6–15; Galen, *Dissection of the Uterus.* In this regard Soranus and Galen benefited from the anatomical work of Herophilus as well as their own practices of dissection and vivisection. In spite of noting these advances, Caldwell cautions that the idea of a wandering womb remained persistent in the Roman era as evidenced by magical incantations and charms that were meant to cure this ailment ("Gynecology," 362–64).
75. See also Dean-Jones, *Women's Bodies*, 64.
76. See *b. Ket.* 10a where a husband and rabbi use the metaphor of a "door" to describe a new bride's hymen, and a "house" as the description of her uterus. The commonness of this metaphor is highlighted by Cynthia Baker, *Rebuilding the House of Israel: Archaeologies of Gender in Jewish Antiquity,* Divinations (Stanford, CA: Stanford University Press, 2002). King notes that Aristotle also uses the metaphors of gates

or doors, houses, and an oven to describe the uterus in *Gen. an.* 4.1.764a12–20 (*Hippocrates' Woman*, 37). See also Hippocrates, *Nat. puer* 5.92.

77. Baker, *Rebuilding the House of Israel*, 34; emphasis original. The association between women and cities is well known; see, for example, Isaiah 54; 60–66. This metaphor continues in additional Second Temple Jewish and early Christian literatures as well (Revelation; *Shepherd of Hermas*; *4 Ezra*).
78. Baker, *Rebuilding the House of Israel*, 52; emphasis original.
79. Ibid., 35; emphasis original. Unlike Greco-Roman sources, the rabbis do not offer a full description of female genitalia but comment on them in passing, generally stressing the need for wives to maintain their cleanliness (see also Ilan, *Jewish Women*, 100–5). King highlights the jar metaphor as part of her argument that the Pandora myth should be seen as the primary context for Hippocratic medicine (*Hippocrates' Woman*, 35). Dean-Jones, however, suggests that the wineskin (*askos*) is "uppermost in the minds of the Hippocratics" because of its flexibility to expand to accommodate the collection of menstrual blood and a growing fetus" (*Women's Bodies*, 65, n. 80).
80. Baker, *Rebuilding the House of Israel*, 52.
81. King, *Hippocrates' Woman*, 27–28.
82. King, *Hippocrates' Woman*, 28. The perceived affinity between the top and bottom of the female body among ancient medical authors is widely recognized among classicists; see: Demand, *Birth, Death, and Motherhood*, 18, 64; Dean-Jones, *Women's Bodies*, 73–74.
83. Soranus, *Gyn.* 1.3.6–12; Hippocrates, *Mul.* 1.2, 40, 85.
84. King, *Hippocrates' Woman*, 28; Ps.-Aristotle, *On Sterility* 634b35; 636b17–18; 637a21–35. See also Hippocrates, *Nat. mul.* 8.425; *Gen.* 5.477; Soranus, *Gyn.* 1.12.44.
85. King examines a range of Hippocratic works, such as *Diseases of Women*, *Epidemics*, and *Aphorisms*, which explicitly tie nosebleeds to menses (*Hippocrates' Woman*, 69–74). *Aphorisms* 5.32–3 claims: "A nosebleed is a good thing if the menstrual period is suppressed."
86. An additional indication of a central passageway in the female body is reflected in the belief that breastmilk was composed of the excess menstrual blood used to nourish a fetus. Unused by the growing fetus, such excess menstrual blood was believed to be pressed upward into the breasts where it was stored for use after parturition (Lev. Rab. 14.3; Aristotle, *Gen. an.* 4.8.776a31–776b4; Hippocrates, *Glands* 16.572; *Nat. puer.* 10.513–14). This subject is the topic for Chapter 4 in this book.
87. Quoted from Flemming, *Medicine*, 222.
88. Demand, *Birth, Death, and Motherhood*, 64.
89. King, *The Disease of Virgins: Green Sickness, Chlorosis and the Problems of Puberty* (London: Routledge, 2004), 50–51. See also Dean-Jones, who writes that for the Hippocratics, "motherhood was generally viewed as the ultimate solution to

women's problems, and easing normal menstruation was no exception" (*Women's Bodies*, 126). Demand writes that, "only the birth of a child gave her [a wife] full status as a *gynē*—woman-wife" (*Birth, Death, and Motherhood*, 17). Flemming likewise describes Soranus's "relentlessly reproductive message" in spite of the fact that he is one of the few to view menstruation and pregnancy as unhealthful for women (*Medicine*, 236–37; cf. *Gyn.* 1.6.27–11.42).

90. Hippocrates, *DYG* 36–37; translated by King, *Disease of Virgins*, 51. For a full critical edition and translation of the Hippocratic text, see Rebecca Flemming and Ann Ellis Hanson, "Hippocrates' 'Peri Parthenîon' (Diseases of Young Girls): Text and Translation," *Early Science and Medicine* 3 (1998): 241–52.
91. King, *Hippocrates' Woman*, 78–85; eadem, *Disease of Virgins*, 50–51.
92. Reflecting on Rufus of Ephesus's *Girls' Regimen* and *Women's Regimen*, Flemming explains that the "intrinsic instability of the female body . . . is driven by a flawed interaction between the body and its environment. . . . Thus, for women the struggle is to establish the somatic balance with which men are, by definition, endowed and so dietetically need only to maintain and reinforce" (*Medicine*, 222–23; cf. 160).
93. Aristotle, *Gen. an.* 4.1.766a.20; Galen, *PHP* 9.3.25–26.
94. Aristotle and several rabbinic texts acknowledge the dangers of early marriage and especially early pregnancies. Aristotle argues that children conceived by young parents are weaker than those conceived in the "prime" of life (*Gen. an.* 4.2.766b28–34). Rabbis were so convinced of the dangers faced by young brides that they permitted the use of contraceptives when girls were married young, a practice that is otherwise restricted to times of a woman's nursing an infant so as not to endanger the production of breastmilk. In both instances, contraceptives are limited to instances where lives were endangered by pregnancy above expected bounds (Ilan, *Jewish Women*, 67).
95. See also Dixon, *Roman Mother*, 21.
96. See Chapter 5 § "Molding Princes for Rome: Maternal Power in the Augustan Age."
97. There is an emphasis on mothers in Jewish literature stretching from Genesis and its various retellings, to the well-known story of the mother of seven sons in 2/4 Maccabees. Some comparable Greek and Roman examples include Thetis (mother of Achilles), Hecuba (mother of Hector), Venus (mother of Aeneas), Cornelia Gracchus, Volumnia (mother of Coriolanus), and Pomponia (mother of Scipio Africanus).
98. For example, Wilson's recent study on masculinity in Luke-Acts argues that Luke makes use of masculine ideologies even as he undermines them with characteristically un-masculine portraits of his main male characters (*Unmanly Men*).

CHAPTER 3

1. Citing a few more recent examples of works devoted to Mary will suffice to demonstrate this point: Andrew T. Lincoln, *Born of a Virgin? Reconceiving Jesus in the*

Bible, Tradition, and Theology (Grand Rapids: Eerdmans, 2013); F. Scott Spencer, *Salty Wives, Spirited Mothers, and Savvy Widows: Capable Women of Purpose and Perseverance in Luke's Gospel* (Grand Rapids: Eerdmans, 2012), 55–100; Amy-Jill Levine with Maria Mayo Robbins, ed., *A Feminist Companion to Mariology* (London: T&T Clark, 2005); Beverly Roberts Gaventa and Cynthia L. Rigby, eds., *Blessed One: Protestant Perspectives on Mary* (Louisville: Westminster John Knox, 2002); Beverly Roberts Gaventa, *Mary: Glimpses of the Mother of Jesus* (Minneapolis: Fortress, 1999).

2. For these reasons, it is not surprising to encounter symbolic readings of Mary throughout Christian tradition. The *Protoevangelium of James* offers Mary's early life story, conception, and birth of Jesus, placing special emphasis on her virginal status throughout. Building on Paul's christological construction of Jesus as the "Second Adam" in Romans 5, for example, Justin Martyr (*Dial.* 100), Irenaeus of Lyons (*Haer.* 3.22), and Tertullian (*Carn. Chr.* 17) famously characterize Mary as a new Eve whose righteous submission to God acts contrasts Eve's disobedience, and thus, brings life instead of death to humanity. See also Jaroslav Pelikan, *Mary Through the Centuries: Her Place in the History of Culture* (New Haven: Yale University Press, 1996); George H. Tavard, *The Thousand Faces of the Virgin Mary* (Collegeville, MN: Liturgical Press, 1996).
3. Luke 11:27–28; John 2:1–12; 19:25–27; Mark 3:31–35; Matt 12:46–50.
4. Families and households were not only made up of biologically related persons in the Roman world. Rather, they included blood-related kin as well as any slaves or additional properties and even significant clients. Kinship networks, therefore, regularly expanded beyond biological connections to entire villages and social groups who worked for each other's best interests along hierarchical lines. Sharon Betsworth, *Children in Early Christian Narratives*, LNTS 521 (London: Bloomsbury/T&T Clark, 2015), 6–20; Marianne Blickenstaff, "*While the Bridegroom Is with Them": Marriage, Family, Gender, and Violence in the Gospel of Matthew*, JSNTSup 292 (London: T&T Clark, 2005), 113–22; Carolyn Osiek and David L. Balch, *Families in the New Testament World: Households and House Churches* (Louisville: Westminster John Knox, 1997).
5. Blickenstaff, *While the Bridegroom Is with Them*, 144.
6. Ibid., 132–33.
7. As Blickenstaff writes of Matthew, this story "does not want people to have children. Instead, they are to become *like* children, that is, incapable of procreation" (Ibid., 154; emphasis original). Candida R. Moss and Joel S. Baden, *Reconceiving Infertility: Biblical Perspectives on Procreation and Childlessness* (Princeton: Princeton University Press, 2015), 200–28.
8. "Children of God" (*tekna tou theou*) appears again in John 5:12 and 11:52 (as well as 1 John 3:1, 2, 10; 5:2); *gennaō* is used in reference to being "born" or "begotten" of God in John 3:3, 4 (2x), 5, 6 (2x), 7, 8 and elsewhere in John 8:41; 9:2, 19, 20, 32, 34; 16:21 (2x); 18:37 (as well as 1 John 2:29; 3:9 [2x]; 4:7; 5:1 [3x], 4, 18 [2x]). The

repetition of vocabulary demonstrates the significance of the theme in Johannine works and will be discussed further below.

9. Annette Weissenrieder writes, "Surprising as it may seem, we must establish here from the outset that the *clear distinction* we make between philosophy on the one hand and medicine on the other, between theoretical and empirical-practical implications, absolutely did not exist in this form in antiquity" ("Spirit and Rebirth in the Gospel of John," *R&T* 21 [2014]: 61, n 5). For this reason, authors classified as either "medical" or "philosophical" in contemporary studies were understood to be *both* in the ancient world and, as such, will be explored in the following section without that distinction imposed.
10. Seim, "Motherhood and the Making of Fathers," 99.
11. Richard Latimore (trans.) *Aeschylus I: Oresteia*, ed. David Grene and Richard Latimore (Chicago: Chicago University Press, 1953).
12. Athena's mother, Metis, was the Titan goddess of wisdom and cunning. Hesiod explains that Zeus swallowed her out of fear for the offspring she would bear him—"thoughtful children" who could equal their father's intellect and threaten his reign (Hesiod, *Theog.* 886–900). See also Philo's praise for "Sabbath." Like Athena, she is personified as female, but nevertheless considered "motherless," and therefore the superior day (*Vit. Mos.* 2.209–10).
13. The head was considered one primary location for production of semen: "the greatest part of the seed flows from the head past the ears into the spinal marrow" (*Gen.* 2.473). Aristotle, likewise, views the head as the source of semen, even though he argues that semen is a blood product rather than that of the marrow or brain (*Gen. an.* 5.3.783b9–784a12). Lesley Ann Dean-Jones, *Women's Bodies in Classical Greek Science* (Oxford: Clarendon, 1996), 84–85; James Wilberding, "Embryology," in *A Companion to Science, Technology, and Medicine in Ancient Greece and Rome*, ed. Georgia L. Irby, BCAW (Malden, MA: Wiley-Blackwell, 2016), 1:333–34.
14. *Eumenides* 658–61 has also been tied to "preformationism," the belief that male semen contains a full human being in miniature, which is fed and incubated by the female until it grows too large for her womb to hold (Clare K. Rothschild, "Embryology, Plant Biology, and Divine Generation in the Fourth Gospel," in Ahearne-Kroll, Holloway, and Kelhoffer, *Women and Gender in Ancient Religions*, 125–51; Wilberding, "Embryology," 1:332–33). While Apollo mentions the begetter's "seed" (*sperma*), he does not describe *what exactly the seed is composed of or contains*, leaving it open to a number of interpretations.
15. Charlotte Elisheva Fonrobert suggests that the rabbis resemble Hippocratic theory most closely (*Menstrual Purity: Rabbinic and Christian Reconstructions of Gender*, Contraversions [Stanford, CA: Stanford University Press, 2000], 63; see *b. Nid.* 31a). More recently, however, Gwynn Kessler has suggested that the rabbis more often offer a one-seed theory focusing on male contribution in a manner that is more similar to Aristotle (*Conceiving Israel: The Fetus in Rabbinic Narratives*,

Divinations [Philadelphia: University of Pennsylvania Press, 2009], 113–14; see Lev. Rab. 14).

16. Translations are from Paul Potter's LCL volumes: Hippocrates vol. 8 (1995) and vol. 10 (2012).
17. This theory has negative implications as well. Since a woman's pleasure is assumed in the conception of *any* child, she is culpable in instances of rape when she conceives. Moreover, a woman's inability to conceive can also be blamed on her not "wanting" to become pregnant and, in effect, rejecting her femininity (*Gen.* 5.477; cf. *Nat. puer.* 2.490; Galen, *UP* 14.10–11 [2.318–20]).
18. Troy W. Martin, "Paul's Pneumatological Statements and Ancient Medical Texts," in *The New Testament and Early Christian Literature*, ed. John Fotopoulos, NovTSup 122 (Leiden: Brill, 2006), 107. Martin cites Hippocrates, *Flat.* 3.1–4, which states: "Now bodies, of men and of animals generally, are nourished by three kinds of nourishment, and the names thereof are solid food, drink, and wind (*pneuma*)" (Jones, LCL).
19. Weissenrieder, "Spirit and Rebirth," 67, n. 22; emphasis added.
20. *Gen. an.* 1.17.721b6–724a14 for Aristotle's discussion and refutation of pangenesis; on sexual differentiation see *Gen. an.* 4.1.763b20–766b27.
21. Aristotle, *Gen. an.* 1.19.727a1–4; 1.19.726b31–20.729a33 is Aristotle's discussion of menstrual blood.
22. Translations of Aristotle's *Generation of Animals* are from A. L. Peck's 1942 LCL volume.
23. Here we find another difference from the Hippocratic position, which asserts that it is better for the womb to be empty at the time of conception lest the seeds contributed are drowned out by the excess menstrual blood (*Nat. puer.* 4.495).
24. Aristotle, *Gen. an.* 2.3.737a22–29. See 2.4.740a35–6.745b21 for his overview of embryonic development.
25. The sex of a fetus was also believed by some to be influenced by the uterine "chamber" in which a fetus developed; the right chamber (as the "stronger" side) resulted in a male, and the left resulted in a female (Hippocrates, *Nat. puer.* 7.540; Aristotle, *Gen. an.* 1.3.716b32–33; Galen, *Sem.* 2.5.1–76; *UP* 14.7 [2.302–10]). Similar conclusions were drawn concerning the right and left testicles of men. Dean-Jones, *Women's Bodies*, 65–69, 166–70; Flemming, *Medicine*, 308–10.
26. *Gen. an.* 2.7.745b27–29, 746a2–4; emphasis added. Galen writes at length on the connection of the uterus to the breasts (*UP* 14.8 [2.310–13]).
27. Ancient medical authors argued that children born in the seventh and ninth months were most likely to survive, interpreting the eighth month of pregnancy as particularly dangerous for both fetus and mother (Hippocrates, *Oct.*; Aristotle, *Gen. an.* 4.4.772b9–11). See Dean-Jones, *Women's Bodies*, 209–11.
28. Galen describes his theory of conception and generation in *UP* as outlined here, but he also offers summaries and explanations in *Natural Faculties*; *On the*

Formation of the Fetus; *On Seeds*. See also the summary offered by Wilberding, "Embryology," 336–37.

29. Yurie Hong, "Collaboration and Conflict: Discourses of Maternity in Hippocratic Gynecology and Embryology," in *Mothering and Motherhood in Ancient Greece and Rome*, ed. Lauren Hackworth Petersen and Patricia Salzman-Mitchell (Austin: University of Texas, 2012), 80.
30. Hong notes that this is in contrast to the gynecological focus of the *Diseases of Women*, in which "the female body takes center stage in the texts while the fetus is a supporting player" whose actions often resemble, rather than combat, the uterus (Ibid., 80–81). Nevertheless, maternal passivity, particularly in childbirth, is also assumed in *Mul.* 1.33–34 (Ibid., 84).
31. Flemming, *Medicine*, 98.
32. Soranus, *Gyn.* 1.12.44 includes the closing of the "mouth" of the vagina as a sign of pregnancy, which a woman might feel as a "shivering sensation" after sex.
33. The author of the *Nature of the Child* uses the analogy of a chick hatching from an egg to explain why "a fetus is born when its nourishment runs out" (19.536). Aristotle also suggests that lack of food is one factor prompting childbirth in *Gen. an.* 4.8.777a22–26.
34. Translation from Hong, "Collaboration and Conflict," 81–82. See also Hippocrates, *Nat. puer.* 30.2–9.
35. Nancy Demand, *Birth, Death, and Motherhood in Classical Greece* (Baltimore: Johns Hopkins University Press, 1994), 19.
36. Ibid.
37. Flemming, *Medicine*, 295–96. Flemming argues that the unique nature of female anatomy is admitted by the fact that Galen offers a discussion of the penis in his *On the Dissection of Muscles* (28–31 [18b.995–99 Kühn]), but must devote an entirely separate work to the uterus, appropriately titled *Dissection of the Uterus*. See also Galen, *AA* 12.2, 7–9; *On the Movement of Muscles* 3.
38. Euripides, *Medea* 235–36, 248–51 (Kovacs, LCL). The entire speech stretches from lines 214 to 266.
39. Quoted in Hong, "Collaboration and Conflict," 85.
40. For more on the connection between blood and breastmilk, see Chapter 4.
41. Helen King, "Sacrificial Blood: The Role of the *Amnion* in Ancient Gynecology," *Helios* 13 (1987): 117–26; eadem, *Hippocrates' Woman: Reading the Female Body in Ancient Greece* (London: Routledge, 1998), 92–97; Nicole Loraux, *Tragic Ways of Killing a Woman* (Cambridge: Harvard University Press, 1987); Dean-Jones, *Woman's Bodies*, 101–3.
42. Dean-Jones, *Women's Bodies*, 102; [Ps.]-Aristotle, *Hist. an.* 7.1.581b1–2; Hippocrates, *Mul.* 2.113.
43. Lev 12:1–5; *t. Nid.* 4.7; *b. Nid.* 30b.
44. King, *Hippocrates' Woman*, 95–96.

45. King notes the appearance of this term particularly in Homeric literature, cf. *Od.* 3.444 (Ibid., 95).
46. On the conflation of amniotic fluid and lochial flow in Aristotelian and Hippocratic texts, see King, "Sacrificial Blood," 117–18, 120–22.
47. Helen King, *Hippocrates' Woman*, 92–97; eadem, "Sacrificial Blood," 120. King also notes similarities in the dressing of brides for marriage and for sacrificial victims before their slaughter. As in marriage, it is the man who "cuts" the victim, starting the flow of blood just he does through defloration. Initiating this flow of blood, the man then steps back in ritual sacrifices, allowing a woman to collect the flowing blood in the *amneion*. In the same way, the woman fulfills her function with her husband and with the polis with flowing and collecting blood throughout her reproductive life. See also, Dean-Jones, *Women's Bodies*, 101–3.
48. Flemming, *Medicine*, 317.
49. Turid Karlsen Seim, "Motherhood and the Making of Fathers in Antiquity: Contextualizing Genetics in the Gospel of John," in *Women and Gender in Ancient Religions*, ed. Stephen P. Ahearne-Kroll, Paul A. Holloway, and James A. Kelhoffer, WUNT 263 (Tübingen: Mohr Siebeck, 2010), 99–123.
50. See Chapter 5 § "Molding Princes for Rome: Maternal Power in the Augustan Age."
51. Kessler, *Conceiving Israel*, 113. See Gen 12–50; Exod 23:36; Judg 13; 1 Sam 1–2; Isa 54–66; Job 10:8–10; Ps 139:13–16.
52. The *Protoevangelium of James* places special emphasis on Mary's purity and virginity in conceiving and even in birthing Jesus. This concern makes sense in a context concerned about what a mother contributes to the formation of her child. Since Jesus is pure, his mother must also have been pure in her provision of any material or seed. Jennifer A. Glancy, *Corporal Knowledge: Early Christian Bodies* (Oxford: Oxford University Press, 2010), 81–134.
53. Stephen P. Ahearne-Kroll, "'Who Are My Mother and My Brothers?' Family Relations and Family Language in the Gospel of Mark," *JR* 81 (2001): 19; E. Elizabeth Johnson, "'Who Is My Mother?' Family Values in the Gospel of Mark," Gaventa and Rigby, *Blessed One*, 38–40.
54. Although some have suggested that Jesus's mother is the "Mary" described as the mother of James and Joses in this verse, Joel Marcus notes that it would be "extraordinary" for Mark to identify her this way instead of through Jesus (*Mark 8–16*, AB27a [New Haven: Yale University Press, 2009], 2:1060).
55. Raymond E. Brown, *The Gospel According to John*, 2 vols., AB 29–29a (Garden City, NY: Doubleday, 1966–1970), 1:99; Joseph A. Grassi, "The Role of Jesus' Mother in John's Gospel: A Reappraisal," *CBQ* 48 (1986): 78; Judith Lieu, "The Mother of the Son in the Fourth Gospel," *JBL* 117 (1998): 69; Adeline Fehribach, "The 'Birthing' Bridegroom: The Portrayal of Jesus in the Fourth Gospel," in *A Feminist Companion to John*, 2 vols., ed. Amy-Jill Levine with Marianne Blickenstaff (London: Sheffield Academic, 2003), 2:127; Turid Karlsen Seim,

"Descent and Divine Paternity in the Gospel of John: Does the Mother Matter?" *NTS* 51 (2005): 373.

56. Katherine Doob Sakenfeld, "Tamar, Rahab, Ruth, and the Wife of Uriah: The Company Mary Keeps in Matthew's Gospel," in Gaventa and Rigby, *Blessed One*, 21–31.
57. Gaventa, *Mary*, 43.
58. Joel B. Green, "Blessed Is She Who Believed: Mary, Curious Exemplar in Luke's Narrative," in Gaventa and Rigby, *Blessed One*, 9; Gaventa, *Mary*, 51–55; Spencer, *Salty Wives*, 74–75; Seim, *Double Message*, 198–208.
59. Adele Reinhartz, "'And the Word Was Begotten': Divine Epigenesis in the Gospel of John," *Sem* 85 (1999): 83–103; Seim, "Descent and Divine Paternity"; eadem, "Motherhood and the Making of Fathers."
60. Rothschild, "Embryology"; Weissenrieder, "Spirit and Rebirth." Gitte Buch-Hansen engages extensively with Reinhartz and Seim, but interprets the Spirit in John in light of Stoic thought, especially as it is expressed through Philo's idea of a "second generation/begetting" (*"It Is the Spirit that Gives Life": A Stoic Understanding of Pneuma in John's Gospel*, BZNW 173 [Berlin: de Gruyter, 2010], esp. 177–216).
61. Mark 1:11; Matt 3:17; Luke 3:22; John 1:34. There is a significant text-critical issue in John 1:34: Does John call Jesus the "Son of God" or "the elect one of God"? Recent work by Tze-Ming Quek ("A Text-Critical Study of John 1.34," *NTS* 55 [2009]: 22–34) has pushed scholars to take the latter option more seriously and may indicate the influence of Isa 42 on John's narrative.
62. Kessler, *Conceiving Israel*, 113.
63. Ibid. See Lev 12:2 (Lev. Rab. 14); Job 10:9–12; *1 En.* 15:4; Wis Sol 7:1–2; 4 Macc 13:20; Philo, *QG* 3.47; *Creation* 132. Kessler considers Lev. Rab. 14 to be more indicative of a general rabbinic perspective on procreation than the oft-cited *b. Nid.* 31a. Overall, she argues, the rabbis are not overly concerned with precise generative theories, but on emphasizing God's role as Creator and his permanent connection to Israel (*Conceiving Israel*, 115). Nevertheless, Michael Satlow explains that "the small amount of data on semen in Jewish literature from the Second Temple period appears to follow Aristotle's embryology" ("'Wasted Seed,' The History of a Rabbinic Idea," *HUCA* 65 [1990]: 157; see also Pieter van der Horst, "Sarah's Seminal Emission: Hebrews 11:11 in the Light of Ancient Embryology," in *Greeks, Romans, and Christians*, eds. David L. Balch, Everett Ferguson, Wayne A. Meeks [Minneapolis: Fortress, 1991], 296–301; Buch-Hansen, *It Is the Spirit*, 105–58, 191–97).
64. Weissenrieder also provides an overview of Jewish understandings of God's giving life by breathing the spirit upon creation in various LXX texts, especially Gen 2:7, and Philonic interpretations ("Spirit and Rebirth," 70–75; eadem, "Die lebendige Wirkung des Geistes in Gen 2,7/LXX. Das Bedeutungsspecktrum von נפח/ἐμφυσάω und נשמה/πνοή in Lichte antiker medizinischer Quellen," *JSCS* 46 [2013]: 11–29).

65. Apollo regards successful pregnancy as natural "unless some god interferes" (Aeschylus, *Eum.* 661) and the Hippocratic author of *Nature of Women* indicates that to understand "human affairs" (lit. "human-making," *anthrōpoisin*), a physician must first take into account the "divine" (1.312). In his *On the Formation of the Fetus* and *On my own Opinions*, Galen also admits that his theories do not completely explain the origin of life in a fetus (see Flemming, *Medicine*, 299–301).
66. Gaventa highlights the repetition of the phrase "the child and his mother" in Matthew's account, which she argues "reflects a powerful connection between the two" (*Mary*, 43).
67. Kessler, *Conceiving Israel*, 112.
68. See Chapter 2 § "Jars and Houses: Constructing the Female Body."
69. The only other instances of Luke describing characters as "filled with a holy Spirit" occurs in 1:67 and in 4:1 with Zechariah and Jesus. Jesus's connection to the holy Spirit is affirmed again at his baptism in 3:22 before he is led out into the wilderness "full of a holy Spirit" (4:1). The description reemerges in Acts as a description for those given prophetic utterance or divine insight (2:4; 4:8, 31; 9:17; 11:24; 13:9), for the seven deacons (6:3), especially Stephen (6:5; 7:55).
70. Charles H. Talbert, "Miraculous Conceptions and Births in Mediterranean Antiquity," in *The Historical Jesus in Context*, ed. Amy-Jill Levine, Dale C. Allison Jr., John Dominic Crossan, Princeton Readings in Religions (Princeton: Princeton University Press, 2006), 83–84.
71. Gaventa, *Mary*, 54.
72. N. Clayton Croy and Alice E. Connor, "Mantic Mary? The Virgin Mother as Prophet in Luke 1.26–56 and the Early Church," *JSNT* 34 (2011): 254–76; Mary F. Foskett, *A Virgin Conceived: Mary and Classical Representations of Virginity* [Bloomington: Indiana University Press, 2002], 130–31; Gaventa, *Mary*, 58; Betsworth, *Children in Early Christian Narratives*, 105.
73. Dale B. Martin, *The Corinthian Body* (New Haven: Yale University Press, 1995), 239–41. Croy and Connor also note this connection ("Mantic Mary," 265).
74. Croy and Connor, "Mantic Mary," 262–66.
75. Ibid., 270.
76. Pondering is highlighted as a paradigmatic aspect of Mary's character by Joseph A. Fitzmyer, who writes that Mary's "treasuring and pondering is part of the picture of the 'believing woman,' 'the handmaid of the Lord' " (*The Gospel According to Luke*, AB28 [Garden City, NY: Doubleday, 1981], 398) and François Bovon concludes that "Mary, the paragon of faith, must understand them [the words] correctly" (*Luke 1*, trans. Christine M. Thomas, Hermeneia [Minneapolis: Fortress, 2002], 92); see also Green, "Blessed Is She," 11; Spencer, *Salty Wives*, 84–88. Gaventa, on the other hand, is more open to its ambiguous possibilities (*Mary*, 61–62).
77. Luke moves the Beelzebub controversy from the story of his family in his Gospel (Mark 3:20-30). Instead, it surfaces in 11:14–23 just prior to the woman's comments concerning Jesus's mother in 11:27.

78. Luke does not use the word *logos* to describe what Mary hears or what God does in Luke 1–2. Instead, he prefers the term *rhema* in the opening chapters (1:37–38, 65; 2:15, 17, 19, 50–51), but switches in 8:21 and 11:28 to *logos*. The use of *rhema* mimics Gen 18:14 (LXX), thus reinforcing the tie to the matriarchal narratives. Ancient interpreters, however, were not bothered by this semantic variance. Jennifer Glancy (*Corporal Knowledge*, 93–94) notes the interpretation of Mary's being impregnated by hearing the word of God in contrast to Eve's deception by Satan's words, which was also frequently sexualized in the history of reception (see Chapter 2). Glancy's observation of this tradition resonates with the spermatic overtones that were also a part of *logos* language in conception as outlined in the previous section and which will recur in the discussion of the Pastoral Epistles in Chapter 5.
79. Brown, *Gospel*, 1:102–3; Gaventa, *Mary*, 89; Francis J. Moloney argues that Mary's acceptance of Jesus's authority makes her the first to believe in Jesus's words in the Gospel (*Belief in the Word: Reading John 1–4* [Minneapolis: Fortress, 1993], 83). Gaventa, however, also notes the "tension" evoked by Jesus's phrase in 2:4 (*Mary*, 83–85).
80. On maternal expectations of mourning, see Paul A. Holloway, "Gender and Grief: Seneca's *Ad Marciam* and *Ad Helviam matrem*," in Ahearne-Kroll, Holloway, and Kelhoffer, *Women and Gender in Ancient Religions*, 299–321. Many commentators note Jesus's filial responsibility in John 19 (Gaventa, *Mary*, 89–95) even if they favor a simultaneously symbolic reading concerning a new family of God (Gail R. O'Day, *John*, NIB [Nashville: Abingdon, 2006], 832) or Mary's status as the new Eve (Brown, *Gospel*, 2:923–27).
81. Jdg 11:12; 1 Kings 17:18.
82. John Chrysostom, *Hom. Joh.* 21.3.
83. Gaventa, *Mary*, 93.
84. Of all the women in the Gospel, it is only Mary Magdalene who receives the honor of being addressed by name after Jesus's resurrection in John 20:16. Yet, even this address is ambiguous. It enables her recognition of Jesus, but he also warns her that his primary objective remains his return to his Father (20:16–17).
85. Reinhartz, "And the Word Was Begotten"; Seim, "Divine Descent"; eadem, "Motherhood and the Making of Fathers."
86. *monogenēs para patros*, 1:16. The majority opinion pushes against a connection to *gennaō*, arguing that *monogenēs* infers unique-ness. This word is used as a description for only-children in ancient texts (Luke 7:12; 8:42; 9:38; see also Jdg 11:34; Pss 22:20; 24:16; 34:17; Heb 11:17). Seim and Reinhartz both offer the suggestion that the semantic range of *monogenēs* could warrant a translation of the term as "begotten only by" in addition to "unique one" to emphasize Jesus's sole parentage by the Father (Reinhartz, "And the Word Was Begotten," 93; Seim, "Descent and Divine Paternity," 365–66).
87. Conway, *Behold the Man: Jesus and Greco-Roman Masculinity* (Oxford: Oxford University Press, 2008), 145; emphasis added.
88. Ibid.

89. Buch-Hansen turns to Philo's idea of a "second generation/begetting" instead of Aristotelian theory alone to argue against the need for a virginal conception in John. According to Buch-Hansen, Jesus is like Moses, when he is "begotten" a second time by God's Spirit and without need for a mother at his baptism (John 1:32–34). Thus, Jesus provides the model for a second generation for his disciples (John 3:1–21). Jesus, however, remains superior to them due to his ascent and resultant transformation into the Holy Spirit who regenerates his followers (*It Is the Spirit*, 175–76, 301–4, 402–4).
90. On the biographical nature of the Gospels, see Charles H. Talbert, *What Is a Gospel?* (Philadelphia: Fortress, 1977); Richard Burridge, *What Are the Gospels? A Comparison with Graeco-Roman Biography*, 2d ed. (Grand Rapids: Eerdmans, 2004). For a review of commonplaces (*topoi*) used in the construction of characters in biographical and other literatures, see Alicia D. Myers, *Characterizing Jesus: A Rhetorical Analysis on the Fourth Gospel's Use of Scripture in Its Presentation of Jesus*, LNTS 458 (London: T&T Clark, 2012), 43–75.
91. Myers, "Gender, Rhetoric, and Recognition: (Re)defining Masculinity in the Gospel of John," *JSNT* 38 (2015): 203–7.
92. Ahearne-Kroll, "Who Are My Mother and My Brothers," 2–9; Blickenstaff, *While the Bridegroom Is with Them*, 117–22.
93. Blickenstaff, *While the Bridegroom Is with Them*, 144–47.
94. Susan Haber, "Living and Dying for the Law: The Mother-martyrs of 2 Maccabees," *Women in Judaism* 4/1 (2006): 1–15 [Online: http://wjudaism.library.utoronto.ca/index.php/ wjudaism/article/view/247/320].
95. See also Num 11:12; Isa 45:9–10; 46:3–4; 66:10–13; L. Juliana M. Claassens, *Mourner, Mother, Midwife: Reimagining God's Delivering Presence in the Old Testament* (Louisville: Westminster John Knox, 2012).
96. Weissenrieder, "Spirit and Rebirth," 80–81; Fehribach, "The 'Birthing' Bridegroom," 104–29; Caroline Bynum, *Jesus as Mother: Studies in the Spirituality of the High Middle Ages* (Berkeley: University of California Press, 1982), 113–35.
97. 1 John 2:29; 3:1, 2, 9, 10; 4:7; 5:1, 2, 4, 18; 2 John 13; 3 John 4.

CHAPTER 4

1. Use and development of milk images can be found in, for example, *Od. Sol.* 8; 19; 35; 40; Ireneaus of Lyons; Clement of Alexandria; Origen of Alexandria; Gregory of Nyssa; Augustine of Hippo; Ephrem the Syrian. On these interpretations of milk imagery see Gail Paterson Corrington, "The Milk of Salvation: Redemption by the Mother in Late Antiquity and Early Christianity," *HTR* 82 (1989): 393–420; John David Penniman, *Raised on Christian Milk: The Symbolic Power of Nourishment in Early Christianity*, Synkrisis Series (New Haven: Yale University Press, 2017).
2. Robin M. Jensen traces various maternal images in the patristic and early church traditions as well as architecture in "*Mater Ecclesia* and *Fons Aeterna*: The Church

and Her Womb in Ancient Christian Tradition," in *A Feminist Companion to Patristic Literature*, ed. Amy-Jill Levine (London: T&T Clark, 2008), 137–55.

3. On God as nurse and nourisher in Hebrew Scripture, see L. Juliana M. Claassens, *The God Who Provides: Biblical Images of Divine Nourishment* (Nashville: Abingdon, 2004), 1–22.
4. "Nurture" (*trophē*) and related ideas of education, training, and upbringing are listed as commonplaces in Theon, *Prog.* 110; Ps.-Hermogenes, *Prog.* 16; Aphthonius the Sophist, *Prog.* 22R–40; Nicolaus the Sophist, *Prog.* 52; Quintilian, *Inst.* 3.7; *Rhet. Her.* 3.6.10–11; Cicero, *Inv.* 1.24.34; 2.59.177; *Part. or.* 22.74–75. See also Hippocrates, *Nutriment*; Galen, *On the Properties of Foodstuffs*; idem, *The Soul's Dependence on the Body*. For more on the *topos* of nourishment, education, and food in particular, as character (and gender) forming, see the discussion below and Alicia D. Myers, "'In the Father's Bosom': Breastfeeding and Identity Formation in John's Gospel," *CBQ* 76 (2014): 486–87; Penniman, *Raised on Christian Milk*, 23–51.
5. Larissa Bonfante, "Nursing Mothers in Classical Art," in *Naked Truths: Women, Sexuality, and Gender in Classical Art and Archaeology*, ed. Ann Olga Kolosk-Ostrow and Claire L. Lyons (London: Routledge, 1997), 174–95.
6. Aristotle, *Gen. an.* 4.8.776a20–776b4. Galen, in contrast, argues that milk does not begin to collect in the breasts until the eighth month (*UP* 14.8).
7. *Gen. an.* 4.8.777a4–8; emphasis original. Aristotle is refuting Empedocles's assertion that milk was decomposed blood.
8. Some Hippocratic authors argue that instead of simple menstrual discharge, breast milk was a distillation of foods consumed by a pregnant woman (*Nat. puer.* 10.513). While this is a different reading than Aristotle and other Hippocratics, the author nevertheless emphasizes the unique role of heat in the creation of milk *and* he suggests that this same substance is consumed by a fetus in utero in 10.514. Thus, like others, this Hippocratic author finds continuity between what infants consume in the womb and after birth.
9. On the common belief of a multi-chambered uterus in women, see Chapter 2. Translations of Galen's *Usefulness of Parts* are taken from Margaret Tallmadge May, *Galen: On the Usefulness of the Parts of the Body* (Ithaca, NY: Cornell University Press, 1968).
10. For this reason, Galen advises excess flux to be drawn off through the breasts (*MMG* 1.15 [XI 54 K]). Rebecca Flemming notes that this application is meant to draw the uterus upward as well (*Medicine and the Making of Roman Women: Gender, Nature, and Authority from Celsus to Galen* [Oxford: Oxford University Press, 2000], 346–47).
11. On the presence of "soul" (*psychē*) in milk, and its ability to shape souls, in Greco-Roman literatures see Penniman, *Raised on Christian Milk*, 25–36 as well as the discussion of 1 Thess 2:7–8.
12. Citing Galen, *De marcone* 9 (6.701 Kühn) and *MM* 6.6 (474.75 Kühn), Julie Laskaris notes his recommendation for "men suckling directly from the woman as

the best way to get the milk" ("Nursing Mothers in Greek and Roman Medicine," *AJA* 112 [2008]: 462). See also Flemming (*Medicine*, 349–50) who cites Galen, *Hipp. Aph.* 5.37, 38; Bonfante, "Nursing Mothers," 174–95; Anthony Corbeill, *Nature Embodied: Gesture in Ancient Rome* (Princeton: Princeton University Press, 2003), 67–106.

13. Amy Richlin, "Pliny's Brassiere," in *Roman Sexualities*, ed. Judith P. Hallett and Marilyn B. Skinner (Princeton: Princeton University Press, 1997), 202–4.
14. Ibid., 205. Galen writes that "the best milk is just about the most wholesome of any foods we consume," but "unwholesome milk" causes bad humors, and even death (*Alim. Fac.* 6.685–6; Owen Powell, trans. and ed., *Galen: On the Properties of Foodstuffs Introduction, Translation, and Commentary* [Cambridge: Cambridge University Press, 2003], 125).
15. Translations of Aulus Gellius's *Attic Nights* are taken from J. C. Rolfe's 1927 LCL volume with some slight adjustments.
16. Favorinus makes use of a well-worn trope by assuming vanity as the motivation for acquiring wet nurses or having an abortion (Seneca, *Helv.* 16.3; Juvenal 6.592–602). In contrast, Soranus's detailed instructions on the selection of wet nurses demonstrates a concern to find quality milk and reputable women to care for infants, who might require wet nurses for a variety of reasons unrelated to the "vanity" of a young, noblewoman.
17. *b. Ber.* 31b reflects a similar sentiment that the purpose of women's breasts are for feeding their own young. While praying for a son, Hannah cries out: "Master of the Universe, everything that you created in a woman has a purpose: eyes to see and ears to hear, a nose to smell, a mouth to speak, hands to do work, legs to walk with, breast to nurse with them. These breasts that You have put over my heart, are they not to nurse [with]? Give me a son, so that I may nurse with them" (quoted in Judith Z. Abrams, *Judaism and Disability: Portrayals in Ancient Texts from the Tanach through the Bavli* [Washington, DC: Gallaudet University Press, 1998], 115–16).
18. Socio-economic class is prominent in Favorinus's discourse. Aulus Gellius sets the scene by explaining that "the father was of senatorial rank and of a family of high nobility" (12.1.3). He also comments, "'But it makes no difference,' they say, 'if provided it [the infant] be nourished and live, by whose milk that is effected.' Why then does not he who affirms this, if he is so dull in comprehending natural feeling, think that it also makes no difference in whose body and from whose blood a human being is formed and fashioned?" (12.1.10–11).
19. *Noct. att.* 12.1.20. Favorinus conflates *Il.* 16.33–35 with *Aen.* 4.365–66, using a text about Achilles and another about Aeneas to characterize the Greek warrior. For other uses of this *topos* concerning Achilles, see Pseudo-Hermogenes, *Prog.* 16; Libanius, *Prog.* Encomium 3.2.
20. Soranus, in his extended discussion on the use of *nutrices* warns his readers: "by nature the nursling becomes similar to the nurse" (*Gyn.* 2.19.88).

21. Perhaps this position explains Favorinus's addressing the mother-in-law not as *mater* (mother) or *matrona* (married woman/wife), but the more generic *mulier* (female), like the other "unnatural women" (*prodigiosae mulieres*) he describes. Her crime is the attempted interruption of the "natural" use of her own daughter's breasts (12.1.5).
22. Such a fact should not be taken to communicate that fathers (and other male family members/household members) played no role in a young child's life. Suzanne Dixon notes that in many upper-class households, a father could have as much responsibility as a mother *if* they hired *nutrices* for actual nursing and close care (Quintilian, *Inst.* 6.1–14; Dixon, *Roman Mother*, 27–30).
23. A hired nurse is to refrain from sex, lest she be distracted by the "diversion of sexual pleasure and moreover spoils and diminishes the milk or suppresses it entirely by stimulating menstrual catharsis through the uterus or bringing about conception" since milk is converted menstrual blood (2.19.88; see also 2.21.90–2.27.96).
24. Plutarch's authorship of *Lib. ed.* is doubtful, but the author will be referred to as "Plutarch" for ease of reference and due to its traditional inclusion in the corpus of his works. In *Lib. ed.*, Plutarch acknowledges that some women are not able to nurse (on account of "weakness") or because they desire to have more children immediately. In every other case, however, he opposes the hiring of wet nurses.
25. Tal Ilan, *Jewish Women in the Greco-Roman Palestine* (Peabody, MA: Hendrickson, 1996), 120–21.
26. Cynthia Chapman, "'Oh that you were like a brother to me, one who had nursed at my mother's breasts': Breast Milk as a Kinship-Forging Substance," *JHebS* 12 (2012): article 7, 38. Tal Ilan notes Josephus's interpretation that Moses refused to be nursed by an Egyptian, thus forcing the hiring of his own mother in *Ant.* 2.9.5.226 (Ilan, *Jewish Women*, 120). Mishnah *Avodah zarah* 2.1 forbids a non-Jewish woman from nursing a Jewish child even though it permits a non-Jewish woman to act as her midwife (see also *t. Nid.* 2.5). See also Penniman, *Raised on Christian Milk*, 53–70.
27. Keith R. Bradley, *Discovering the Roman Family: Studies in Roman History* (Oxford: Oxford University Press, 1991), 27; Dixon, *Roman Mother*, 32–24; 154–61.
28. Fittingly this discussion is in the midst of Cato's education of his son, to which Plutarch emphasizes Cato's deep commitment rather than turning care over to slaves (20.1–6). On affection through breastfeeding, also see Plutarch, *Am. prol.* 3.496a–496c.
29. Homer, *Il.* 22.77–89.
30. Chariton, *Chaer.* 3.5. In this scene, Chaereas's mother quotes Hecuba's exclamation from *Il.* 22.82–83.
31. Penniman, *Raised on Christian Milk*, 57; see also Susan Haber, "Living and Dying for the Law: The Mother-martyrs of 2 Maccabees," *Women in*

Judaism: A Multidisciplinary Journal 4/1 (2006): 6–8 [Online: http://wjudaism.library.utoronto.ca/index.php/wjudaism/article/view/247/320].

32. Euripides, *Or.* 969, 1206–7 (Way, LCL). See also Aeschylus, *Cho.* 523–50, 928; Homer, *Od.* 19.435–36, 467–91.
33. Gail Labovitz, "'These Are the Labors': Constructions of the Woman Nursing Her Child in the Mishnah and Tosefta," *Nashim* 3 (2000): 15–42. Labovitz notes a contrast of perspectives concerning nursing women between the Mishnah and the Babylonian Talmud and Tosefta. She argues that the Mishnah constructs a nursing woman as one focused on the welfare of her husband and his household, while the Babylonian Talmud and *tannaitic* materials in the Tosefta push attention to the welfare of the child. Nevertheless, both traditions emphasize the importance of a nursing mother.
34. Seneca, *Ep.* 45.13–33. Antony Corbeill, "Dining Deviants in Roman Political Invective," in *Roman Sexualities* (ed. Judith P. Hallett and Marilyn B. Skinner; Princeton: Princeton University Press, 1997), 99–128.
35. Translation from Dixon, *Roman Mother*, 115.
36. Translation of *t. Nid.* 2.3 taken from Labovitz, "These Are the Labors," 29. Labovitz suggests that this debate centers on issues of purity concerning when a husband can resume having sex with his wife once she begins to menstruate again while nursing (*m. Nid.* 1.3–5; *t. Nid.* 1.5, 10; 2.1–7).
37. One short funerary inscription from Athens reads: "Good Athenadora, wife of Thaumasius, filled with God's influence. She bore children and nursed them when they were infants. Earth took this young mother and keeps her, though the children need her milk" (*Kaibel* 176.G; Mary R. Lefkowitz and Maureen B. Fant, eds., *Women's Life in Greece and Rome: A Sourcebook in Translation* [Baltimore: Johns Hopkins University Press, 1992], 20).
38. Translations from W. Peterson's LCL volume.
39. *Dial.* 28.7; emphasis added.
40. Bradley, *Discovering the Roman Family*, 13–36. Soranus's extensive attention to wet nurses illustrates the pervasive practice of their employment, though he does admit that mother's milk is to be preferred (*Gyn.* 2.18.87). Whether or not a slave mother could nurse her own child was not a priority—indeed, Plutarch's example of Cato Major's wife implies that her slaves' children received *better* nourishment at her own breast rather than at that of their biological mothers.
41. Jesus's placement of his mother in the beloved disciple's household is often cited as a display of filial concern for his mother. It also continues the motif of distancing biological families since Jesus puts her with a non-blood relative rather than having her remain with her biological family, which seems to have included several brothers (2:12; 6:42; 7:1–9).
42. This portion of the chapter is a development of ideas first published in Myers, "In the Father's Bosom," 481–97.

43. BDAG; LSJ; Francis J. Moloney, "'In the Bosom of' or 'Turned towards' the Father?" *AusBR* 31 (1983): 64–65; Martin O'Kane, "'The Bosom of Abraham' (Luke 16:22): Father Abraham in the Visual Imagination," *BibInt* 15 (2007): 489–93.
44. "Heart" (NRSV, NLT); "side" (CEB, NAB); "closest relationship/fellowship" (NIV, TNIV, NET); "bosom" (NAS, NKJV).
45. O'Kane, "The Bosom of Abraham," 485, see also pp. 489–93.
46. Claassens, *God Who Provides*, 2–7.
47. Jacob Cherian, "The Moses at Qumran: The מורה הצדק as the Nursing-Father of the יחד," in *The Bible and the Dead Sea Scrolls*, vol. 2, The Second Princeton Symposium on Judaism and Christian Origins (Waco, TX: Baylor University Press, 2006), 351–61.
48. Wayne A. Meeks, *The Prophet-King: Moses Traditions and Johannine Christology*, NovTSup 14 (Leiden: Brill, 1967); Stan Harstine, *Moses as a Character in the Fourth Gospel: A Study in Ancient Literary Techniques*, JSNTSup 229 (Sheffield: Sheffield Academic, 2002); Alicia D. Myers, *Characterizing Jesus: A Rhetorical Analysis on the Fourth Gospel's Use of Scripture in Its Presentation of Jesus*, LNTS 458 (London: T&T Clark, 2012).
49. Chapman, "Breast Milk as Kinship-Forging Substance," 38.
50. This interpretation does not displace the associations between God's gift of wisdom and Torah as "bread" and the bread images in John 6. Instead, recognizing the breastmilk traditions that are also associated with manna adds another layer of depth while also repeating a consistent connection between nourishment and education in Jewish traditions. For more on the connections between John 6 and exodus traditions, see Peder Borgen, *Bread from Heaven: An Exegetical Study of the Concept of Manna in the Gospel of John and the Writings of Philo*, NovTSup 10 (Leiden: Brill, 1965); Myers, *Characterizing Jesus*, 104–12.
51. J. Albert Harrill, "Cannibalistic Language in the Fourth Gospel and Greco-Roman Polemics of Factionalism (John 6:52–66)," *JBL* 127 (2008): 133–58.
52. George L. Parsenios traces written and iconographic interpretations that depict the beloved disciple as "tak[ing] on the role of Christ" (*First, Second and Third John*, PNTC [Grand Rapids: Baker, 2014], 48–51). Although Parsenios identifies John 19:25–27 as the source for these interpretations, the nursing of the disciple at Jesus's breast likewise indicates his formation to reflect Jesus.
53. Paul A. Holloway, "Gender and Grief: Seneca's *Ad Marciam* and *Ad Helviam matrem*," in *Women and Gender in Ancient Religions*, ed. Stephen P. Ahearne-Kroll, Paul A. Holloway, and James A. Kelhoffer, WUNT 263 (Tübingen: Mohr Siebeck, 2010), 299–321.
54. Gaventa, *Our Mother Saint Paul* (Louisville: Westminster John Knox, 2007); Susan Eastman, *Recovering Paul's Mother Tongue: Language and Theology in Galatians* (Grand Rapids: Eerdmans, 2007); Margaret Aymer, "'Mother Knows Best': The Story of Mother Paul Revisited," in *Mother Goose, Mother Jones, Mommie Dearest: Biblical Mothers and Their Children*, ed. Cheryl A. Kirk-Duggan and Tina

Pippin, SemeiaSt 61 (Atlanta: SBL, 2009), 187–98; Ulrich Schmidt, "1 Thess 2.7b, c: 'Kleinkinder, die wie eine Amme Kinder versorgen,'" *NTS* 55 (2009): 116–20; Jennifer Houston McNeel, *Paul as Infant and Nursing Mother: Metaphor, Rhetoric, and Identity in 1 Thessalonians 2:5–8*, ECL 12 (Atlanta: SBL Press, 2014); Penniman, *Raised on Christian Milk*, 74–75.

55. Abraham Malherbe, "Gentile as a Nurse: The Cynic Background of I Thess ii," *NovT* 12 (1970): 203–17; Trevor J. Burke, "Pauline Paternity in 1 Thessalonians," *TynBul* 51 (2000): 59–80; Gaventa, *Our Mother*, 21–25, 43–50; Aymer, "Mother Knows Best"; McNeel, *Paul as Infant*, 61–98.
56. Susan M. Elliott, *Cutting Too Close for Comfort: Paul's Letter to the Galatians in its Anatolian Context*, JSNTSup 248 (London: T&T Clark, 2003); James R. Edwards, "Galatians 5:12: Circumcision, the Mother Goddess, and the Scandal of the Cross," *NovT* 53 (2011): 319–37.
57. While the focus here is certainly *mostly* on the male believers in Galatia, there is room for considering the female perspective as well, depending on what role mothers had in the circumcisions of their sons (see Haber, "Living and Dying for the Law," 2–4).
58. The connection to Sarah is clear in the text, and is implied in the reference to Isa 54:1, which makes use of the theme of a barren woman blessed with children common in the Hebrew Bible. Nevertheless, that Paul leaves her unnamed is significant rhetorically. Leaving this slot "blank," he can fill it himself—as he claims to do in Gal 4:19–20. Interestingly, Paul has also emphasized his legitimate Jewish heritage earlier in the letter (1:15; 2:15). Being born from Paul, then, integrates the Galatians into the "Israel of God" since they have a Jewish "mother" in him (6:16).
59. On anxieties surrounding proof of paternity see Turid Karlsen Seim, "Motherhood and the Making of Fathers in Antiquity: Contextualizing Genetics in the Gospel of John," in Ahearne-Kroll, Holloway, and Kelhoffer, *Women and Gender in Ancient Religions*, 99–123.
60. Among those who promote a two-seed theory are the Hippocratics, Soranus, and Galen. Chapter 3 § "Seeds, Bloods, and Spirit: Ancient Embryologies."
61. Gaventa comments that the passivity of Paul's labor "until Christ *is formed* in you" appears "flawed," but that it is appropriate on theological grounds (*Our Mother*, 37). Yet, it also should be noted that ancients predominantly *assumed* maternal passivity in labor (Hippocrates, *Nat. puer.* 19.532). Paul's passivity, therefore, reflects ancient parturitive theories *as a part of* his theological instruction.
62. There is a significant text-critical issue in 1 Thess 2:7 concerning whether or not Paul wrote "infants" (*nēpioi*) or "gentle" (*ēpioi*). See McNeel, *Paul as Infant*, 35–60.
63. Gaventa, *Our Mother*, 27.
64. Malherbe, "Gentle as a Nurse," 211–14; Burke, "Paul's Paternity," 75; Gaventa, *Our Mother*, 23–25; Otto Merk, "1 Thessalonians 2:1–12: An Exegetical-Theological Study," in *The Thessalonians Debate: Methodological Discord or Methodological*

Synthesis, ed. Karl P. Donfried and Johannes Beutler (Grand Rapids: Eerdmans, 2000), 106–7; McNeel, *Paul as Infant*, 77–80.

65. Penniman, *Raised on Christian Milk*, 32. For more on the "nutritive soul," see *Raised on Christian Milk*, 46–49. See also the analysis of Favorinus above.

66. Ibid., 32.

67. Penniman's comment that "[f]rom Paul's body flows a stream of pneumatic words, *no different* than the *spiritus*-carrying milk that flows from a mother," therefore, needs nuancing (Ibid., 73; emphasis added). Paul's word, his "milk," *is* different even if it is compared to breastmilk and makes use of its physiological constructions in the ancient Mediterranean world.

68. The following two sections have been developed from material previously published in Alicia D. Myers, "*Pater Nutrix*: Milk Metaphors and Character Formation in Hebrews and 1 Peter," in *Making Sense of Motherhood: Biblical and Systematic Perspectives*, ed. Beth Stovell (Eugene, OR: Wipf & Stock, 2016), 81–99.

69. Philo, *Every Good Person*, 160 (Colson, LCL). To this quotation, Gaventa (*Our Mother*, 43–44) also adds Philo, *Prelim. Studies* 19; *Agr.* 9; *Migr.* 29; *Dreams* 2.10.

70. Ron Guzmán and Michael W. Martin ("Is Hebrews 5:11–6:20 Really a Digression?" *NovT* 57 [2015]: 295–310) argue that while the vast majority of interpreters regard 5:11–6:12/20 a digression, only 5:11–14 adheres to the technical descriptions of a *digressio*. They do acknowledge the coherence of 5:11–6:20 as a deliberative section meant to prompt the audience onward in their education (303).

71. Harold W. Attridge, *Hebrews*, Hermeneia (Philadelphia: Fortress, 1989), 158–62; Craig R. Koester, *Hebrews*, AB 36 (Garden City, NY: Doubleday, 2001), 308–10; Peter S. Perry, "Making Fear Personal: Hebrews 5.11–6.12 and the Argument from Shame," *JSNT* 32 (2009): 104–5; James W. Thompson, *Hebrews*, PCNT (Grand Rapids: Baker, 2008), 120–22, 128–33.

72. Furthermore, the description of Sarah's "casting of seed" (*katabolēn spermatos*) in Heb 11:11 also indicates the author's awareness of common embryological and physiological theories on the milieu (Pieter van der Horst, "Sarah's Seminal Emission: Hebrews 11:11 in the Light of Ancient Embryology," in *Greeks, Romans, and Christians*, eds. David L. Balch, Everett Ferguson, and Wayne A. Meeks [Minneapolis: Fortress, 1991], 287–302).

73. The charge of milk-dependency corresponds to characterizations of effeminacy for those eating "luxurious" diets discussed above (Seneca, *Ep.* 45.13–33).

74. John A. L. Lee, "Hebrews 5:14 and ΕΞΙΣ: A History of Misunderstanding," *NovT* 39 (1997), 155; emphasis original. See also Mark Kiley, "A Note on Hebrews 5:14," *CBQ* 42 (1980): 501–3.

75. Lee, "Hebrews 5:14," 158 citing Aristotle, *Rhet.* 1362b.13; *Cat.* 8b.28. See also Hippocrates, *Nutriment* 34.3 that states, "Nourishment (*trophē*) is sometimes into growth and being, sometimes into being only, as it is with old men; sometimes in addition it is into strength. The condition (*diathesis*) of the athlete is not natural (*phusei*); a healthy state (*hexis hugeinē*) is superior to all" (Jones, LCL).

76. Lee, "Hebrews 5:14," 155; see also Plato, *Laws* 2.666a.7.
77. As Gaventa, Eastman, and McNeel argue for Paul's use of maternal imagery, Philip L. Tite also argues that "the function of metaphor within 1 Peter is not simply one of ornamental illustration of theological points"; rather, these metaphors are a key part of the persuasive power of the letter ("Nurslings, Milk and Moral Development in the Greco-Roman Context: A Reappraisal of the Paraenetic Utilization of Metaphor in 1 Peter 2.1–3," *JSNT* 31 [2009]: 372).
78. "Obedience" (*hypakoē*) is a recurring word in this section of 1 Peter (1:2, 14, 22).
79. The new begetting image continues in 2:9–12 which quotes Hosea 2:23 and alludes to the larger context of Hosea 1–3. Like the offspring of Hosea and Gomer, and the house of Israel that they represent, the audience of 1 Peter experiences a transition in birth/household status when their Father (Hosea or God) accepts them (1 Peter 2:10). The election by God as their Father results not only in a lifestyle change for the audience of 1 Peter, but an ethnic change as well (2:12). Once again, breastmilk impacts ethnic status.
80. The instrumental use of *dia logou zōntos theou kai menontos* (*through* the living and remaining word of God) in 1:23 reflects the corresponding use of the preposition in 1:3, where the believers are "begotten anew into a living hope *through* the resurrection of Jesus Christ from death" (*di anastaseōs Iēsou Christou ek nekrōn*).
81. These verses are a quotation of Isa 40:6–8 and use *rhēma* instead of *logos* for "word." Following verse 23, verses 24–25 explain the "remaining" presence of God's word, whether termed *logos* or *rhēma*. While Karen Jobes interprets the word change to indicate a different type of "word" being implied here (preached versus regenerating), she also admits these words are often "synonymous" ("Got Milk? Septuagint Psalm 33 and the Interpretation of 1 Peter 2:1–3," *WTJ* 63 [2002]: 3). Her desire to separate the two stems from not being able to reconcile the seed and milk metaphors in the passage, which rely on ancient physiological theories not explored in her article.
82. Jobes, "Got Milk," 4.
83. Tite, "Nurslings," 390.
84. Paul J. Achtemeier, *1 Peter*, Hermeneia (Minneapolis: Fortress, 1996), 145–46; M. Eugene Boring, *1 Peter*, ANTC (Nashville: Abingdon, 1999), 93; Duane F. Watson and Terrance Callan, *First and Second Peter*, PNTC (Grand Rapids: Baker, 2012), 44–45.
85. Dan G. McCartney, "λογικος in 1 Peter 2,2," *ZNW* 82 (1991), 128–32; Lewis R. Donelson, *I & II Peter and Jude*, NTL (Louisville: Westminster John Knox, 2010), 57; Watson and Callan understand the "spiritual milk" as a "corrective for the vice of deceit and involves verbal communication" (45).
86. Against this general trend are the studies of Tite, "Nurslings" and Troy W. Martin, "Christians as Babies: Metaphorical Reality in 1 Peter," in *Reading 1–2 Peter and Jude: A Resource for Students*, ed. Eric F. Mason and Troy W. Martin, RBS 77 (Atlanta: SBL, 2014), 107–12. Martin translates the phrase as "logical, undiluted milk" (109).

87. Tite translates the phrase as "high-quality word-like milk" to emphasize its connection to the practices of locating an ideal wet nurse in the Roman world ("Nurslings," 393, see also 377–86).
88. Tite, "Nurslings," 391. See *Od. Sol.* 8:12–18; 19:1–11; 35:5; 40:1. This is not to suggest there are no similarities between these *Odes* and 1 Peter; both reflect ancient physiological theories and understandings of breastmilk. In *Od. Sol.* 8, for example, the connection between formation in utero is paralleled with continued formation at God's breast. The result is a deep intimacy between God and the singer of the *Ode*. From this formation not only can God recognize "Solomon," but Solomon likewise recognizes God as the one who formed and nurtured him. Martin, in contrast to Tite, understands both God *and* Christ to be figured as male: God is the Father and Christ's blood/word of God is his sperm ("Christians as Babies," 110–11). The collapsing of word with Christ's blood, however, Martin overlooks the instrumental role of Jesus's crucifixion and resurrection in 1 Peter (1:3, 23), as well as the role of maternal blood in embryological and parturitive theories.
89. Jobes, "Got Milk," 8.
90. J. Francis ("'Like Newborn Babes'—The Image of the Child in 1 Peter 2:2–3," *StudBib* 3 [1978]: 113) also notes a similarity between "supernatural begetting" in 1 Peter and Johannine literature (John 1:12–13; 1 John 3:9).
91. On the contrasts between NT and Greco-Roman masculinities see Maud W. Gleason, "By Whose Gender Standards (if Anybody's) Was Jesus a Real Man?" in *New Testament Masculinities*, ed. Stephen D. Moore and Janice Capel Anderson, SemSt 45 (Atlanta: SBL, 2003), 325–27; Jennifer A. Glancy, *Corporal Knowledge: Early Christian Bodies* (Oxford: Oxford University Press, 2010), 24–47; Brittany E. Wilson, *Unmanly Men: Refigurations of Masculinity in Luke-Acts* (Oxford: Oxford University Press, 2015).

CHAPTER 5

1. See Chapter 2 § "Jars and Houses: Constructing the Female Body."
2. Feminine virtue was an important topic in the Roman world. Plutarch devotes an entire work to it, appropriately titled *Women's Virtues*. See also the discussion of women's competitions for honor in Zeba Crook, "Honor, Shame and Social Status Revisited," *JBL* 128 (2009): 591–611.
3. Suzanne Dixon, *The Roman Mother* (Norman: University of Oklahoma Press, 1987); Emily A. Hemelrijk, *Matrona Docta: Educated Women in the Roman Élite from Cornelia to Julia Domna*, Routledge Classical Monographs (London: Routledge, 1999). On legal independence (*sui iuris*), see Judith Evans Grubbs, *Women and the Law in the Roman Empire: A Sourcebook on Marriage, Divorce, and Widowhood* (London: Routledge, 2002), 20–21.
4. *Eth. nic.* 9.7.1168a24–27. All quotations from Rackham, LCL unless otherwise noted.

5. Dixon, *Roman Mother*, 44–47.
6. On *pater potestas* and *manu* in marriage practices of the Roman world, see Grubbs, *Women and the Law*, 20–23.
7. Plutarch frequently cites the maternal ancestry of his biographical subjects (*Alex.* 2.1; *Alc.* 1.1–2; *Ant.* 2.1; *Sol.* 1.2; *Per.* 3.1–2; *Cor.* 1.2–4; etc.) and notes the attachment that remains between sons and mothers, especially if those mothers were widows who remained unmarried (*Cor.* 4.3–4; *TG* 1.1–5). Dixon (*Roman Mother*, 15) cites Plutarch, *Cat. Min.* 3.1 and Tacitus, *Agr.* 4. On the sustained relationships between fathers and the daughters who continued their paternal lines, see Judith P. Hallett, *Fathers and Daughters in Roman Society: Women and the Elite Family* (Princeton: Princeton University Press, 1984), 62–149, esp. 133–49.
8. Women were, nevertheless, required to have a male guardian (*tutela mulierum*). This practice also eventually ended by the early fourth century (Grubbs, *Women and the Law*, 23–36, 43).
9. Susan E. Hylen, *A Modest Apostle: Thecla and the History of Women in the Early Church* (Oxford: Oxford University Press, 2015), 35–36.
10. Dixon, *Roman Mother*, 51–60. A funerary inscription dedicated to Murdia, from Rome in the first cent BCE, notes her equal care for her children in spite of her being a step-mother to many of them. The author praises Murdia, since "she made all her sons equal heirs after she gave a bequest to her daughter. A mother's love is composed of her affection for her children and equal distribution to each child" (*CIL* VI.10230 = *ILS* 8394.L; Mary R. Lefkowitz and Maureen B. Fant, eds., *Women's Life in Greece and Rome: A Sourcebook in Translation* [Baltimore: Johns Hopkins University Press, 1992], 17).
11. This most often translated into children being reared in their father's household. Thus, having divorced her first husband at her father's request, the pregnant Livia birthed Drusus, who was promptly taken to his biological father's house after she delivered the child in the Imperial Palace (Tacitus, *Ann.* 1.10; 5.1; Suetonius, *Aug.* 62, 69; *Tib.* 4; *Claud.* 1).
12. Dixon, *Roman Mother*, 65–67.
13. Messalus explains: "The object of this rigorous system (*disciplina ac severitas*) was that the natural disposition of every child, while still sound at the core and untainted, not warped as yet by any vicious tendencies, might at once lay hold with the heart and soul on virtuous accomplishments, and whether its bent was towards the army, or the law, or the pursuit of eloquence, might make that its sole aim and drink up its fullness" (Tacitus, *Dial.* 28.7).
14. Eleanor Winsor Leach, "Venus, Thetis and the Social Construction of Maternal Behavior," *The Classical Journal* 92 (1997): 366–68.
15. See a more detailed analysis of these narratives in Rebecca Langlands, *Sexual Morality in Ancient Rome* (Cambridge: Cambridge University Press, 2002), 84–109.
16. Plutarch, *Cor.* 35.3. Translations from Perrin, LCL unless otherwise noted.

17. In his biography of Gaius, Plutarch writes that the people of Rome "honored Cornelia as much as for her children as for her father" (*GG* 4.4 [Perrin, LCL]). The *populares* were figured as legendary defenders of the plebians; their primary opponents were the *optimates*, defenders of the patricians. Suzanne Dixon, *Cornelia: Mother of the Gracchi*, Women of the Ancient World (London: Routledge, 2007).
18. Dixon, *Cornelia*, 52–53.
19. Translation from Dixon, *Cornelia*, 51. See also Plutarch, *TG* 1.1–6; Corrado Petrocelli, "Cornelia the Matron," in *Roman Women*, ed. Augusto Fraschetti, trans. Linda Lappin (Chicago: University of Chicago Press, 2001), 58.
20. Plutarch, *GG* 19. See also Seneca, *Marc.* 16.3 (in contrast to the ever-mourning Octavia at *Marc.* 2.3–5); *Helv.* 17.3.
21. Livy 27.37; 5.25. Milnor reviews women's roles in the proscriptions (*Gender, Domesticity, and the Age of Augustus: Inventing Private Life*, Oxford Studies in Classical Literature and Gender Theory [Oxford: Oxford University Press, 2005], 186–238) as well as the attention given to repeal of the *lex Oppia*, which inspired women to come to the forum in support of its repeal (pp. 154–85; Livy 34). When a similar tax limiting female displays of luxury was again proposed, the Roman matron Hortensia convinced the men through her own speech in the forum (Appian, *Bell. civ.* 4.32–34). Hortensia's ability is praised by Quintilian, who argues that her example demonstrates the importance of women's education for the good of their children (*Inst.* 1.1.6; Valerius Maximus 8.4.3; Milnor, *Gender*, 221–26).
22. Milnor, *Gender*, 32.
23. Ibid. Langlands notes the importance of performed "purity" (*pudicitia*) by Roman matrons, who also worshipped a goddess so named (*Sexual Morality in Ancient Rome*, 37–77).
24. The *leges Iuliae* included the *lex Iulia de maritandis ordinbus* and the *lex Iulia de adulteriis* (Grubbs, *Women and the Law*, 83–85).
25. Also called the "right of (three) children"; Grubbs, *Women and the Roman Law*, 37–43.
26. Hylen, *Modest Apostle*, 32–36; Grubbs, *Roman Women and the Law*, 37.
27. Milnor, *Gender*, 145.
28. Ibid., 147–49; Dionysius of Halicarnassus, *Rom. ant.* 2.1–29, esp. 2.24.2.
29. Translation from Milnor, *Gender*, 144.
30. Ibid., 145; Langlands, *Sexual Morality*, 329–32. See Tacitus, *Ann.* 3.22–24.
31. Milnor, *Gender*, 151.
32. On common constructions of stepmothers in Mediterranean antiquity see Patricia A. Watson, *Ancient Stepmothers: Myth, Misogyny and Reality*, Mnemosyne 143 (Leiden: Brill, 1995).
33. Translations of Tacitus's *Annals* are from J. Jackson's 1925 LCL volumes.
34. The irony here is surely not lost on Tacitus, since Caligula succeeded Tiberius (*Ann.* 5.1; 6.45–50).

35. Britannicus was Claudius's natural son, through his wife Messalina. While Britannicus acts as Tacitus's tragic foil for Nero and Agrippina, Messalina's famously adulterous behavior—for which she was eventually executed—was perhaps sufficient reason for Claudius to prefer Nero to his own son as successor (*Ann.* 11.26–38).
36. On Livia's sustained popularity see Dixon, *Roman Mother*, 97. Livia fashioned herself as the ideal Roman matron in part by sponsoring the cult of Concordia, which symbolized not only the political and civil concord of Rome, but also family harmony (Beth Severy, *Augustus and the Family at the Birth of the Roman Empire* [London: Routledge, 2003], 131–38).
37. Tacitus explicitly identifies Agrippina's ambition with gender deviancy writing, "From this moment it [Rome] was a changed state, and all things moved at the fiat of a woman—but not a woman who, as Messalina, treated in wantonness the Roman Empire as a toy. It was a tight-drawn, almost *masculine tyranny*" (*Ann.* 12.7; emphasis added).
38. Anna Rebecca Solevåg, *Birthing Salvation: Gender and Class in Early Christian Childbearing Discourse*, BIS 121 (Leiden: Brill, 2013).
39. Stephen D. Moore and Janice Capel Anderson, eds., *New Testament Masculinities*, SemSt 45 (Atlanta: SBL, 2003); Colleen M. Conway, *Behold the Man: Jesus and Greco-Roman Masculinity* (Oxford: Oxford University Press, 2008); Brittany E. Wilson, *Unmanly Men: Refigurations of Masculinity in Luke-Acts* (Oxford: Oxford University Press, 2015); Alicia D. Myers, "Gender, Rhetoric, and Recognition: (Re) defining Masculinity in the Gospel of John," *JSNT* 38 (2015): 191–218.
40. I have limited my examination of extracanonical writings to these works due to their relative chronological proximity to the NT (ca. 150–211 CE), their popularity and lasting influence in Christian traditions, as well as their attention to the topic of mothers.
41. Most scholars agree that the Pastoral Epistles are pseudonymous letters written in Paul's name after his death (ca. 100 CE). For this reason, I am using the title "Pastor" to refer to the author these letters. Solevåg, *Birthing Salvation*, 85–87; Marianne Bjelland Kartzow, *Gossip and Gender: Other of Speech in the Pastoral Epistles*, BZNW 164 (Berlin/New York: de Gruyter, 2009), 3–5; Jennifer A. Glancy, "Protocols of Masculinity in the Pastoral Epistles," in Moore and Anderson, *New Testament Masculinities*, 235–64.
42. Stanley E. Porter ("What does it Mean to be 'Saved by Childbirth' [1 Timothy 2.15]?" *JSNT* 49 [1993]: 93–94) and Solevåg (*Birthing Salvation*, 91–135) argue for elements of eschatological salvation; Moyer Hubbard ("Kept Safe Through Childbearing: Maternal Mortality, Justification By Faith, and the Social Setting of 1 Timothy 2:15," *JETS* 55 [2012]: 743–62) and Christopher R. Hutson ("'Saved through Childbearing' The Jewish Context of 1 Timothy 2:15," *NovT* [2014]: 392–410) argue for "being kept safe through/during childbearing"; Annette Weissenrieder ("What Does σωθήσεται δὲ διὰ τῆς τεκνογονίας

'To Be Saved by Childbearing' Mean [1 Timothy 2:15]? Insights from Ancient Medical and Philosophical Texts," *Early Christianity* 5 [2014]: 313–36) advocates for a combination of healthful and eschatological salvation by means of childbearing, while Matthias Becker ("Ehe als Sanatorium: Plutarchs *Coniugalia Praecepta* und die Pastoralbriefe," *NovT* 52 [2010]: 241–66) highlights the connection between Plutarch's *Conjungal Precepts* and 1 Timothy in presenting marriage as a way to heal *vitium feminae* (feminine vice). Kenneth L. Waters, Sr. ("Saved Through Childbearing: Virtues as Children in 1 Timothy 2:11–15," *JBL* 123 [2004]: 703–35) takes a very different route by offering an allegorical reading of the passage, wherein the virtues of remaining "in faith, and love, and holiness with temperance" are the children by whose birth a woman is saved.

43. The majority of scholars opt for the more common instrumental *dia* ("by means of" or "through"). Only those arguing for the reading of "being kept safe" must opt for the much more rare (though possible) temporal *dia* ("during"). See Hubbard, "Kept Safe," 756–57; Hutson, "Saved Through Childbearing," 408; as well as Weissenrieder's response ("What Does," 313, n. 3 and 315, n. 11).
44. Most scholars note the technical use of *teknogonia* as a reference to the specific act of childbirth in the larger culture, as well as 1 Timothy's own preference for *teknotropheō* as the general description of "childrearing" in 5:10 (e.g., Weissenrieder, "What Does," 327–31). However, some scholars struggling to make sense of the verse due to the very real dilemmas of maternal death in childbirth, infertile couples, as well as miscarried and still-birthed children, attempt to solve this crisis by claiming *teknogonia* refers to general maternal or parental activities (e.g., Douglas J. Moo, "Interpretation of 1 Timothy 2:11–15: A Rejoinder," *TJ* 2 [1981]: 205–6; Luke Timothy Johnson, *Letters to Paul's Delegates: 1 Timothy, 2 Timothy, Titus* [Valley Forge, PA: Trinity Press International, 1996], 133–34).
45. Solevåg, *Birthing Salvation*, 88.
46. See especially Chapter 2 § "Jars and Houses: Constructing the Female Body."
47. Hippocrates, *Nat. mul.* 2.315; 3.316; 8.324; 35.379; 43.388–89; 53.395; 67.402.
48. Weissenrieder, "What Does," 322–25.
49. See Chapter 2 § "Pandora and Eve: Hellenistic Interpretations on the Origins of 'Woman.'" On the social and economic aspects of women's adornment see Alicia J. Batten, "Neither Gold nor Braided Hair (1 Timothy 2.9; 1 Peter 3.3): Adornment, Gender, and Honor in Antiquity," *NTS* 55 (2009): 484–501.
50. Vita Daphna Arbel, *Forming Femininity in Antiquity: Eve, Gender, and Ideology in the Greek* Life of Adam and Eve (Oxford: Oxford University Press, 2012), 34–36; *LAE* [Latin] 18.1–21.3.
51. 1 Sam 1:3–18; Luke 1:6–7; Silicus Italicus, *Pun.* 13.613–19; Aeschylus, *Eum.* 661.
52. Tal Ilan, *Jewish Women in Greco-Roman Palestine* (Peabody, MA: Hendrickson, 1996), 111–16.

53. Hutson, "Saved through Childbearing," 399–403. He also traces the connections made between these three commandments and Eve's sin in Gen. Rab. 17.8 and the Palestinian Talmud (*Šabb.* 2.6.1–2).
54. See Chapter 2 § "Jars and Houses: Constructing the Female Body"; Cynthia Baker, *Rebuilding the House of Israel: Archaeologies of Gender in Jewish Antiquity*, Divinations (Stanford, CA: Stanford University Press, 2002), 34.
55. See also Silicus Italicus, *Pun.* 13.613–19.
56. Josephus, *Ant.* 2.9.4; Josephus highlights Jocabed's righteousness along with that of her husband in 2.9.3–4. In Exod 1:19 the Hebrew midwives describe the ease of delivery for the Hebrew women in contrast to Egyptian women. *Asen. Isa.* 11.7–14; *Prot. Jas.* 18–20. Jennifer A. Glancy, *Corporal Knowledge* (Oxford: Oxford University Press, 2010), 81–136.
57. Isa 26:17–18; Jer 4:31; 49:22 (30:16 LXX); Mic 4:10; John 16:21; Rom 8:21. See also Beverly Roberts Gaventa, *Our Mother Saint Paul* (Louisville: Westminster John Knox, 2007), 56–58.
58. On the overlaps between Rev 12 and various ancient myths see David L. Balch, "'A Woman Clothed with the Sun' and the 'Great Red Dragon' Seeking to 'Devour her Child' (Rev 12:1, 4) in Roman Domestic Art," in *The New Testament and Early Christian Literature in Greco-Roman Context*, ed. John Fotopoulos, NovTSup 122 (Leiden: Brill, 2006), 287–314.
59. The salvation birthed and experienced by this woman is contrasted with the destruction of the "Babylon the Great," who is the only woman called a "mother" in Revelation (17:5). This "whore" births multiple prostitutes rather than a single savior. She, and her uncontrolled sexuality, act as a conduit for chaos. Order/life is only firmly secured when she is destroyed by the Masculine Divine in Revelation's salvific narrative (Rev 18–19). The whore Babylon is replaced by the "bride of the Lamb," the "new Jerusalem," who dresses in "fine linen, bright and clean" (19:8) and who is a virginal bride, intact and ready to submit to her Lord's rule (Rev 21). For a counter-reading of Babylon's whore-motherhood see Stephanie Buckhanon Crowder, *When Momma Speaks: The Bible and Motherhood from a Womanist Perspective* (Louisville: Westminster John Knox, 2016), 34–35, 109.
60. Solevåg, *Birthing Salvation*, 96–100.
61. Glancy, "Protocols of Masculinity," 238–49; Mary Rose D'Angelo, "'Knowing How to Preside Over His Own Household': Imperial Masculinity and Christian Asceticism in the Pastorals, *Hermas*, and Luke-Acts," in Moore and Anderson, *New Testament Masculinities*, 271–78; Solevåg, *Birthing Salvation*, 106–10.
62. Solevåg, *Birthing Salvation*, 110–12.
63. The Pastor could encourage a connection between these women and Eve by linking "the devil" who holds as "captives" (*ezōgrēmenoi*) those resisting God's will in 2:24–26 just prior to mentioning the "captivation" (*aichmalōzontes*) of silly women in 3:6. See Kartzow, *Gossip and Gender*, 137. Kartzow also includes extensive evidence

on the association between women, gossip, and sexual promiscuity in the ancient Mediterranean world (pp. 67–116).

64. Ephesians's interpretation of Gen 1–2 reflects other Jewish interpretations that understood marriage as the restoration of the once whole *adam* (Gen 1:26–27; 2:18–25) described in Chapter 2.

65. The connections between the NT household codes and household ideals from the larger Greco-Roman world, both Roman and Jewish, have been explored extensively and are also reflected in the discussion of Roman matrons above. David L. Balch, *Let Wives Be Submissive: The Domestic Code in 1 Peter*, SBLMS 26 (Chico, CA: Scholars Press, 1981); Benjamin G. Wold, "Family Ethics in *4QInstruction* and the New Testament," *NovT* 50 (2008): 286–300; Margaret Y. MacDonald, "Beyond Identification of the Topos of Household Management: Reading the Household Codes in Light of Recent Methodologies and Theoretical Proposals in the Study of the New Testament," *NTS* 57 (2009): 65–90.

66. First Peter 1:18 contrasts the "perishable" (*phthartois*) nature of "silver and gold" (*argyriō ē chrysiō*) and the believers' previous "conduct" (*anastrophēs*) with the "honorable blood of Christ" (see also 1:7). This blood participates in the regeneration and rebirth of these believers by means of "not perishable but imperishable seed" (*ouk ek sporas phthartēs all aphthartou*, 1:23) so that they can be holy in their "conduct" (*anastrophē*, 1:15). In 1 Peter 3:1–3, the author again incorporates these ideas by highlighting "gold" (*chrysiōn*) in contrast to "imperishableness" (*aphthartō*) of a woman/wife's submissive "conduct" (*anastrophēs*). This combination of ideas in 1 Peter 3 participates in the author's larger equation of submission with imitating Christ so that virtuous women/wives resemble Christ just as the slaves of 2:18–25.

67. Chapter 4 § "Longing for the Pure, Word-like Milk: 1 Peter."

68. Betsy J. Bauman-Martin, "Women on the Edge: New Perspectives on Women in the Petrine *Haustafel*," *JBL* 123 (2004): 265; see also pp. 273–74.

69. Ibid., 272.

70. For recent overviews on the dates and manuscript traditions of these writings see Solevåg, *Birthing Salvation*, 137–41, 199–203; Richard I. Pervo, *The Acts of Paul: A New Translation with Introduction and Commentary* (Eugene, OR: Cascade Books, 2014), 41–78.

71. Gail P. C. Streete contrasts the ready acceptance of Perpetua and Felicitas in contrast to the debates surrounding Thecla ("Buying the Stairway to Heaven: Perpetua and Thecla as Early Christian Heroines," in *A Feminist Companion to the New Testament Apocrypha*, ed. Amy-Jill Levine with Maria Mayo Robbins [Cleveland: Pilgrim, 2006], 186–205). Thecla's ambiguous legacy, artistic representations, and the popularity of her shrine in Seleucia indicate her lasting influence. Steven J. Davis, *The Cult of Saint Thecla: A Tradition of Women's Piety in Late Antiquity* (Oxford: Oxford University Press, 2001); Elizabeth A. Castelli, *Martyrdom and Memory: Early Christian Culture Making*, Gender, Theory, and Religion (New York: Columbia University Press, 2004), 134–71; Hylen, *Modest Apostle*, 91–113.

72. Translations from Pervo, *Acts of Paul*, with some minor adjustments.
73. Thecla displays a love-sickness that is common in Hellenistic novels. Susan A. Calef, "Thecla 'Tried and True' and the Inversion of Romance," in Levine and Robbins, *A Feminist Companion to the New Testament Apocrypha*, 169–70; Matt Jackson-McCabe, "Women and Eros in Greek Magic and the *Acts of Paul and Thecla*," in *Women and Gender in Ancient Religions*, ed. Stephen P. Ahearne-Kroll, Paul A. Holloway, James A. Kelhoffer, WUNT 263 (Tübingen: Mohr Siebeck, 2010), 267–78; B. Diane Lipsett, *Desiring Conversion: Hermas, Thecla, Aseneth* (Oxford: Oxford University Press, 2011), 58–64.
74. Calef, "Thecla Tried and True," 172.
75. On the importance of Thecla's chastity, as well as its anti-social stance, see Virginia Burrus, *Chastity as Autonomy: Women in the Stories of the Apocryphal Acts* (Lewiston, NY: Mellen, 1987), 53–60; Hylen, *Modest Apostle*, 79–81.
76. Johannes Vorster, "Construction of Culture through the Construction of Person: The Construction of Thecla in the *Acts of Thecla*," in Levine and Robbins, *A Feminist Companion to the New Testament Apocrypha*, 110–11.
77. Streete suggests that Paul fears that he might give in to the temptation of Thecla's beauty and acts "cowardly" toward her ("Buying the Stairway to Heaven," 198–99).
78. On the ambiguity of Thecla's transformation: Lipsett, *Desiring Conversion*, 84–85; Hylen, *Modest Apostle*, 71–90; Cornelia B. Horn, "Suffering Children, Parental Authority and the Quest for Liberation?: A Tale of Three Girls in the *Acts of Paul (and Thecla)*, the *Act(s) of Peter*, the *Acts of Nerseus and Achilleus*, and the *Epistle of Pseudo-Titus*," in Levine and Robbins, *A Feminist Companion to the New Testament Apocrypha*, 121–30.
79. Hylen, *Modest Apostle*, 88–89.
80. See also the positive presentation of Paul's disciple, the householder and father, Onesiphorus. Nevertheless, after days praying and fasting in a tomb with Paul and their parents, Onesiphorus's two boys require physical salvation in the form of food and cry out, "we're hungry" (23). This plot device enables the boys to find Thecla in the marketplace and reunite her with Paul while underscoring the connection between children and worldly requirements.
81. Horn, "Suffering Children," 126.
82. Romans believed that children solidified marital harmony (*concordia*) and fellowship (Plutarch, *Coniugalia Praecepta*; Andrew S. Jacobs, "'Her Own Proper Kinship': Marriage, Class and Women in the Apocryphal Acts of the Apostles," in Levine and Robbins, *A Feminist Companion to the New Testament Apocrypha*," 24–40; Becker, "Ehe als Sanatorium," 243–49).
83. Translations of *Acts of Andrew* are from Dennis R. MacDonald, *The Acts of Andrew*, Early Christian Apocrypha 1 (Santa Rosa, CA: Polebridge, 2005).
84. Jacobs notes the transformation of Maximilla's bedroom from a site of conjugal relations to a "Christian meeting-place" or "sacred *syngeneia*, i.e., kinship" ("Her

Own Proper Kinship," 37–40). In this way, the *Acts of Andrew* rejects Roman conjugal ethics for the new family of believers.

85. On the Platonic overtones see Solevåg, *Birthing Salvation*, 145–48; Caroline T. Schroeder, "The Erotic Asceticism of the *Passion of Andrew*: The Apocryphal *Acts of Andrew*, the Greek Novel, and Platonic Philosophy," in Levine and Robbins, *A Feminist Companion to the New Testament Apocrypha*, 47–59.
86. Commenting on the contrast between Maximilla and Stratocles, Solevåg writes, "By means of the imagery of childbearing, the women in the text have in fact been relegated to the sidelines. It seems that the reproductive capacity to regenerate in the believing community belongs exclusively to men, not to women" (*Birthing Salvation*, 173).
87. Compare Andrew's manly courage in the face of his death (Acts Andr. 55). Solevåg, *Birthing Salvation*, 151–61.
88. Outi Lehtipuu writes, "If virginity and continence are preconditions of salvation, Maximilla clearly sacrifices her slave girl and denies her salvation. Yet the author of the *Acts of Andrew* takes no notice of this; for him, Euclia is just an insignificant pagan slave, a useful instrument for Maximilla in her pursuit of a virtuous and pure life" ("The Example of Thecla and the Example(s) of Paul: Disputing Women's Role in Early Christianity," in Ahearne-Kroll, Holloway, and Kelhoffer, *Women and Gender in Ancient Religions*, 363). See also Solevåg, *Birthing Salvation*, 158–68, 189–95.
89. Anna Rebecca Solevåg, "Adam, Eve, and the Serpent in the Acts of Andrew," in *Hidden Truths from Eden: Esoteric Readings of Genesis 1–3*, ed. Caroline Vander Stichele and Susanne Scholz, SemSt 76 (Atlanta: SBL Press, 2014), 12–14.
90. Solevåg, *Birthing Salvation*, 180–86.
91. On the textual history associated with the *Martyrdom of Perpetua and Felicitas* see Jan N. Bremmer and Marco Formisano, "Perpetua's Passions: A Brief Introduction," in *Perpetua's Passions: Multidisciplinary Approaches to the* Passio Perpetuae et Felicitatis, ed. Jan N. Bremmer and Marco Formisano (Oxford: Oxford University Press, 2012), 2–7.
92. Scholars generally agree that Perpetua wrote the section attributed to her (e.g., Bremmer and Formisano, "Introduction," 5; Walter Ameling, "*Femina Liberaliter Instituta*—Some Thoughts on a Martyr's Liberal Education," in Bremmer and Formisano, *Perpetua's Passions*, 78–102).
93. Hanne Sigismund-Nielson, "Vibia Perpetua—An Indecent Woman," in Bremmer and Formisano, *Perpetua's Passions*, 114–16.
94. Translations and numbering of the *Martyrdom of Perpetua and Felicitas* are from Joseph Furrell and Craig Williams, trans., "The Passion of Saints Perpetua and Felicity," in Bremmer and Formisano, *Perpetua's Passions*, 14–23.
95. Sigismund-Nielson, "Vibia Perpetua," 107–10.
96. In 1.iii the intentions of Perpetua's father called the "ruses of Satan." Perpetua subsequently experiences a vision after each encounter with her father. In two of

these dream visions she defeats symbols of Satan: first, a dragon, whose head she tramples; second, an Egyptian, whom she kicks in the face and she kills by stepping on his head. In these scenes, Perpetua enacts the promise of Gen 3:15 (LXX) that Eve's offspring ("seed," *spermatos*) will strike or guard (*tērēsei*) the serpent's head, while his offspring (*spermatos*) will strike the heel.

97. Sigismund-Nielson, "Vibia Perpetua," 110.
98. As Candida Moss notes ("Blood Ties: Martyrdom, Motherhood, and Family in the *Passion of Perpetua and Felicity*," in Ahearne-Kroll, Holloway, and Kelhoffer, *Women and Gender in Ancient Religions*, 203–5), neither Perpetua nor Felicitas abandon their children. Instead, their children also become part of God's household through God's miraculous provision and their rearing by another who is explicitly identified as a believer. In 15.vii, the audience is told Felicitas's daughter is raised by a "sister" (*soror*), and in 3.v Perpetua secures care for her son from her mother and brother, who was identified as a catechumen in 2.ii. Moss argues that Perpetua's mother is also a Christian since Perpetua writes that her father is "the only one in my whole family who would not rejoice at my martyrdom" (3.v; 5.vi).
99. Jan N. Bremmer, "Felicitas: The Martyrdom of a Young African Woman," in Bremmer and Formisano, *Perpetua's Passions*, 43.
100. Solevåg, *Birthing Salvation*, 207; Lesley Ann Dean-Jones, *Women's Bodies in Classical Greek Science* (Oxford: Clarendon, 1996), 209–11. See also Hippocrates, *Oct.*; Aristotle, *Gen. an.* 4.4.772b9–11.
101. See Chapter 3 § "A Necessary Sacrifice: Childbirth, Combat, and Blood-letting."
102. Sigismund-Nielson, "Vibia Perpetua," 114–17.
103. Jacobs describes the women of the Apocryphal Acts as "apostolic homewreckers" ("Her Own Proper Kinship," 18–19).
104. Hylen, *Modest Apostle*, 73–85; Solevåg, *Birthing Salvation*, 177–89; Craig Williams, "Perpetua's Gender: A Latinist Reads the *Passio Perpetuae et Felicitatis*," in Bremmer and Formisano, *Perpetua's Passions*, 54–77.
105. In the *Acts of Peter*, for example, the paralysis of Peter's daughter is meant as salvation for her and men who would be tempted by her virginal beauty (Horn, "Suffering Children," 130–37). The chastity of Perpetua and Felicitas is guaranteed by the narrative due to their martyrdom. Thecla's continued unmarried existence, in contrast, brings condemnation for her from Western Church Fathers, most notably, Tertullian (Streete, "Buying the Stairway," 196).

CHAPTER 6

1. Chapter 2 § "[Hu]man or Un[hu]man: Masculinity in the Greco-Roman World."
2. Flemming, *Medicine and the Making of Roman Women: Gender, Nature, and Authority from Celsus to Galen* (Oxford: Oxford University Press, 2000), 119.
3. Virgin and chaste women are the topic of much reflection, as in the cases of Thecla and Maxmilla, since their faithfulness to God (or gods) results in their

realignment of the married and maternal ideal of womanhood. These women can convey gender liminal traits (i.e., Thecla's wearing of a garment "styled" like a man's), but they remain at least potentially female, and therefore, feminine. For this reason, the sustained virginity of such women was a source of some concern—hence, Paul's concern for Thecla and the various stories of the Roman Vestal virgins, whose intact virginity was tied to the intact safety of Rome (e.g., Mary F. Foskett, *A Virgin Conceived: Mary and Classical Representations of Virginity* [Bloomington: Indiana University Press, 2002], 55–58).

4. Dale B. Martin, "Contradictions of Masculinity: Ascetic Inseminators and Menstruating Men in Greco-Roman Culture," in *Generation and Degeneration: Tropes of Reproduction in Literature and History from Antiquity through Early Modern Europe*, ed. Valeria Finucci and Kevin Brownlee (Durham, NC: Duke University Press, 2001), 81–108.
5. Commenting on Gregory of Nyssa's use of feminine imagery in his own theology, Virginia Burrus comments, "Gregory continually makes himself female so as ultimately to become more male" (*"Begotten, Not Made": Conceiving Manhood in Late Antiquity*, Figurae: Reading Medieval Culture [Stanford, CA: Stanford University Press, 2000], 187). The same can be said for the feminized Savior, apostles, and teachers in the NT and *Acts of Andrew*.
6. This book has focused on women and female bodies in the soteriological scheme of the NT and other early Christian literature. The conclusions offered here, however, do not indicate that conveying salvation as a type of masculinization is not equally difficult for "men" or those occupying male bodies, all of whom likewise must negotiate gender debates and embodied spaces in these theological conversations. For further discussions see Burrus, *Begotten Not Made*; Stephen D. Moore, *God's Gym: Divine Male Bodies of the Bible* (London: Routledge, 1996).
7. Emily A. Hemelrijk, *Matrona Docta: Educated Women in the Roman Élite from Cornelia to Julia Domna*, Routledge Classical Monographs (London: Routledge, 1999).
8. B. J. Brooten, *Women Leaders in Ancient Synagogues: Inscriptional Evidence and Background Issues*, BJS 36 (Chico, CA: Scholars Press, 1982); Ross Shepard Kraemer, *Unreliable Witnesses: Religion, Gender, and History in the Greco-Roman Mediterranean* (Oxford: Oxford University Press, 2011), 179–241. Some women were also called "mother of the synagogue," which parallels the masculine title, "father of the synagogue" to denote their leadership status. See, esp. Kraemer, *Unreliable Witnesses*, 232–41 where she emphasizes the impossibility of knowing exactly what happened in ancient synagogues, thus making it impossible to identify precisely who could hold "leadership" roles (and what said roles would entail). What is clear, however, from these inscriptions is that women were thus honored. Kraemer's observation also extends to early Christian communities, whose awareness, use, and conformity to any sort of institutionalized norm (such as the Pastoral Epistles) cannot be confirmed. Indeed, from the exploration of

texts in this book, we see a variety of practices and constructions described in literature, all of which offer only a glimpse of the scope of potential practices and constructions in developing Christian communities.

9. Kristina Milnor, *Gender, Domesticity, and the Age of Augustus: Inventing Private Life*, Oxford Studies in Classical Literature and Gender Theory (Oxford: Oxford University Press, 2005), 27–34; Jodi Vandenberg-Daves, *Modern Motherhood: An American History* (New Brunswick, NJ: Rutgers University Press, 2014), 189–90, 280–86.
10. See, for example, Douglas J. Moo, "Interpretation of 1 Timothy 2:11–15: A Rejoinder," *TJ* 2 [1981]: 198–222; Wayne Grudem, *Evangelical Feminism and Biblical Truth: An Analysis of More than 100 Disputed Questions* (Wheaton, IL: Crossway, 2012). Dale B. Martin criticizes the dominant narrative of "Christian values" in American Christianity in *Sex and the Single Savior: Gender and Sexuality in Biblical Interpretation* (Louisville: Westminster John Knox, 2006), 122. Candida R. Moss and Joel S. Baden address the persistent stigma of childlessness in *Reconceiving Infertility: Biblical Perspectives on Procreation and Childlessness* (Princeton: Princeton University Press, 2015), 1–20.
11. Rebecca Jo Plant, *Mom: The Transformation of Motherhood in Modern America* (Chicago: University of Chicago Press, 2010), 116–17.
12. Vandenberg-Daves, *Modern Motherhood*, 173.
13. Plant, *Mom*, 10.
14. Vandenberg-Daves, *Modern Motherhood*, 178–79.
15. Ibid., 181.
16. Ibid., 181–82.
17. Ibid., 201, 241–42.
18. Tracing the history of family assistance and welfare laws, Vandenberg-Daves writes, "American society had long resisted both the idea that mothering was work and the notion that the paid labor of mothers was necessary to many families. The idea of women supporting children outside of marriage was also anathema" (Ibid., 217). Patricia Hill Collins, *From Black Power to Hip Hop: Racism, Nationalism, and Feminism* (Philadelphia: Temple University Press, 2006), 71.

Bibliography

Abrams, Judith Z. *Judaism and Disability: Portrayals in Ancient Texts from the Tanach through the Bavli*. Washington, DC: Gallaudet University Press, 1998.

Achtemeier, Paul J. *1 Peter*. Hermeneia. Minneapolis: Fortress, 1996.

Ahearne-Kroll, Stephen P. "'Who Are My Mother and My Brothers?' Family Relations and Family Language in the Gospel of Mark." *JR* 81 (2001): 1–25.

Ameling, Walter. "*Femina Liberaliter Instituta*—Some Thoughts on a Martyr's Liberal Education." Pages 78–102 in *Perpetua's Passions: Multidisciplinary Approaches to the* Passio Perpetuae et Felicitatis. Edited by Jan N. Bremmer and Marco Formisano. Oxford: Oxford University Press, 2012.

Anderson, Gary A., and Michael E. Stone. *A Synopsis of the Books of Adam and Eve*. EJL 5. Atlanta: Scholars Press, 1994.

Arbel, Vita Daphna. *Forming Femininity in Antiquity: Eve, Gender, and Ideology in the Greek* Life of Adam and Eve. Oxford: Oxford University Press, 2012.

Attridge, Harold W. *Hebrews*. Hermeneia. Philadelphia: Fortress, 1989.

Aymer, Margaret. "'Mother Knows Best': The Story of Mother Paul Revisited." Pages 187–98 in *Mother Goose, Mother Jones, Mommie Dearest: Biblical Mothers and Their Children*. Edited by Cheryl A. Kirk-Duggan and Tina Pippin. SemeiaSt 61. Atlanta: SBL, 2009.

Baker, Cynthia. *Rebuilding the House of Israel: Archaeologies of Gender in Jewish Antiquity*. Divinations. Stanford, CA: Stanford University Press, 2002.

Balch, David L. *Let Wives Be Submissive: The Domestic Code in 1 Peter*. SBLMS 26. Chico, CA: Scholars Press, 1981.

_____. "'A Woman Clothed with the Sun' and the 'Great Red Dragon' Seeking to 'Devour her Child' (Rev 12:1, 4) in Roman Domestic Art." Pages 287–314 in *The New Testament and Early Christian Literature in Greco-Roman Context*. Edited by John Fotopoulos. NovTSup 122. Leiden: Brill, 2006.

Batten, Alicia J. "Neither Gold nor Braided Hair (1 Timothy 2.9; 1 Peter 3.3): Adornment, Gender, and Honor in Antiquity." *NTS* 55 (2009): 484–501.

Bauman-Martin, Betsy J. "Women on the Edge: New Perspectives on Women in the Petrine *Haustafel*." *JBL* 123 (2004): 253–79.

Becker, Matthias. "Ehe als Sanatorium: Plutarchs *Coniugalia Praecepta* und die Pastoralbriefe." *NovT* 52 (2010): 241–66.

Betsworth, Sharon. *Children in Early Christian Narratives*. LNTS 521. London: Bloomsbury/T&T Clark, 2015.

Blickenstaff, Marianne. *"While the Bridegroom Is with Them": Marriage, Family, Gender, and Violence in the Gospel of Matthew*. JSNTSup 292. London: T&T Clark, 2005.

Bonfante, Larissa. "Nursing Mothers in Classical Art." Pages 174–95 in *Naked Truths: Women, Sexuality, and Gender in Classical Art and Archaeology*. Edited by Ann Olga Kolosk-Ostrow and Claire L. Lyons. London: Routledge, 1997.

Borgen, Peder. *Bread from Heaven: An Exegetical Study of the Concept of Manna in the Gospel of John and the Writings of Philo*. NovTSup 10. Leiden: Brill, 1965.

Boring, M. Eugene. *1 Peter*. ANTC. Nashville: Abingdon, 1999.

Bovon, François. *Luke 1*. Translated by Christine M. Thomas. Hermeneia. Minneapolis: Fortress, 2002.

Boyarin, Daniel. *Carnal Israel: Reading Sex in Talmudic Culture*. The New Historicism 25. Berkeley: University of California Press, 1993.

Bradley, Keith R. *Discovering the Roman Family: Studies in Roman History*. Oxford: Oxford University Press, 1991.

Bremmer, Jan N. "Felicitas: The Martyrdom of a Young African Woman." Pages 35–53 in *Perpetua's Passions: Multidisciplinary Approaches to the* Passio Perpetuae et Felicitatis. Edited by Jan N. Bremmer and Marco Formisano. Oxford: Oxford University Press, 2012.

Bremmer, Jan N., and Marco Formisano. "Perpetua's Passions: A Brief Introduction." Pages 1–13 in *Perpetua's Passions: Multidisciplinary Approaches to the* Passio Perpetuae et Felicitatis. Edited by Jan N. Bremmer and Marco Formisano. Oxford: Oxford University Press, 2012.

Brooten, B. J. *Women Leaders in Ancient Synagogues: Inscriptional Evidence and Background Issues*. BJS 36. Chico, CA: Scholars Press, 1982.

Brown, Raymond E. *The Gospel According to John*. 2 vols. AB 29–29a. Garden City, NY: Doubleday, 1966–1970.

Buch-Hansen, Gitte. *"It Is the Spirit that Gives Life": A Stoic Understanding of Pneuma in John's Gospel*. BZNW 173. Berlin: de Gruyter, 2010.

Buchanan, Lindal. *Rhetorics of Motherhood*. Studies in Rhetorics and Feminism. Carbondale: Southern Illinois University Press, 2013.

Burke, Trevor J. "Pauline Paternity in 1 Thessalonians." *TynBul* 51 (2000): 59–80.

Burridge, Richard. *What Are the Gospels? A Comparison with Graeco-Roman Biography*. 2d ed. Grand Rapids: Eerdmans, 2004.

Burrus, Virginia. *"Begotten, Not Made": Conceiving Manhood in Late Antiquity*. Figurae: Reading Medieval Culture. Stanford, CA: Stanford University Press, 2000.

_____. *Chastity as Autonomy: Women in the Stories of the Apocryphal Acts*. Lewiston, NY: Mellen, 1987.

Butler, Shane. "Notes on a *Membrum Disiectum*." Pages 236–55 in *Women and Slaves in Greco-Roman Culture: Differential Equations*. Edited by Sandra R. Joshel and Sheila Murnaghan. New York: Routledge, 1998.

Bynum, Caroline. *Jesus as Mother: Studies in the Spirituality of the High Middle Ages*. Berkeley: University of California Press, 1982.

Caldwell, Lauren. "Gynecology." Pages 360–70 in vol. 1 of *A Companion to Science, Technology, and Medicine in Ancient Greece and Rome*. Edited by Georgia L. Irby. BCAW. Malden, MA: Wiley Blackwell, 2016.

Calef, Susan A. "Thecla 'Tried and True' and the Inversion of Romance." Pages 163–85 in *A Feminist Companion to the New Testament Apocrypha*. Edited by Amy-Jill Levine with Maria Mayo Robbins. Cleveland: Pilgrim, 2006.

Castelli, Elizabeth A. *Martyrdom and Memory: Early Christian Culture Making*. Gender, Theory, and Religion. New York: Columbia University Press, 2004.

Chapman, Cynthia. "'Oh that you were like a brother to me, one who had nursed at my mother's breasts': Breast Milk as a Kinship-Forging Substance." *JHebS* 12 (2012): article 7.

Cherian, Jacob. "The Moses at Qumran: The מורה הצדק as the Nursing-Father of the יחד." Pages 351–61 in *The Bible and the Dead Sea Scrolls*. Vol. 2: The Second Princeton Symposium on Judaism and Christian Origins. Waco, TX: Baylor University Press, 2006.

Claassens, L. Juliana M. *The God Who Provides: Biblical Images of Divine Nourishment*. Nashville: Abingdon, 2004.

_____. *Mourner, Mother, Midwife: Reimagining God's Delivering Presence in the Old Testament*. Louisville: Westminster John Knox, 2012.

Clark, Elizabeth A. "Antifamilial Tendencies in Ancient Christianity." *JHS* 5 (1995): 356–80.

_____. *History, Theory, Text: Historians and the Linguistic Turn*. Cambridge: Harvard University Press, 2004.

Collins, Patricia Hill. *From Black Power to Hip Hop: Racism, Nationalism, and Feminism*. Philadelphia: Temple University Press, 2006.

Conte, Gian Biagio. *The Rhetoric of Imitation: Genre and Poetic Memory in Virgil and Other Latin Poets*. Edited by Charles Segal. Ithaca, NY: Cornell University Press, 1986.

Conway, Colleen M. *Behold the Man: Jesus and Greco-Roman Masculinity*. Oxford: Oxford University Press, 2008.

Corbeill, Anthony. "Dining Deviants in Roman Political Invective." Pages 99–128 in *Roman Sexualities*. Edited by Judith P. Hallett and Marilyn B. Skinner. Princeton: Princeton University Press, 1997.

_____. *Nature Embodied: Gesture in Ancient Rome*. Princeton: Princeton University Press, 2003.

Corrington, Gail Patterson. "The Milk of Salvation: Redemption by the Mother in Late Antiquity and Early Christianity." *HTR* 82 (1989): 393–420.

Crook, Zeba. "Honor, Shame and Social Status Revisited." *JBL* 128 (2009): 591–611.

Crowder, Stephanie Buckhanon. *When Momma Speaks: The Bible and Motherhood from a Womanist Perspective*. Louisville: Westminster John Knox, 2016.

Croy, N. Clayton, and Alice E. Connor. "Mantic Mary? The Virgin Mother as Prophet in Luke 1.26–56 and the Early Church." *JSNT* 34 (2011): 254–76.

D'Angelo, Mary Rose. "'Knowing How to Preside Over His Own Household': Imperial Masculinity and Christian Asceticism in the Pastorals, *Hermas*, and Luke-Acts." Pages 265–96 in *New Testament Masculinities*. Edited by Stephen D. Moore and Janice Capel Anderson. SemSt 45. Atlanta: SBL, 2003.

Davis, Steven J. *The Cult of Saint Thecla: A Tradition of Women's Piety in Late Antiquity*. Oxford: Oxford University Press, 2001.

Dean-Jones, Lesley. *Women's Bodies in Classical Greek Science*. Oxford: Clarendon: 2001.

DeConick, April D. *Holy Misogyny: Why the Sex and Gender Conflicts in the Early Church Still Matter*. New York: Continuum, 2011.

Demand, Nancy. *Birth, Death, and Motherhood in Classical Greece*. Baltimore: Johns Hopkins University Press, 1994.

Dixon, Suzanne. *Cornelia: Mother of the Gracchi*. Women of the Ancient World. London: Routledge, 2007.

______. *The Roman Mother*. Norman: University of Oklahoma Press, 1987.

Donelson, Lewis R. *I & II Peter and Jude*. NTL. Louisville: Westminster John Knox, 2010.

Eastman, Susan. *Recovering Paul's Mother Tongue: Language and Theology in Galatians*. Grand Rapids: Eerdmans, 2007.

Edwards, James R. "Galatians 5:12: Circumcision, the Mother Goddess, and the Scandal of the Cross." *NovT* 53 (2011): 319–37.

Elliott, Susan M. *Cutting Too Close for Comfort: Paul's Letter to the Galatians in its Anatolian Context*. JSNTSup 248. London: T&T Clark, 2003.

Fehribach, Adeline. "The 'Birthing' Bridegroom: The Portrayal of Jesus in the Fourth Gospel." Pages 104–29 in vol. 2 of *A Feminist Companion to John*. Edited by Amy-Jill Levine with Marianne Blickenstaff. London: Sheffield Academic, 2003.

Fitzmyer, Joseph A. *The Gospel According to Luke*. AB 28. Garden City, NY: Doubleday, 1981.

Flemming, Rebecca. *Medicine and the Making of Roman Women: Gender, Nature, and Authority from Celsus to Galen*. Oxford: Oxford University Press, 2000.

Flemming, Rebecca, and Ann Ellis Hanson. "Hippocrates' 'Peri Partheniôn' (Diseases of Young Girls): Text and Translation." *Early Science and Medicine* 3 (1998): 241–52.

Fonrobert, Charlotte Elisheva. *Menstrual Purity: Rabbinic and Christian Reconstructions of Gender*. Contraversions. Stanford, CA: Stanford University Press, 2007.

Foskett, Mary F. *A Virgin Conceived: Mary and Classical Representations of Virginity*. Bloomington: Indiana University Press, 2002.

Francis, J. "'Like Newborn Babes'—The Image of the Child in 1 Peter 2:2–3." *StudBib* 3 (1978): 111–17.

Furrell, Joseph, and Craig Williams, trans. "The Passion of Saints Perpetua and Felicity." Pages 14–23 in *Perpetua's Passions: Multidisciplinary Approaches to the* Passio Perpetuae et Felicitatis. Edited by Jan N. Bremmer and Marco Formisano. Oxford: Oxford University Press, 2012.

Gaventa, Beverly Roberts. *Mary: Glimpses of the Mother of Jesus*. Minneapolis: Fortress, 1999.

_____. *Our Mother Saint Paul*. Louisville: Westminster John Knox, 2007.

Gaventa, Beverly Roberts and Cynthia L. Rigby, eds. *Blessed One: Protestant Perspectives on Mary*. Louisville: Westminster John Knox, 2002.

Glancy, Jennifer A. *Corporal Knowledge: Early Christian Bodies*. Oxford: Oxford University Press, 2010.

_____. "Protocols of Masculinity in the Pastoral Epistles." Pages 235–64 in *New Testament Masculinities*. Edited by Stephen D. Moore and Janice Capel Anderson. SemSt 45. Atlanta: SBL, 2003.

_____. *Slavery in Early Christianity*. Minneapolis: Fortress, 2006.

Gleason, Maud W. "By Whose Gender Standards (if Anybody's) Was Jesus a Real Man?" Pages 325–28 in *New Testament Masculinities*. Edited by Stephen D. Moore and Janice Capel Anderson. SemSt 45. Atlanta: SBL, 2003.

_____. *Making Men: Sophists and Self-Presentation in Ancient Rome*. Princeton: Princeton University Press, 1995.

Grassi, Joseph A. "The Role of Jesus' Mother in John's Gospel: A Reappraisal." *CBQ* 48 (1986): 67–80.

Graver, Margaret. "Dog-Helen and Homeric Insult." *Classical Antiquity* 14 (1995): 41–61.

Green, Joel B. "Blessed is She Who Believed: Mary, Curious Exemplar in Luke's Narrative." Pages 9–20 in *Blessed One: Protestant Perspectives on Mary*. Edited by Beverly Roberts Gaventa and Cynthia L. Rigby. Louisville: Westminster John Knox, 2002.

Grubbs, Judith Evans. *Women and the Law in the Roman Empire: A Sourcebook on Marriage, Divorce, and Widowhood*. London: Routledge, 2002.

Grudem, Wayne. *Evangelical Feminism and Biblical Truth: An Analysis of More than 100 Disputed Questions*. Wheaton, IL: Crossway, 2012.

Guzmán, Ron, and Michael W. Martin. "Is Hebrews 5:11–6:20 Really a Digression?" *NovT* 57 (2015): 295–310.

Haber, Susan. "Living and Dying for the Law: The Mother-martyrs of 2 Maccabees." *Women in Judaism* 4/1 (2006): 1–15 [Online: http://wjudaism.library.utoronto.ca/index.php/wjudaism/article/view/247/320].

Hallett, Judith P. *Fathers and Daughters in Roman Society: Women and the Elite Family*. Princeton: Princeton University Press, 1984.

Harrill, J. Albert. "Cannibalistic Language in the Fourth Gospel and Greco-Roman Polemics of Factionalism (John 6:52–66)." *JBL* 127 (2008): 133–58.

Harstine, Stan. *Moses as a Character in the Fourth Gospel: A Study in Ancient Literary Techniques*. JSNTSup 229. Sheffield: Sheffield Academic, 2002.

Hemelrijk, Emily A. *Matrona Docta: Educated Women in the Roman Élite from Cornelia to Julia Domna*. Routledge Classical Monographs. London: Routledge, 1999.

Holloway, Paul A. "Gender and Grief: Seneca's *Ad Marciam* and *Ad Helviam matrem*." Pages 299–321 in *Women and Gender in Ancient Religions*. Edited by Stephen P. Ahearne-Kroll, Paul A. Holloway, and James A. Kelhoffer. WUNT 263. Tübingen: Mohr Siebeck, 2010.

Hong, Yurie. "Collaboration and Conflict: Discourses of Maternity in Hippocratic Gynecology and Embryology." Pages 71–96 in *Mothering and Motherhood in Ancient Greece and Rome*. Edited by Lauren Hackworth Petersen and Patricia Salzman-Mitchell. Austin: University of Texas, 2012.

Horn, Cornelia B. "Suffering Children, Parental Authority and the Quest for Liberation?: A Tale of Three Girls in the *Acts of Paul (and Thecla)*, the *Act(s) of Peter*, the *Acts of Nerseus and Achilleus*, and the *Epistle of Pseudo-Titus*." Pages 118–45 in *A Feminist Companion to the New Testament Apocrypha*. Edited by Amy-Jill Levine with Maria Mayo Robbins. Cleveland: Pilgrim, 2006.

Horst, Pieter van der. "Sarah's Seminal Emission: Hebrews 11:11 in the Light of Ancient Embryology." Pages 287–302 in *Greeks, Romans, and Christians*. Edited by David L. Balch, Everett Ferguson, Wayne A. Meeks. Minneapolis: Fortress, 1991.

Hubbard, Moyer. "Kept Safe Through Childbearing: Maternal Mortality, Justification By Faith, and the Social Setting of 1 Timothy 2:15." *JETS* 55 (2012): 743–62.

Hutson, Christopher R. "'Saved through Childbearing' The Jewish Context of 1 Timothy 2:15." *NovT* (2014): 392–410.

Hylen, Susan E. *A Modest Apostle: Thecla and the History of Women in the Early Church*. Oxford: Oxford University Press, 2015.

Ilan, Tal. *Jewish Women in Greco-Roman Palestine*. Peabody, MA: Hendrickson, 1996.

Jackson-McCabe, Matt. "Women and Eros in Greek Magic and the *Acts of Paul and Thecla*." Pages 267–78 in *Women and Gender in Ancient Religions*. Edited by Stephen P. Ahearne-Kroll, Paul A. Holloway, James A. Kelhoffer. WUNT 263. Tübingen: Mohr Siebeck, 2010.

Jacobs, Andrew S. "'Her Own Proper Kinship': Marriage, Class and Women in the Apocryphal Acts of the Apostles." Pages 18–46 in *A Feminist Companion to the New Testament Apocrypha*. Edited by Amy-Jill Levine with Maria Mayo Robbins. Cleveland: Pilgrim, 2006.

Jacques, Heather A. K., and H. Lorraine Radtke. "Constrained by Choice: Young Women Negotiate the Discourses of Marriage and Motherhood." *Feminism and Psychology* 22 (2012): 443–61.

Jauss, H. R. *Aesthetic Experience and Literary Hermeneutics*. Minneapolis: University of Minnesota Press, 1982.

Jensen, Robin M. "*Mater Ecclesia* and *Fons Aeterna*: The Church and Her Womb in Ancient Christian Tradition." Pages 137–55 in *A Feminist Companion to Patristic Literature*. Edited by Amy-Jill Levine. London: T&T Clark, 2008.

Jobes, Karen H. "Got Milk? Septuagint Psalm 33 and the Interpretation of 1 Peter 2:1–3." *WTJ* 63 (2002): 1–14.

Johnson, E. Elizabeth. "'Who Is My Mother?' Family Values in the Gospel of Mark." Pages 32–46 in *Blessed One: Protestant Perspectives on Mary*. Edited by Beverly Roberts Gaventa and Cynthia L. Rigby. Louisville: Westminster John Knox, 2002.

Johnson, Luke Timothy. *Letters to Paul's Delegates: 1 Timothy, 2 Timothy, Titus*. Valley Forge, PA: Trinity Press International, 1996.

Jones, Jane Clare. "Idealized and Industrialized Labor: Anatomy of a Feminist Controversy." *Hypatia* 27 (2012): 99–117.

Jones-Lewis, Molly. "Physicians and 'Schools.'" Pages 386–401 in vol. 1 of *A Companion to Science, Technology, and Medicine in Ancient Greece and Rome*. Edited by Georgia L. Irby. BCAW. Malden, MA: Wiley Blackwell, 2016.

Kahl, Brigitte. "No Longer Male: Masculinity Struggles Behind Galatians 3.28?" *JSNT* 79 (2000): 37–49.

Kartzow, Marianne Bjelland. *Gossip and Gender: Other of Speech in the Pastoral Epistles*. BZNW 164. Berlin/New York: de Gruyter, 2009.

Kessler, Gwynn. *Conceiving Israel: The Fetus in Rabbinic Narratives*. Divinations. Philadelphia: University of Pennsylvania Press, 2009.

Kiley, Mark. "A Note on Hebrews 5:14." *CBQ* 42 (1980): 501–3.

King, Helen. *The Disease of Virgins: Green Sickness, Chlorosis and the Problems of Purity*. London: Routledge, 2004.

———. *Hippocrates' Woman: Reading the Female Body in Ancient Greece*. London: Routledge, 1998.

———. *The One-Sex Body on Trial: The Classical and Early Modern Evidence*. The History of Medicine in Context. London: Ashgate, 2013.

———. "Sacrificial Blood: The Role of the *Amnion* in Ancient Gynecology." *Helios* 13 (1987): 117–26.

King, Karen L., ed. *Women and Goddess Traditions in Antiquity and Today*. SAC. Minneapolis: Fortress, 1997.

Koester, Craig R. *Hebrews*. AB 36. Garden City, NY: Doubleday, 2001.

Kraemer, Ross Shepard. *Unreliable Witnesses: Religion, Gender, and History in the Greco-Roman Mediterranean*. Oxford: Oxford University Press, 2011.

Labovitz, Gail. "'These Are the Labors': Constructions of the Woman Nursing Her Child in the Mishnah and Tosefta." *Nashim* 3 (2000): 15–42.

Langlands, Rebecca. *Sexual Morality in Ancient Rome*. Cambridge: Cambridge University Press, 2002.

Laqueur, Thomas W. *Making Sex: Body and Gender from the Greeks to Freud*. Cambridge: Harvard University Press, 1992.

Laskaris, Julie. "Nursing Mothers in Greek and Roman Medicine." *AJA* 112 (2008): 459–64.

Leach, Eleanor Winsor. "Venus, Thetis and the Social Construction of Maternal Behavior." *The Classical Journal* 92 (1997): 347–71.

Lee, John A. L. "Hebrews 5:14 and ΕΞΙΣ: A History of Misunderstanding." *NovT* 39 (1997): 151–76.

Lefkowitz, Mary R., and Maureen B. Fant, eds. *Women's Life in Greece and Rome: A Sourcebook in Translation*. Baltimore: Johns Hopkins University Press, 1992.

Lehtipuu, Outi. "The Example of Thecla and the Example(s) of Paul: Disputing Women's Role in Early Christianity." Pages 349–378 in *Women and Gender in Ancient Religions*. Edited by Stephen P. Ahearne-Kroll, Paul A. Holloway, and James A. Kelhoffer. WUNT 263. Tübingen: Mohr Siebeck, 2010.

Levine, Amy-Jill, with Maria Mayo Robbins, ed. *A Feminist Companion to Mariology*. London: T&T Clark, 2005.

Lieu, Judith. "The Mother of the Son in the Fourth Gospel." *JBL* 117 (1998): 61–77.

Lincoln, Andrew T. *Born of a Virgin? Reconceiving Jesus in the Bible, Tradition, and Theology*. Grand Rapids: Eerdmans, 2013.

Lipsett, B. Diane. *Desiring Conversion: Hermas, Thecla, Aseneth*. Oxford: Oxford University Press, 2011.

Loraux, Nicole. *Tragic Ways of Killing a Woman*. Cambridge: Harvard University Press, 1987.

MacDonald, Dennis R. *The Acts of Andrew*. Early Christian Apocrypha 1. Santa Rosa, CA: Polebridge, 2005.

MacDonald, Margaret Y. "Beyond Identification of the Topos of Household Management: Reading the Household Codes in Light of Recent Methodologies and Theoretical Proposals in the Study of the New Testament." *NTS* 57 (2009): 65–90.

Malherbe, Abraham. "Gentile as a Nurse: The Cynic Background of I Thess ii." *NovT* 12 (1970): 203–17.

Marcus, Joel. *Mark 8–16*. AB 27a. New Haven: Yale University Press, 2009.

Martin, Dale B. "Contradictions of Masculinity: Ascetic Inseminators and Menstruating Men in Greco-Roman Culture." Pages 81–108 in *Generation and Degeneration: Tropes of Reproduction in Literature and History from Antiquity through Early Modern Europe*. Edited by Valeria Finucci and Kevin Brownlee. Durham, NC: Duke University Press, 2001.

_____. *The Corinthian Body*. New Haven: Yale University Press, 1995.

_____. *Sex and the Single Savior: Gender and Sexuality in Biblical Interpretation*. Louisville: Westminster John Knox, 2006.

Martin, Troy W. "Christians as Babies: Metaphorical Reality in 1 Peter." Pages 99–112 in *Reading 1–2 Peter and Jude: A Resource for Students*. Edited by Eric F. Mason and Troy W. Martin. RBS 77. Atlanta: SBL, 2014.

_____. "Paul's Pneumatological Statements and Ancient Medical Texts." Pages 105–26 in *The New Testament and Early Christian Literature*. Edited by John Fotopoulos. NovTSup 122. Leiden: Brill, 2006.

McCartney, Dan G. "λογικος in 1 Peter 2,2." *ZNW* 82 (1991): 128–32.

McNeel, Jennifer Houston. *Paul as Infant and Nursing Mother: Metaphor, Rhetoric, and Identity in 1 Thessalonians 2:5-8*. ECL 12. Atlanta: SBL Press, 2014.

Meeks, Wayne A. *The Prophet-King: Moses Traditions and Johannine Christology*. NovTSup 14. Leiden: Brill, 1967.

Merk, Otto. "1 Thessalonians 2:1–12: An Exegetical-Theological Study." Pages 89–113 in *The Thessalonians Debate: Methodological Discord or Methodological Synthesis*. Edited by Karl P. Donfried and Johannes Beutler. Grand Rapids: Eerdmans, 2000.

Meyers, Carol. *Rediscovering Eve*. Oxford: Oxford University Press, 2013.

Milnor, Kristina. *Gender, Domesticity, and the Age of Augustus: Inventing Private Life*. Oxford Studies in Classical Literature and Gender Theory. Oxford: Oxford University Press, 2005.

Moloney, Francis J. *Belief in the Word: Reading John 1–4*. Minneapolis: Fortress, 1993.

_____. "'In the Bosom of' or 'Turned towards' the Father?" *AusBR* 31 (1983): 63–71.

Moo, Douglas J. "Interpretation of 1 Timothy 2:11–15: A Rejoinder." *TJ* 2 (1981): 198–222.

Moore, Stephen D. *God's Gym: Divine Male Bodies of the Bible*. London: Routledge, 1996.

Moore, Stephen D., and Janice Capel Anderson, eds. *New Testament Masculinities*. SemSt 45. Atlanta: SBL, 2003.

Moss, Candida R. "Blood Ties: Martyrdom, Motherhood, and Family in the *Passion of Perpetua and Felicity*." Pages 189–208 in *Women and Gender in Ancient Religions*. Edited by Stephen P. Ahearne-Kroll, Paul A. Holloway, and James A. Kelhoffer. WUNT 263. Tübingen: Mohr Siebeck, 2010.

Moss, Candida R., and Joel S. Baden. *Reconceiving Infertility: Biblical Perspectives on Procreation and Childlessness*. Princeton: Princeton University Press, 2015.

Myers, Alicia D. *Characterizing Jesus: A Rhetorical Analysis on the Fourth Gospel's Use of Scripture in Its Presentation of Jesus*. LNTS 458. London: T&T Clark, 2012.

_____. "Gender, Rhetoric, and Recognition: (Re)defining Masculinity in the Gospel of John." *JSNT* 38 (2015): 191–218.

_____. "'In the Father's Bosom': Breastfeeding and Identity Formation in John's Gospel." *CBQ* 76 (2014): 481–97.

_____. "*Pater Nutrix*: Milk Metaphors and Character Formation in Hebrews and 1 Peter." Pages 81–99 in *Making Sense of Motherhood: Biblical and Systematic Perspectives*. Edited by Beth Stovell. Eugene, OR: Wipf & Stock, 2016.

Neusner, Jacob. *Genesis Rabbah: The Judaic Commentary to the Book of Genesis A New American Translation*. Vol. 1. BJS 104. Atlanta: Scholars Press, 1985.

O'Brien, Joan. "Nammu, Mami, Eve, and Pandora: 'What's in a Name?'" *The Classical Journal* 79 (1983): 35–45.

O'Day, Gail R. *John*. NIB. Nashville: Abingdon, 2006.

O'Kane, Martin. "'The Bosom of Abraham' (Luke 16:22): Father Abraham in the Visual Imagination." *BibInt* 15 (2007): 489–93.

O'Reilly, Andrea, ed. *Maternal Theory: Essential Readings*. Toronto: Demeter, 2007.

Osiek, Carolyn, and David L. Balch. *Families in the New Testament World: Households and House Churches*. Louisville: Westminster John Knox, 1997.

Parker, Holt N. "The Teratongenic Grid." Pages 47–65 in *Roman Sexualities*. Edited by Judith P. Hallett and Marilyn B. Skinner. Princeton: Princeton University Press, 1997.

Parsenios, George L. *First, Second, and Third John*. PNTC. Grand Rapids: Baker, 2014.

Pelikan, Jaroslav. *Mary Through the Centuries: Her Place in the History of Culture*. New Haven: Yale University Press, 1996.

Penniman, John David. *Raised on Christian Milk: The Symbolic Power of Nourishment in Early Christianity*. Synkrisis Series. New Haven: Yale University Press, 2017.

Perry, Peter S. "Making Fear Personal: Hebrews 5.11–6.12 and the Argument from Shame." *JSNT* 32 (2009): 99–125.

Pervo, Richard I. *The Acts of Paul: A New Translation with Introduction and Commentary*. Eugene, OR: Cascade Books, 2014.

Petrocelli, Corrado. "Cornelia the Matron." Pages 34–65 in *Roman Women*. Edited by Augusto Fraschetti. Translated by Linda Lappin. Chicago: University of Chicago Press, 2001.

Plant, Rebecca Jo. *Mom: The Transformation of Motherhood in Modern America*. Chicago: University of Chicago Press, 2010.

Porter, Stanley E. "What does it Mean to be 'Saved by Childbirth' [1 Timothy 2.15]?" *JSNT* 49 (1993): 87–102.

Quek, Tze-Ming. "A Text-Critical Study of John 1.34." *NTS* 55 (2009): 22–34.

Rabbinowitz, Peter. "Truth in Fiction: A Reexamination of Audiences." *Critical Inquiry* 4 (1977): 121–41.

_____. "Whirl without End: Audience Oriented Criticism." Pages 81–100 in *Contemporary Literary Theory*. Edited by G. Douglas Atkins and Laura Morrow. Amherst: University of Massachusetts Press, 1988.

Reinhartz, Adele. "'And the Word Was Begotten': Divine Epigenesis in the Gospel of John." *Sem* 85 (1999): 83–103.

Rich, Adrienne. *Of Woman Born: Motherhood as Experience and Institution*. Repr. New York: Norton, 1995.

Richlin, Amy. "Pliny's Brassiere." Pages 197–221 in *Roman Sexualities*. Edited by Judith P. Hallett and Marilyn B. Skinner. Princeton: Princeton University Press, 1997.

Rocca, Julius. "Anatomy and Physiology." Pages 345–59 in vol. 1 of *A Companion to Science, Technology, and Medicine in Ancient Greece and Rome*. Edited by Georgia L. Irby. BCAW. Malden, MA: Wiley Blackwell, 2016.

Rothschild, Clare K. "Embryology, Plant Biology, and Divine Generation in the Fourth Gospel." Pages 125–51 in *Women and Gender in Ancient Religions*. Edited by Stephen P. Ahearne-Kroll, Paul A. Halloway, and James A. Kelhoffer. WUNT 263. Tübingen: Mohr Siebeck, 2010.

Sakenfeld, Katherine Doob. "Tamar, Rahab, Ruth, and the Wife of Uriah: The Company Mary Keeps in Matthew's Gospel." Pages 21–31 in *Blessed One: Protestant*

Perspectives on Mary. Edited by Beverly Roberts Gaventa and Cynthia L. Rigby. Louisville: Westminster John Knox, 2002.

Satlow, Michael L. "'Try to be a Man': The Rabbinic Construction of Masculinity." *HTR* 89 (1996): 19–40.

_____. "'Wasted Seed,' The History of a Rabbinic Idea." *HUCA* 65 (1990): 137–75.

Schmidt, Ulrich. "1 Thess 2.7b, c: 'Kleinkinder, die wie eine Amme Kinder versorgen.'" *NTS* 55 (2009): 116–20.

Schroeder, Caroline T. "The Erotic Asceticism of the *Passion of Andrew*: The Apocryphal *Acts of Andrew*, the Greek Novel, and Platonic Philosophy." Pages 47–59 in *A Feminist Companion to the New Testament Apocrypha*. Edited by Amy-Jill Levine with Maria Mayo Robbins. Cleveland: Pilgrim, 2006.

Seim, Turid Karlsen. "Descent and Divine Paternity in the Gospel of John: Does the Mother Matter?" *NTS* 51 (2005): 361–75.

_____. "Motherhood and the Making of Fathers in Antiquity: Contextualizing Genetics in the Gospel of John." Pages 99–123 in *Women and Gender in Ancient Religions*. Edited by Stephen P. Ahearne-Kroll, Paul A. Holloway, and James A. Kelhoffer. WUNT 263. Tubingen: Mohr Siebeck, 2010.

Severy, Beth. *Augustus and the Family at the Birth of the Roman Empire*. London: Routledge, 2003.

Sigismund-Nielson, Hanne. "Vibia Perpetua—An Indecent Woman." Pages 103–17 in *Perpetua's Passions: Multidisciplinary Approaches to the* Passio Perpetuae et Felicitatis. Edited by Jan N. Bremmer and Marco Formisano. Oxford: Oxford University Press, 2012.

Solevåg, Anna Rebecca. "Adam, Eve, and the Serpent in the Acts of Andrew." Pages 9–28 in *Hidden Truths from Eden: Esoteric Readings of Genesis 1–3*. Edited by Caroline Vander Stichele and Susanne Scholz. SemSt 76. Atlanta: SBL Press, 2014.

———. *Birthing Salvation: Gender and Class in Early Christian Childbearing*. BIS 121. Leiden: Brill, 2013.

Soskice, Janet Martin. *The Kindness of God: Metaphor, Gender, and Religious Language*. Oxford: Oxford University Press, 2007.

Spencer, F. Scott. *Salty Wives, Spirited Mothers, and Savvy Widows: Capable Women of Purpose and Persistence in Luke's Gospel*. Grand Rapids: Eerdmans, 2012.

Streete, Gail. P. C. "Buying the Stairway to Heaven: Perpetua and Thecla as Early Christian Heroines." Pages 186–205 in *A Feminist Companion to the New Testament Apocrypha*. Edited by Amy-Jill Levine with Maria Mayo Robbins. Cleveland: Pilgrim, 2006.

Talbert, Charles H. "Miraculous Conceptions and Births in Mediterranean Antiquity." Pages 79–86 in *The Historical Jesus in Context*. Edited by Amy-Jill Levine, Dale C. Allison Jr., John Dominic Crossan. Princeton Readings in Religions. Princeton: Princeton University Press, 2006.

_____. *Reading Luke-Acts in its Mediterranean Milieu*. NovTSup 107. Leiden: Brill, 2003.

_____. *What Is a Gospel?* Philadelphia: Fortress, 1977.

Tavard, George H. *The Thousand Faces of the Virgin Mary*. Collegeville, MN: Liturgical Press, 1996.

Taylor, Erin N., and Lora Ebert Wallace. "For Shame: Feminism, Breastfeeding Advocacy, and Maternal Guilt." *Hypatia* 27 (2012): 76–98.

Temkin, Oswei, trans. *Soranus' Gynecology*. Baltimore: Johns Hopkins University Press, 1956.

Thompson, James W. *Hebrews*. PCNT. Grand Rapids: Baker, 2008.

Tite, Philip L. "Nurslings, Milk and Moral Development in the Greco-Roman Context: A Reappraisal of the Paraenetic Utilization of Metaphor in 1 Peter 2.1–3." *JSNT* 31 (2009): 371–400.

Trible, Phyllis. *God and the Rhetoric of Sexuality*. Philadelphia: Fortress, 1978.

Vandenberg-Daves, Jodi. *Modern Motherhood: An American History*. New Brunswick: Rutgers University Press, 2014.

Vorster, Johannes. "Construction of Culture through the Construction of Person: The Construction of Thecla in the *Acts of Thecla*." Pages 98–117 in *A Feminist Companion to the New Testament Apocrypha*. Edited by Amy-Jill Levine with Maria Mayo Robbins. Cleveland: Pilgrim, 2006.

Walters, Jonathan. "Invading the Roman Body: Manliness and Impenetrability in Roman Thought." Pages 29–46 in *Roman Sexualities*. Edited by Judith P. Hallett and Marilyn B. Skinner. Princeton: Princeton University Press, 1997.

Waters, Kenneth L., Sr. "Saved Through Childbearing: Virtues as Children in 1 Timothy 2:11–15." *JBL* 123 (2004): 703–35.

Watson, Duane F., and Terrance Callan. *First and Second Peter*. PNTC. Grand Rapids: Baker, 2012.

Watson, Patricia A. *Ancient Stepmothers: Myth, Misogyny and Reality*. Mnemosyne 143. Leiden: Brill, 1995.

Weissenrieder, Annette. "Die lebendige Wirkung des Geistes in Gen 2,7/LXX. Das Bedeutungsspecktrum von נפה/ἐμφυσάω und נשמה/πνοή in Lichte antiker medizinischer Quellen." *JSCS* 46 (2013): 11–29.

_____. "Spirit and Rebirth in the Gospel of John." *R&T* 21 (2014): 58–85.

_____. "What Does σωθήσεται δὲ διὰ τῆς τεκνογονίας 'To Be Saved by Childbearing' Mean [1 Timothy 2:15]? Insights from Ancient Medical and Philosophical Texts." *Early Christianity* 5 (2014): 313–36.

Wilberding, James. "Embryology." Pages 329–41 in vol. 1 of *A Companion to Science, Technology, and Medicine in Ancient Greece and Rome*. Edited by Georgia L. Irby. BCAW. Malden, MA: Wiley-Blackwell, 2016.

Williams, Craig. "Perpetua's Gender: A Latinist Reads the *Passio Perpetuae et Felicitatis*." Pages 54–77 in *Perpetua's Passions: Multidisciplinary Approaches to the* Passio Perpetuae et Felicitatis. Edited by Jan N. Bremmer and Marco Formisano. Oxford: Oxford University Press, 2012.

Wilson, Brittany E. *Unmanly Men: Refigurations of Masculinity in Luke-Acts*. Oxford: Oxford University Press, 2015.

Wold, Benjamin G. "Family Ethics in *4QInstruction* and the New Testament." *NovT* 50 (2008): 286–300.

Wolkow, B. M. "The Mind of a Bitch: Pandora's Motive and Intent in the *Erga*." *Hermes* 135 (2007): 247–62.

Zeitlin, Froma I. *Playing the Other: Gender and Society in Classical Greek Literature.* Women in Culture and Society. Chicago: University of Chicago Press, 1996.

Index

www.ingramcontent.com/pod-product-compliance
Ingram Content Group UK Ltd.
Pitfield, Milton Keynes, MK11 3LW, UK
UKHW041356190726
13851UKWH00014B/129